African Science

African Science

WITCHCRAFT, VODUN, AND
HEALING IN SOUTHERN BENIN

Douglas J. Falen

THE UNIVERSITY OF WISCONSIN PRESS

The University of Wisconsin Press
728 State Street, Suite 443
Madison, Wisconsin 53706
uwpress.wisc.edu

Gray's Inn House, 127 Clerkenwell Road
London EC1R 5DB, United Kingdom
eurospanbookstore.com

Printed in the United States of America

This book may be available in a digital edition.

Library of Congress Cataloging-in-Publication Data
Names: Falen, Douglas J., author.
Title: African science : witchcraft, Vodun, and healing in southern Benin /
Douglas J. Falen.
Description: Madison, Wisconsin : The University of Wisconsin Press, [2018] |
Includes bibliographical references and index.
Identifiers: LCCN 2018011398 | ISBN 9780299318901 (cloth : alk. paper)
Subjects: LCSH: Witchcraft—Benin. | Vodou—Benin. | Benin—Religion.
Classification: LCC BL2470.D3 F35 2018 | DDC 299.6/96683—dc23
LC record available at https://lccn.loc.gov/2018011398

ISBN 9780299318949 (pbk. : alk. paper)

*To all my Beninese friends
and the others who shared their lives and stories.*

I hope this book does justice to your vision of your world.

Contents

Illustrations

Acknowledgments

I am grateful first and foremost to all my Beninese friends and informants who opened the door to their lives and let me in. I thank them for their hospitality, shared meals, and willingness to look beyond our differences to find friendship and a common humanity in us all. Their ideas and words were the inspiration for this book, and I have tried to tell their stories in a way that they would appreciate. Although I can never adequately repay them all for what they have given me, I pledge to donate my royalties from the sale of this book to friends, informants, and members of their families who are struggling to eat, to stay healthy, and to send their children to school.

I express special thanks to my longtime friend and brother, Chams Linkpon, for his encouragement, candor, introductions, and translation help over the years. Now that he lives in the United States, I experience a great void in my visits to Benin. I am deeply indebted to Hippolyte Behanzin, a confidant and fellow researcher who freely shared his insights and passions with me. Special thanks go to my close friends Romain Togni and Germain Gblangoun, who were always available to offer their insights, introduce me to people, and house me. Other people who made important contributions to my research include Gabin Djimasse, Hounon Fulbert Dahwenou, Chimène Ahouanmagnagahou, Dah Agossouza, Toussaint Mekpo, and Romeo Atingli. I also express gratitude to Maureen Klein, who joined me for a field season as a research assistant and helped collect some of the data used in this book. I am grateful to Timothy Landry, Marcy O'Neil, and anonymous reviewers for feedback that contributed to important improvements in this work. All photographs that appear throughout the text were taken by me.

The research on which this book is based was funded through support from Agnes Scott College, and I am fortunate to work at an institution that maintains a commitment to faculty research.

Note on Fon Transcription and Pronunciation

The Fon language, known as Fɔ̀gbè by its speakers, is the most widely spoken language in southern Benin. It is related to other nearby languages in the Gbe family, spoken in Benin, Togo, and Ghana (Ethnologue n.d.). The colonial language of French is still the official language of government and education, so few Fon speakers actually read and write in their native language. My transcription style uses R. P. B. Segurola's (1963) orthography, with the exception of certain words that have an established academic spelling or are proper names, such as Vodun and Fon. In some cases, I have transcribed words that are not found in the dictionary; therefore, these spellings may not adhere to a standardized spelling. Below is a guide of the International Phonetic Alphabet (IPA) characters used to transcribe the Fon language. All letters not indicated here follow standard American English pronunciation. Nouns are pluralized by adding the postposition morpheme lɛ, as in vǐ lɛ (child plural). For readability, plural Fon words are written in singular form within the text. All translations are mine unless otherwise indicated.

Consonants

c   as in *ch*urch
gb   as in ru*gb*y, also at the beginning of a word
h   rounded, voiced *h*
kp   as in ba*ckp*ain, also at the beginning of a word
x   fricative, voiceless *h*, as in Ba*ch*
ɖ (Ð)   retroflex *d*, with the tongue back and toward the middle of the palate
ñ   as in ca*ny*on

Vowels

a   as in f*a*ther
e   as in f*ai*l

ɛ	as in pet
i	as in sleep
ɔ	as in caught
u	as in food

Nasal vowels show a tilde (˜) above the letter, as in ã, ɛ̃, ɔ̃, or ĩ. Tones are marked as follows on all vowels:

é	high tone
e	middle tone
è	low tone
ě	rising tone
ê	falling tone (rare)

African Science

Introduction

The American media's stereotypic depiction of Africa as the land of safari wildlife, dismal poverty, and rampant corruption has always been problematic, as has its negative portrayal of African religions. But the media's treatment of witchcraft is more than a simplistic stereotype. True, the characterization of Africa as the unquestioned home of witchcraft unfortunately can foster distorted, exotic, and unflattering images of Africans, but such labels do more than objectify and reify dynamic peoples and their cultures. These labels also suggest a profound intellectual and spiritual chasm by evoking ideas of an "irrational," "primitive" people inhabiting the "dark continent." The media reports of supernatural fears, child witches, and evangelical exorcisms encourage Westerners to think of Africans as fundamentally different from themselves, as incapable of rational thought, and as guided by a terror provoked by imaginary evil powers. At the same time, these stories capture something meaningful about contemporary Africa—the fact that witchcraft is one of the most troubling, challenging, and powerful phenomena on the continent and a defining and perplexing feature for both Africans and foreigners. This book explores the supernatural ideas and practices commonly known as "witchcraft" (àzě in the Fon language) in the southern region of the Republic of Benin and their links to notions of science, magic, healing, and the indigenous Vodun religion. While the popular media and much academic writing posit an incompatibility between Western and African worldviews, Beninese people see similarities across categories and cultures. For my Beninese friends and informants, witchcraft is a universal phenomenon that encompasses science, religion, and moral philosophy. In reporting on these connections, along with accounts of my own experiences, I hope to offer outsiders a view from within the Beninese occult world, thereby reducing the divisive foreignness with which Westerners treat African occult practices and beliefs.

Finding the Occult in Benin

One sweltering afternoon in July 2008, I was finishing an interview in the town of Bohicon when I received a call from my friend Odette, who worked at a radio station in Abomey. She said frantically, "Douglas, come down to the station quickly! They've caught some witches, and they're going to put them on the air!" I was ten kilometers away, but I quickly jumped on a *zemijā* (mototaxi) and headed for Abomey. When I arrived at the radio station, there was already a crowd of twenty to thirty people, many of them staff of the station, but several others wandered in off the street. A small dejected woman of about sixty years old sat on a chair in the hot sun, along with two quiet girls around seven and ten years old. As usual during tense and emotional moments, several people were speaking at once, and I had trouble making sense of the situation. I found Odette, and she and one of the journalists filled me in on what was happening. They told me that the woman and girls were witches and that one of the men talking to the crowd was the son of the delegate (a municipal official) from a nearby village. The delegate's son and several other people were responsible for bringing the three accused witches to the radio station. Apparently, the previous day the woman was passing through the village on her way from Bohicon to another village when night fell, and she needed a place to stay. She inquired at the house of the delegate, whose role obliges him to provide hospitality to strangers in need. He offered to lodge the woman for the night, but while she was arranging her things in preparation to sleep, a small calabash fell out of her clothing. The delegate saw the calabash, immediately recognizing it as the *àzĕ-ká* (witchcraft calabash) carried by witches, and he called others to join him in taking the woman into custody. They questioned her about her activities, and she admitted to being an *àzètɔ́* (witch). Furthermore, she also admitted to initiating two young girls who were distant relatives of hers into the witch society. In the morning, the delegate's son and some others located the two girls and escorted all three of them to the radio station in Abomey. Odette informed me that they had all confessed to being *àzètɔ́* and that they were prepared to go on the radio to discuss their crimes.

Most of the people gathering at the station showed considerable excitement and disgust, recounting pieces of the morning's events while sucking their teeth and commenting on how sad and cruel *àzĕ* can be. After about twenty minutes, several reporters invited the three accused witches and the people who accompanied them behind the building, where they could conduct the interview away from the noise and distraction of the crowd. Since I knew people at the station, and Odette put in a word for me, the reporters allowed me to attend the interview, though I also obtained permission from the three accused *àzètɔ́* to attend the meeting and to record my own copy of the interview that the reporters conducted. When the interview began, the reporter questioned the woman first. She confessed to killing a number of people in her life and to having inducted the two girls into the group. She was timid, frail, and soft-spoken, and the way her eyes scanned, searching left and right, made me think she was anxious and scared. When the girls were interviewed, the older one spoke more, since the younger girl seemed intimidated or confused by the commotion around her. But what the girls confirmed is that they were visited in their dreams by the older woman and that she had led them to the nocturnal feasts where they consumed people's souls. The children confessed to having killed three of their classmates. Everyone in attendance was awed by the confessions and even more stunned by the young age of these supposed witches. When the interview was over one of the reporters called the old woman over to him and grabbed her hand. Though she did not appear completely willing, she complied with the request. The man took a stick and repeatedly hit her hands sharply. The woman flinched and cried out slightly but did not struggle to get free. I was disturbed and turned to another reporter beside me to ask why the man was hitting her. He answered that this was a usual form of punishment and that the accused woman expected this.

Though I saw the three presumed *àzètɔ́* with my own eyes and heard the testimony and confessions with my own ears, I found the experience confusing and unsettling. From the expressions of excitement and alarm among the crowd, I gathered that everyone present viewed this as an especially distressing example of the dangerous and baffling powers of witchcraft. This type of confession and direct confrontation is far from a daily occurrence in Benin, but the event is emblematic of Beninese people's fear of and preoccupations with invisible and incomprehensible evil forces, which they often say are disproportionately wielded by women. The event raises difficult questions about reality and the anthropologist's relationship with the "Other." Encounters like these, with foreign gods and occult practices, constitute some of the most challenging cross-cultural experiences with which anthropologists must contend, because these experiences force us to engage with the lived worlds of people who may appear drastically different from ourselves. Nevertheless, my aim in this work is to explore the Beninese people's concepts of witchcraft and sorcery in their own terms in an attempt to find common ground across cultural difference.

In the formative years of my research among the Fon people in Abomey (1998–2000) I tended to overlook religious and supernatural issues. My lack of interest in religion may appear surprising, given that Benin is known worldwide as the cradle of Voodoo (called Vodun in Benin). How could I go to Benin and avoid investigating secret societies, spirit possession, magical formulae, and mystical powers? At the time, my avoidance of these topics was largely due to my focus on studying gender and marriage relations. Further- more, in my life in the United States, I practiced no religion and had no real exposure to belief in gods or spiritual entities. In short, spiritual concerns seemed peripheral to my task. In my writing that came out of that research, I did take account of spiritual practices, but it was an admittedly brief overview of the religious and supernatural domains of Fon culture.

When I finally began studying occult dimensions of Beninese life, my study was the product of a confluence of factors. In 2006, though I was still con- cerned with gender and marriage, I began a new direction in my fieldwork, looking specifically at the interaction between Christianity and polygynous marriage in Benin (Falen 2008). I immediately discovered that one cannot understand African Christianity without acknowledging the role of witch- craft, since the fear of witches is the principal force driving people toward the varied and proliferating churches in Benin. At the same time, I encoun- tered unsolicited testimonials from my Beninese friends about their children being killed by witches. I also heard countless stories of a novel development whereby children were themselves becoming witches, rather than merely the victims they had been some years earlier. Although witchcraft had always been a topic of discussion, when comparing my experiences with those from before, I found that talk about witchcraft had grown to startling proportions. It became clear that Beninese people were experiencing what Adam Ashforth (2005) calls "spiritual insecurity." Though these influences attracted my inter- est in the occult, I had not yet committed to pursuing it as a topic of research.

As it often happens during fieldwork, it was an unexpected experience and the urging of a Beninese friend that ultimately led me to undertake this study of the occult in southern Benin. In May 2006 I arrived in the Fon ethnic group's cultural capital of Abomey and learned that an elderly friend of mine had recently died and that his family was preparing to hold elaborate funeral ceremonies. He had been an important man in a royal Fon family, bearing the title of Daǎ (an honorific term for a household head). It was through the old man that I became friends with two of his sons. I had previously lived with his son David in a nearby village for about six months in 1999.[1] When I visited in

2006 it was my first time returning to Benin in four years, and I was saddened by the news that met me. Although I had not known the old man intimately, I used to visit him regularly, often dropping by as I passed by his home, offering him a small gift in deference to his age and for the paternal role he played in helping me find a place to live during my research.

After I learned about the funeral, Gaston, the elder of the two sons and a middle-school geography teacher in his forties, immediately invited me to participate in the two-week ceremony, asking me to assume the role of one of the Daǎ's twenty children. He saw this as an opportunity to honor the connection I had enjoyed with the Daǎ's family and to offer me a rare glimpse into Fon royal religious and social life. Although my research activities did not permit me to attend the entirety of the lengthy rituals, over the course of the next ten days, I visited the family almost daily, participating in various events with my adoptive siblings. Gaston loaned me a length of the cloth whose pattern he and his siblings had chosen as the uniform for the funeral ceremonies. Bare-chested and with the cloth wrapped around my waist, I joined the Daǎ's other children dancing to drum rhythms into the early morning hours in front of the assembled family and guests. I listened to griots singing about the departed household leader, and I joined the crowd in viewing his body, adorned with a collection of cloths to accompany him into the afterlife.[2] I followed the others who kneeled before the body, and I participated with the delegations of related families in offering coins during the family prayers.

Over the course of these rites, I was also given access to a few private aspects of religious life. For example, I attended the burial and observed the hidden tomb dug out like a tunnel to the side of the burial pit, since a Daǎ's resting place must never be apparent from the surface. I also heard discussion about the location of a second, private interment of the Daǎ's true power and soul in the form of his nails and hair, which must be buried separately from his body in a location known only to close family members. The importance of secrets, hidden knowledge, and mysterious powers so prevalent in southern Benin became clearer to me during the funeral as I sat talking with Gaston, his siblings, and other friends at moments between the rites. In addition to discussing some less public aspects of funerary traditions, conversations often turned to the occult. Gaston and his brother David, also a schoolteacher, told me about the power to make corpses speak, but only if the person had died from a lightning strike. In fact, they told me that when their father's body was in the morgue awaiting the start of the ceremonies, some thieves came to collect parts of the corpse to use in magical rituals, but lightning struck and killed the thieves. Their bodies were ritually awakened, and they confessed to their attempted crime. David told me he had personally witnessed a corpse made to speak in this manner.

Another magical matter arose at one point during the ceremonies when a rain shower began suddenly, interrupting the scheduled events and generating discussion about what precautions had been taken to prevent this disturbance by the weather. Gaston informed me that he had entrusted the task to one of his brothers, who had hired a specialist to protect the funeral from rain, an especially important responsibility during the rainy season's heavy downpours in the months of May and June. But there were questions about the specialist's skill, and a frustrated Gaston claimed he would have to find somebody else to do the job right. He said he knew an old man from the outlying town of Djidja who mastered the power of leaves and magical spells, the power known as *bŏ* in the Fon language. He eventually introduced me to the man and asked him to provide us with the formula for stopping the rains (see chapter 1). The man showed us several leaves and demonstrated the procedure for invoking their powers and hiding them in a nearby tree. He promised us that rain would never fall until he removed the *bŏ*. The next day, the man's promise was tested, as ominous storm clouds gathered during one of the rituals. A strong wind howled and bent the trees as a few large drops of rain started falling. But within minutes the dark clouds passed, the wind subsided, and no more than a few raindrops ever fell. Gaston said matter-of-factly that what we had just witnessed was impressive but not unusual in Africa. He repeated a common refrain that I have heard many times, that Africans have special knowledge of plants, nature, and mystical forces that allows them to do extraordinary things. But he added that, as an anthropologist, my mission should be to investigate these African secrets and introduce them to America. He claimed that what we had seen were scientifically verifiable properties found in nature and that by recording the formulae in academic publications we could put such knowledge in the hands of humanity. He added that the old man from Djidja was a perfect example of someone possessing this scientific knowledge but that in order to truly control these forces the man is also likely to be a *sorcier* (French for "witch/magician/sorcerer").

Though I had had many discussions about the occult in previous years, Gaston's insistence that I should study it, along with my observations of witchcraft's growing prominence, tipped the balance.[3] Once I had accepted the task, I quickly came to understand that witchcraft, or whatever name we choose to call it, is undeniably the most significant social force in Benin and one that I could no longer ignore. Following this realization, I devoted some time during my 2006 field season to asking people about their beliefs and experiences with the occult. I followed this with more directed interviews during three subsequent month-long field visits in 2008, 2009, and 2012. I concentrated on the two geographic areas where I had the most contacts and experience: the metropole of Cotonou and the rural and semiurban region in and around the towns of Abomey and Bohicon. However, I also visited people in Ouidah and Porto-Novo. During my 2008 visit I interviewed people from a wide range of occupations, ages, and religious backgrounds in order to understand their views of witchcraft, who witches are, and what they do. In my 2009 field season I concentrated my investigation on traditional healers and their efforts to combat and exorcise witchcraft, since the business of healing is integrally related to the growing prevalence of witchcraft fears and accusations. In 2012 I collected information about the relationship of Vodun and witchcraft and about foreign esoteric societies that are often classified as witchcraft. This book is the compilation of findings and perspectives garnered in part through fieldwork and relationships that began in 1996, though most of the specific information was obtained in the more recent field seasons, which produced a total of 141 interviews (as well as numerous informal discussions) with pastors, teachers, business owners, mothers, fathers, farmers, healers, and many others. Although I conducted interviews with rural inhabitants, many informants were educated urbanites whose unambiguous acceptance of witchcraft's existence should call into question Western stereotypes that belief in occult powers is confined to poor, marginalized, unsophisticated, rural individuals. I agree with Peter Geschiere (1997) that, rather than being solely a "traditional" belief confined to rural villages, African witchcraft is also very much a part of the modern urban world.

Secrecy, Occult Fears, and the Discourse of Witchcraft

As elsewhere in Africa, witchcraft and sorcery in the Republic of Benin are unavoidable phenomena and hot topics of conversation (Henry 2008b). But the presence of a foreigner prompts questions about the relationship between researcher and informant and about the ability to penetrate a world of guarded esoteric knowledge. While I believe I was successful at achieving familiarity with local notions of magic and the supernatural, given the dramatic and devastating results of occult activities, it should be unsurprising that people sometimes expressed reticence in discussing these sensitive topics. In particular, women showed greater disinclination to talk about witchcraft. Granted, part of my research focused on healers (most of whom are men), so I spoke with more male than female informants, but I also felt that women either showed less knowledge or were less forthcoming about the details of occult matters. Perhaps their reserve was well founded, since women are more frequently accused of witchcraft, whereas male healers who possess occult knowledge are typically regarded as benevolent (see chapter 1).

Though Westerners might hold a curiosity about exotic magical or occult phenomena, Beninese witchcraft and sorcery are more than quaint folklore. The occult is part of people's everyday lives, but it is extraordinarily serious business that can inspire great fear. Informants were often afraid that by talking about occult powers or by revealing secret knowledge, they might put themselves or me in danger. For example, when I told an auto mechanic in Cotonou about my research, he vehemently declined to participate, saying he knew nothing and had no interest in talking about witchcraft. He explained that he might talk to me later in a different place, but not in public. A Cotonou artist expressed similar reservations, declining even to give me his name for fear that the witches in his family would overhear him and take vengeance. This response was based on the widespread claim that witches have the ability to listen in on distant conversations through use of a supernatural "antenna" that allows them to monitor their enemies' activities. However, not everyone was so tight-lipped. Despite a few misgivings, many other informants were longtime friends offering candid views of the occult, like Gaston, who adopted my research as his own pet project. In general, I found that many people discussed the occult frequently and openly, perhaps reassured by my outsider status that I would not use the knowledge against them.

For those friends who expressed fear, many directed their concerns toward me, suggesting that I should be careful about probing too deeply lest a disgruntled witch feel threatened by my research and take supernatural measures to silence me (see Stoller and Olkes 1987). People cautioned me against asking questions too bluntly and too openly, and even those who recognize Westerners' disbelief in witchcraft suggested that they should still be careful in Africa, especially in Benin. My adoptive Beninese mother, Mouni, stated that associating with healers and ritual specialists put me at risk of contracting witchcraft (as I later learned, several people suspected that I had become a witch). But Gaston responded to Mouni, saying that I was relatively well integrated into Beninese society and that people trusted me enough to allow me to ask questions without launching any magical injunctions against me. Even if his statement were accurate and not mere flattery, I did take pains to avoid arousing animosity, in part for my own protection. But I also trod gingerly on the path of the occult out of respect for people's anxiety and for the sanctity of their supernatural secrets. For example, I have been offered initiation in various religious groups, including the witchcraft society, but I have declined all such invitations in order to preserve my status as an outsider who is less of a threat. Gaston told me that patience is an asset because it helps gain the trust of religious leaders. And Gaston's friend Serge, a Vodun priest, praised me for maintaining a calm detachment, as opposed to intruding in secret societies or seeking to acquire sacred knowledge. Following an interview with a group of religious specialists, Serge approvingly recalled me declaring to them, "Acè bá n ḍe ǎ" (I'm not seeking power). I never asked for demonstrations of witchcraft powers or for magical formulae (though informants occasionally offered these of their own volition); instead, I collected ordinary expressions of discourse about occult ideas and behaviors. Although I did interview healers and some other ritual leaders, the information I gathered does not constitute a practitioner's knowledge; instead, it is probably similar to that accessible to an ordinary Beninese person who takes an interest in the occult.

While the information I report is not necessarily secret, this book is a wide-ranging and systematic assemblage of my observations and people's statements and views about the supernatural. Of course, because people could have been wary about disclosing sacred knowledge to me, they might have intentionally distorted their testimony. Even without intentional subterfuge, discourse is inherently messy and contradictory, challenging our attempts to generalize or establish consensus. Nevertheless, to the extent possible, I consider this an accurate representation of the range of southern Beninese ideas and practices related to witchcraft, magic, and healing. Rather than portray the occult with broad, crude brushstrokes that gloss over gaps between data points, I have attempted to reproduce some of the disordered details. This, I hope, offers a richer portrayal of informants' disagreements and contradictions, but, like a pointillist painting, it also allows the reader to step back and see the larger picture of the occult in Benin.

Terminological Concerns

Beninese people refer to supernatural abilities or mystical forces as magic, science, religion, witchcraft, or sorcery, and they are at the core of life in the Republic of Benin. What I refer to as the occult dimension of these forces occurs in two basic forms, called *bŏ* and *àzě* in the Fon language used throughout the southern part of the country. *Bŏ* are essentially magical charms and formulae, while *àzě* consists of a psychic ability to perform superhuman acts and to consume people's souls. In African studies, the "occult" has been used to refer to evil and negative acts, such as the destructive witchcraft found in

Benin, but also to human sacrifice, zombification, and the trade in body parts. While I might classify these latter practices within the occult, they are not a major part of the discourse in Benin; therefore, my use of "occult" in this work refers mainly to *bŏ* and *àzĕ*. Furthermore, in recognizing the possibility that occult studies will contribute to the exoticism or negative image of Africa, I wish to stress that the morality of *bŏ* and *àzĕ* is viewed with considerable ambivalence; therefore, I do not equate the "occult" with purely malevolent forces (see Ranger 2007; ter Haar and Ellis 2009). It may be problematic to use an all-encompassing term like "religion" to refer to a broad range of magico-religious customs, including both the occult and the worship of deities, but I will show how some of those differences melt away in certain contexts (Meyer 2009; ter Haar and Ellis 2009).

People who wield the power of *bŏ* are called *botɔ́* in Fon, while those possessing *àzĕ* are *àzètɔ́*. Both of these terms can be translated as "witch" or "sorcerer," though *àzĕ* is usually more powerful and more consistent with what I will call witchcraft, and this work will focus especially on *àzĕ*. *Àzĕ* is said to be responsible primarily for killing family members, ruining businesses, and causing illness. The mystical forces of *bŏ* and *àzĕ* invade families and overlap with politics, business, and religion. For many people, occult power is the source of misery, fear, financial ruin, and death. But for others, it is also the source of creativity, pride, religious faith, and spiritual commerce; such people say witchcraft can heal illness or bring luck and success. The occult also bears a key social and cosmological message as a reminder of the presence of both good and evil in the world.

Whenever anthropologists write about their fieldwork using a language different from the one spoken by their informants, they run the risk of distorting people's understandings of their world. In my case, this risk is especially pronounced for the following three reasons. First, during many of my interviews, my informants and I used a combination of French and Fon languages, and I occasionally relied on Beninese friends to translate parts of our discussions in Fon. Therefore, in addition to the usual problems posed by writing a book in a language other than the research language, distortion might arise from the alternation between languages and from the additional filter of translation between Fon and French. Second, as noted above, occult secrets are jealously guarded, which means total consensus is unlikely. Despite some common patterns, there is significant heterogeneity in people's notions of these phenomena, rendering ethnographic accounts potentially reductionist. Third, the topic of the supernatural has a particularly confusing history in the anthropology of Africa, and with good reason. The terminologies and related

conceptualizations of "witchcraft" and "sorcery" in Western academic literature are not always consistent; nor are they necessarily true to African sensibilities (Pels 1998; J. Rush 1974). We cannot be confident that the words we use
to describe African occult practices accurately convey indigenous people's
views. Furthermore, it would be wrong to suggest that members of a society
all agree on the meanings of words they use among themselves. Witchcraft
and sorcery terminology can be confusing within the Fon language, as well as
between Fon, French, and English.

One problem is how to deal with the fact that English has two words, witchcraft and sorcery, whereas Beninese frequently use the French word *la sorcellerie* to translate both witchcraft and sorcery (see Moore and Sanders 2001).
E. E. Evans-Pritchard ([1937] 1976) famously distinguished between witchcraft
and sorcery among the Azande, who have two separate concepts for magical
acts. The first, which Evans-Pritchard labeled witchcraft, was a psychic, involuntary, invisible force that brought harm to people. The second, which he
called sorcery, consisted of intentional, tangible, and learned procedures for
manipulating supernatural forces. While this distinction has long served as
a starting point for anthropological discussions of witchcraft and sorcery in
Africa, in truth the distinction rarely holds up to cross-cultural comparison,
and anthropologists do not always use the terms consistently (Turner 1964).

With respect to Benin, we might ask a number of questions: Is there always
a clearly defined distinction between witchcraft and sorcery in the way that
Evans-Pritchard ([1937] 1976) defined them? How do we discriminate termi-
nologically between benevolent and malevolent magical acts? What is the difference between a witch, a healer, a sorcerer, and a wizard (see Middleton and
Winter 1963a, 3)? And perhaps most importantly, given the African context,
it is worth asking what differences exist between witchcraft and the domains
we label religion, magic, and science. Although I make no claim of having
solved the terminological dilemma or of being able to portray African witchcraft in an "authentic" fashion, I do argue that much academic writing has
failed to represent African supernatural worlds in a way that bridges cultural
gaps or in a way that problematizes simplistic characterizations of "witchcraft." I believe some of these distortions arise from the fact that Western
academic and folk notions tend to distinguish the occult too facilely from religion and science, such that the occult is irrevocably relegated to the domain
of the imaginary (see Pocock 1972).

For one thing, Western views take religion for granted and, in Durkheimian fashion, as something that serves a purpose. Although a similar functionalist approach characterized witchcraft studies of the mid-twentieth century,

a fundamental difference between the treatment of witchcraft and religion is that witchcraft is often singled out as imaginary—an unreal, irrational (and implicitly "primitive") response to life's problems. Contemporary scholars often portray African witchcraft as a sign of tension, disharmony, and social decay, which is in stark contrast to the academic treatment of official religion. Why is "religious" belief portrayed as distinct from "witchcraft" and immune to skepticism? What difference exists between witchcraft and religion, other than the fact that religions typically have institutional and even governmental legitimacy? My aim here is not to question the legitimacy of religion but rather to highlight the fact that distinguishing religion from the occult may contribute to judgmental attitudes about the difference between Africa and the West.

In the West, the idea of magic carries a performative connotation, which suggests illusion, deception, and sleight of hand. A trick, by definition, is something that is unreal and appears to do something recognized as impossible or false. For my Beninese informants, Western magic performances present a conundrum to muddy the waters around witchcraft. There is a divergence of opinion among my informants, with some suggesting that Western magic is equivalent to witchcraft, while others argue that such shows amount to nothing more than commercialized illusions. Despite the usual secrecy enshrouding acts of witchcraft, some informants pointed out that African witches can perform similar demonstrations to prove to me that witchcraft exists. They also noted the magical qualities of the theatrical performances by the Beninese secret society of Zǎgbétɔ́, guardians of the night who transform ducks into turtles beneath a dancing straw tent. Some said the Zǎgbétɔ́ are a money-making theater group that uses illusion, although others contended that the Zǎgbétɔ́ really do have mystical, perhaps witchlike, powers that they cannot fully reveal in public. Although Westerners may perceive the claims about African witches as distinct from magic routines, there is much more ambivalence among Beninese respondents.

Science is another domain that, in comparison to witchcraft, generally goes unquestioned by Westerners. Among academics, science is often viewed as inherently rational, while witchcraft is implicitly portrayed as irrational. Though the existence of witchcraft is continually subjected to scrutiny among scholars, most of them are unlikely to question the reality of science. To the average Western onlooker, witchcraft is based on faith, fear, and imagination, and science is founded on observable, reproducible experimentation. Although Evans-Pritchard (1935, [1937] 1976) made great strides in recognizing the logical and rational basis of Azande occult beliefs, his bias in favor of observable phenomena led him to conclude that sorcery exists, while witch-craft does not. Thus emerged a pattern of depicting witchcraft *belief* as real but witchcraft itself as imaginary (ter Haar 2007). While many academic works explicitly or implicitly declare witchcraft's nonexistence, I have never met a Beninese of any religion, occupation, or educational level who denies its existence. Furthermore, when I asked my Beninese friends and informants a broad question like "what is witchcraft?" a common refrain was that witch-craft is a "science," often likened to Western technological inventions such as cell phones, airplanes, and computers. Some acknowledged a difference between the two systems of knowledge, claiming that white people possess science, whereas Africans possess witchcraft. But in the next breath, most people labeled the former "white people's witchcraft" and the latter "African science" (see Ashforth 2005). According to the Western model, science and witchcraft are incompatible, despite the fact that both rely on specialized training and experimentation, resulting in fantastic acts. It is the ambivalence characterizing both the distinction and the convergence between the notions of the occult and technology that shape the arguments of this book.

In order to unsettle the presumed distinctions between Western domains of belief, when I refer to witchcraft throughout this work, I intentionally in-tersperse indigenous words (*àzě* and *bǒ*) with English terms (witchcraft and sorcery) while also drawing on meanings implied by words like technology, supernatural, occult, mysticism, spirituality, nature, philosophy, magic, med-icine, religion, and yes, even science. I believe that none of these terms alone is sufficient to capture how Beninese people view these forces. To reduce the entire constellation of conceptions to witchcraft runs the risk of essentializing all acts as negative and imaginary. Yet to label everything as science or tech-nology has the opposite effect of suggesting that everything is plain, visible, and true, which would ignore the fact that Beninese people themselves are constantly questioning what is real or unreal, what is natural or supernatural. Occasionally, Beninese claim to know how a particular effect is produced, whereas at other times they do not. By using a variety of English and Fon words and occasionally their French equivalents, I hope to disrupt the com-mon understandings of these terms in English, allowing us to see Beninese concepts, as well as our own, in a new light. As Eduardo Viveiros de Castro argues, "A good translation is one that allows the alien concepts to deform and subvert the translator's conceptual toolbox so that the *intentio* of the orig-inal language can be expressed within the new one" (2004, 5). In casting *àzě* as science, religion, medicine, and magic, I endeavor to convey its multiplic-ity of meanings, as well as the deeply contested sense of these forces in Benin.

African Science

Blurring the lines between religion, science, and magic could make some fervent rationalists and theologians uncomfortable. Indeed, the majority academic opinion holds that witchcraft is imaginary; therefore, the belief in such supernatural forces is irrational. As philosophers Barry Hallen and J. Olubi Sodipo (1997) point out, Western scholars express embarrassment about the history of witches in the West; witches are a mark of shame on an otherwise rational culture. Hallen and Sodipo note that clinical psychologists and other scholars interpret witchcraft confession as a psychological product of frustration among subordinate groups or, worse, of mental illness. Current anthropological scholarship often depicts witchcraft as a metaphor for social turmoil, finding a language that makes sense to our scientific sensibilities but that does not automatically demonstrate an acceptance of native belief as true. In an earlier anthropology, and still in Western folk ideology, magic was portrayed as a crutch for an inferior mind, or at least as an impoverished explanation in the absence of a "true" scientific understanding (Malinowski 1948; Thomas 1971). In a word, witchcraft and magic became "superstition." By contrast, Christianity and other religions of the developed world receive little of this critical attention. But as my informants' testimony shows, the boundary between magic and religion is exceedingly porous, a position advanced by other writers. Randall Styers (2004), for example, notes that, despite repeated attempts, the literature on religion and magic betrays a long history of failed efforts to define these terms and their separate domains. The conundrum is so vexing that Claude Lévi-Strauss concluded, "There is no religion without magic any more than there is magic without at least a trace of religion" (1966, 221). Stanley Jeyaraja Tambiah (1990, 19) tracks the origins of the distinction between magic and religion in Christian theological debates. He notes that when Protestants were distancing themselves from what they saw as the magical rituals of Catholicism, they introduced a distinction between prayer and spell, the former characterizing religion, and the latter being a feature of magic. Tambiah notes that these concepts were later adopted by Edward Burnett Tylor (1871) and James George Frazer (1890) and incorporated into the anthropological canon.

To the question of why academics continue to use the term "magic," Randall Styers argues, "One of the primary functions of magic in this scholarly literature has been to serve as a foil for religion. . . . Magic is 'the bastard sister of religion'" (2004, 6). Styers states that modernity itself has been defined by the creation of discursive boundaries between "primitive" magic on one side and "modern" science and religion on the other. Magical thought is usually attributed to colonized peoples, the former "primitives" and "savages" of an earlier anthropology. The presumed illegitimacy of magic is marshaled in the effort to define the West as "modern" and therefore superior to "traditional" societies.[4] And anthropologists themselves are not immune to these othering tendencies. Byron Good (1994), citing Wilfred Cantwell Smith's (1977) linguistic history of the word "belief," holds that anthropology's language of "belief" implies doubt or falsehood, often in contrast to Western "knowledge" or "truth." This is ironic, given anthropologists' usual mission of withholding judgment of other cultures. But it is also emblematic of our instinct to defend our ontological turf, giving us the satisfaction of presenting our own position as the correct one.

As for magic and science, there is a similar tendency to take the distinction for granted. Academics brought up in a Western scientific paradigm are socialized to regard science as the ultimate source of truth, in contrast to the superstition of magical systems of thought. But philosophers have criticized this tendency. Though controversial, Robin Horton's (1967a) position is that traditional African religious thought holds many similarities to scientific thinking (see also Capra 1975). Addressing African spiritual beliefs, Horton writes:

> How could primitives believe that a visible, tangible object was at once its solid self and the manifestation of an immaterial being? How could a man literally see a spirit in a stone? These puzzles, raised so vividly by Lévy-Bruhl, have never been satisfactorily solved by anthropologists. "Mystical thinking" has remained uncomfortably, indigestibly *sui generis*. And yet these questions of Lévy-Bruhl's have a very familiar ring in the context of European philosophy. Indeed, if we substitute atoms and molecules for gods and spirits, these turn out to be the very questions . . . posed by modern scientific theory in the minds of Berkeley, Locke, Quine, and a whole host of European philosophers from Newton's time onwards. (1967a, 52)

Horton (1967a, 54) goes on to suggest that both scientists and African diviners display similar thought processes and the use of theory in order to explain events. Indeed, my own data tend to confirm Horton's assessment of the resemblance between scientific and magical thought, in that Beninese people are not merely slaves to tradition; instead, they constantly doubt what they see and hear, and they test different ingredients, procedures, and ritual specialists and then evaluate the results. Horton's philosophical approach to science and spirituality is entirely consistent with Beninese people's own theory as evidenced in the supercategory àzě, which combines science, magic, and religion. Following this model, in the way that Karin Barber (1981) contends that African gods are invented by humans in search of concrete results, people are free to abandon any diviner or healer who is unable to satisfy their needs. Thus, even in the supernatural realms, African thought demonstrates a practical, materialistic, and critical approach to life (Mbiti 1969).

Despite these lessons on the similarities between different knowledge systems, Ghanaian philosopher Kwame Anthony Appiah (1992) contends that science exhibits greater emphasis on systematic experimentation, information dissemination, repeatability, and the development of alternative theories. While he acknowledges that scientists are far from totally neutral, he suggests that religious thought is more concerned with meaning and values than is science. He identifies some of the possible factors for these differences in industrial societies' development of social mobility, individualism, and literacy, all of which promote debates over contrasting ideas. Horton (1967b) himself draws a distinction between the "open" scientific outlook and the "closed" outlook of traditional African thought. Although part 1 of Horton's article argues for the similarities between scientific and spiritual thought, part 2 hedged on these claims by declaring that African thought does not allow for self-critique or the abandonment of a failed theory in the way that science does. But like Andrew Apter (1992), I argue that African ritual and spiritual thought *do* allow for self-reflection, critique, and even the abandonment of theory. Within African systems of thought lies the potential for dramatic change and transformation, and this transformative potential is at the heart of àzě. Àzě is constantly reworking the political and religious landscape while also being reworked itself through the articulation with Vodun and other religions and through invention and the borrowing of foreign traditions. What remain more fixed are larger paradigms—and this is true for both African and scientific systems of thought (Appiah 1992). Accordingly, we can recognize that in Africa, whatever experiences people have are unlikely to cause them to forsake their resolve that spiritual and supernatural forces exist.

Scientists are likewise resistant to the abandonment of science and rationality in the face of failed experiments. Thomas Kuhn (1962) was one of the first to introduce the idea that scientists are themselves embedded in a social and psychological mindset that makes them resistant to new paradigms that are inconsistent with their standpoint. Although Kuhn's theories allow for scientific shifts, they remind us that science, like religion, is supported by a degree of faith. Regarding contemporary Western faith in science, Tambiah writes: "A commitment to the notion of nature as the ground of causality can function as a belief system without its guaranteeing a verified 'objective truth' as modern science may define it" (1990, 10). Too little attention is paid to the magical thinking and faith associated with Western science (see Verrips 2003). Many researchers talk about the "occult imaginary," but few interrogate the "scientific imaginary." However, following Kuhn, some scholars in the field of science studies (e.g., Bruno Latour) have questioned science's privileged claim to a single reality. These debates, popularly dubbed the "science wars," reflected the tension between science's positing of an independent natural world and the postmodern argument that science is itself rooted in culture and therefore a social construction (Latour 1988, 1993). There is much about the world and the human body of which doctors and scientists are ignorant. We know little about how drugs operate, how the brain works, or the creation of the universe. And even what we think we know from science is constructed via particular instruments, language, and cultural learning. So while I agree with Horton and Appiah that science and magic may not be identical, there may be more resemblance than people are comfortable with or accustomed to admitting. Those who subscribe to Horton's general message make the case that the boundaries between religion, magic, and science are a product of mythmaking, and the myth is founded on particular social and political agendas related to an enduring discomfort among Westerners with seeing the Self and Other as one.

Horton makes another important point, claiming that academics often overlook examples of overtly magico-spiritual thinking in their own societies. While professional scientists may scoff at magical thinking, they ignore just how much folk culture embraces and celebrates it. Indeed, magical thought was never vanquished in the West, and scholars have observed that societies the world over are experiencing a reenchantment (Geschiere 1997, 2000; Meyer and Pels 2003; Taylor 2008; van Binsbergen 2001). New Age religion and Wicca are some recent examples of the ways that Westerners have embraced the possibility of mystical powers, demonstrating the difficulty in separating magic from religion. Furthermore, popular culture is filled with a fascination with mystical and fantastic powers, from Harry Potter, to Voodoo dolls, to films and television shows about vampires, superheroes, psychics, and time-travelers. Science fiction has always skirted the fringe between magical fiction and scientific reality. For example, the 1960s TV series *Star Trek* anticipated many innovations like cell phones, teleconferencing, voice-activated computers, and noninvasive medical devices. One could argue that inventions that seem purely imaginary today may actually be possible in the future. In fact,

Frances Yates (1964, cited in Tambiah 1990, 29) proposes that magical thought was actually the inspiration and catalyst for the development of the scientific movement during the Enlightenment. Thus, alchemy and other practices that we now consider pseudoscience were very much part of the rich and productive intellectual climate of the Enlightenment. Today, *Star Wars* and other films depict Jedi knights and superheroes with godlike powers, and these characters come closest to Beninese conceptions of àzètɔ́ (witches). Although the figure of the "witch" is a much regretted chapter in the history of Western civilization, one way we might view the witchcraft phenomenon is through reference to images that are pervasive in our society. Just as Darth Vader was seduced by the dark side in *Star Wars*, Beninese worry that religious leaders and others believed to possess àzĕ will turn to evil. The moral messages conveyed by our superhero stories, about the battle between good and evil and the corrupting influence of ultimate power, are the same as those found in accounts of àzètɔ́. But although such characters are generally relegated to a fictional existence in the West, I must stress that my Beninese friends see them as terribly real. Thus, comparison to Western fictional characters may provide an opening to understanding other belief systems, but they cannot take us all the way. This is why I maintain that to understand witchcraft among Beninese, we must also take seriously their claims that science and witchcraft occupy similar domains and that they represent similar modes of knowledge.

Goals of the Book

When one understands the simultaneous juxtaposition and merging of science and witchcraft in Africa, it becomes evident that anthropological studies have missed something in their characterization of occult forces. I believe a key objective of anthropological study is the rapprochement of peoples and cultures, but the divide between Africa and the West remains vast when it comes to witchcraft. In addition to the widespread disbelief in witchcraft expressed in academic discourse, Western news headlines sensationalize the stories of child witches in Africa (Houreld 2009; Karimi 2009; Oppenheimer 2010), and human rights groups argue against the mistreatment of accused witches. Yet in a number of African nations, the acceptance of witchcraft's reality is so pervasive that courts regularly hear witchcraft cases and sentence accused witches (Geschiere and Fisiy 1994). To the average European or American, such events are unimaginable, or perhaps it is more accurate to say they are *only* imaginable, because witchcraft appears so far from reality.

My intent is not to try to convince readers of the existence of witchcraft, nor is my position a claim of authority to define reality. Instead, I hope the contribution of this book is to destabilize common perceptions of witchcraft and shed light on how Beninese people see and experience occult forces. Doing this might help remove some of the stigma and the exotic perception of African people's mystical worlds. Readers might understandably want to know whether I actually "believe" in witchcraft (see Viveiros de Castro 2013). In fact, some Beninese informants interpreted my research as a quest for proof of witchcraft, as if I were a messenger who could show Americans that witchcraft is real. In some ways, this was Gaston's desire, which will have to remain unfulfilled for now, since I did not witness many demonstrations (and I never sought them). Moreover, those informants trying to protect esoteric knowledge might have seen my inquiries as a quest to appropriate their knowledge and power, leading them to distrust me. In any event, I usually explained that I was neither trying to prove witchcraft's reality nor trying to make off with their secrets. In fact, many of my Beninese friends and informants have never seen explicit proof; instead, they have interpreted misfortune, sudden death, incredible coincidence, and confession as sufficient proof of the existence of invisible forces. As for me, after listening to their accounts and testimonials, I am more receptive to these ideas than before. Over a twenty-year span of working in Benin, with the longest stay of two years, I have come to see many Beninese as close friends and even family. And when these rational, trustworthy friends and family declare the existence of something, I am naturally more inclined to take it seriously than if it came from strangers. As to what I believe, I confess that this remains a struggle for me. In my life in the United States, witches are not real; but, as I describe in chapter 3, while in Benin I found myself occasionally fearful of witchcraft as I was drawn into the perspective of my friends. This has made me sympathetic to the notion of alternate realities (Kapferer 2002), but realities that nevertheless can be bridged through human connection, such as that created through ethnographic fieldwork. After a number of years of close contact with a people and their culture, I have not only begun to appreciate the social conditions that permit people to believe something but have also become sensitive to *how* they believe it on a personal, emotional, and embodied level. Yet, like many of my informants, I cannot blindly accept all claims of supernatural power, so I continue to ask questions and wonder what elements of witchcraft, religion, and science are real, false, hidden, or overt. Because ethnography is inherently about storytelling, I attempt to convey these epistemological and ontological struggles through my own and my informants' accounts of our experiences. I acknowledge that reading ethnography is a far cry from doing ethnography, and so I cannot expect my audience to feel the same transformative effects that I have felt over the course of long-term fieldwork. At the same time, I contend that even receiving a glimpse of Beninese life provided in this book might be enough to provoke thought and raise questions that can unsettle some of what readers take for granted.

However, ethnography is also a social science, so my stories are not meant to inspire exotic or voyeuristic reactions; instead, I hope that a reader can view these phenomena through various theoretical lenses and consider the ramifications of the different perspectives for foreigners' ability to respect and empathize with African people. This book employs a variety of theoretical and methodological approaches coming out of the sociological and anthropological traditions. As a social scientist, I cannot deny some of the social functions (or rather the social effects) of occult behaviors and beliefs. For example, the occult may serve as a leveling mechanism when the fears of envy-inspired witchcraft cause more fortunate individuals to downplay their successes (Rosenthal 1998) or to share their wealth with less fortunate family members (Fisiy 1998). Witchcraft may also serve to promote social conformity and to reduce the expression of hostility (Evans-Pritchard [1937] 1976). It is clear that jealousy, envy, and inequality are key components of the fears and suspicions of witchcraft in Africa, and this observation is made readily by ordinary Beninese people. Following the modernity school in witchcraft studies, I acknowledge the idea that witchcraft and occult fears accompany (or symbolize) the spread of capitalism and the resulting inequality and social upheaval (Comaroff and Comaroff 1993; Taussig 1980).[5] Furthermore, given witchcraft's gender imagery and the fact that accusations are unequally directed at women, feminist perspectives suggest that witchcraft may reflect both male fears of a threatened status quo and the patriarchal power to scapegoat women as witches. I also explore the possibility that the occult expresses Africans' frustration with Western-inspired "development" and a postcolonial desire to offer an African alternative to Western ways of knowing (Falen 2007; Smith 2008; West 2005). Despite the value in these theoretical interpretations, we must use our scientific perspectives cautiously. Bruce Kapferer argues that occult beliefs are too often "boxed away into familiar sociological and rational categories: witchcraft as resistance, witchcraft as the folk explanation of misfortune, or witchcraft and sorcery as types of 'social diagnosis' (Moore and Sanders 2001). The practices are domesticated to the analysts' own sensibilities. There is a tendency towards a too easy glossing of the phenomena in question, a brushing aside of dynamics that are not immediately and externally self-evident" (2002, 20). Therefore, although I acknowledge the utility of our theoretical tools for understanding some aspects of witchcraft, this book also takes inspiration from the phenomenological method pioneered by Jeanne Favret-Saada (1980) and Paul Stoller and Cheryl Olkes (1987) and partially adopted by Harry West (2007) and Adam Ashforth (2005). In anthropology the phenomenological approach typically involves privileging experience and the lived worlds of others, as opposed to abstract theorizing in the anthropologist's intellectual tradition (Desjarlais and Throop 2011; Jackson 2013; Katz and Csordas 2003). Phenomenological anthropology often includes a narrative ethnographic writing style that employs engaging first-person accounts to emphasize bodily or emotional experiences within the fieldwork process (Ram and Houston 2015). While this book is not strictly a phenomenological ethnography, I follow these authors in employing some narrative techniques to demonstrate my perceptions and experiences living in a world inhabited by witches. In other words, I take seriously my Beninese friends' expressions of fear or pride and their testimonies about mystical powers because I believe in the necessity of anchoring my analysis in the beliefs of my Beninese friends and informants and in "taking [my] intellectual cues from their concerns" (Jackson 2013, 254). Apter writes: "Whatever the methodological concern—functionalism with authority, Marxism with contradiction and change, structuralism with binary contrast and equivalence, phenomenology with the construction of experience—the interpretation of cultural forms must begin with the people, not the ethnographer" (1991, 223). Therefore, I have determined that, whatever methodological techniques or theoretical interpretations I employ, I should also write this book in a manner such that my Beninese friends would recognize their views and beliefs in my words. As a result, much of my analysis is inspired by Beninese people's claims that witchcraft is a science with important links to religion, philosophy, and global spiritual movements.

In addition to investigating philosophical questions about science and the occult, this book is about the articulation between the occult and organized religions in Benin, including Christianity and the indigenous polytheistic religion of Vodun, found among the Fon- and Ewe-speaking peoples and related ethnic groups of southern Togo and Benin. In some ways, by highlighting the connections between witchcraft and Vodun, I am in danger of feeding exoticism and popular stereotypes about Vodun and its New World cousin, Voodoo. American popular culture in the form of film, TV, music, and video games depicts these African-based religious traditions as equivalent to black magic and witchcraft. A great deal of scholarship has gone into dispelling this unfortunate conflation, particularly with respect to Haitian Vodou (Brown 2001; Desmangles 1992; Herskovits [1937] 1971). Caribbeanist authors have endeavored to distinguish between serving the legitimate spirits, on the one hand, and seeking to manipulate illegitimate supernatural forces, on the other. I must state early on and emphatically that this same distinction exists in Benin, so it would be a fallacy to claim that practicing the Vodun religion is tantamount to casting evil spells. Ordinary adherents of Vodun (known as Voduisants) do not equate their religion with magic, and even less with nefarious actions. Nevertheless, scholars of Afro-Caribbean religion have acknowledged the blurred lines between the Haitian "good" priest (*hungan*) and "evil" priest (*bocor*) (Brown 2001; Herskovits [1937] 1971), and there are also important links between the legitimate and illegitimate spiritual domains in Benin. This book outlines both distinctions and connections between Vodun and the occult, bringing to light the similarities shared by the Vodun religious tradition and New World Vodou. Perhaps because indigenous religions are in retreat in many African countries, other recent works on African occult forces do not delve deeply into the role of indigenous religions in the occult or into the connections between witchcraft and the organized worship of divinities. Vodun is alive and flourishing in southern Benin, opposing and interacting with other religions and supernatural forces.

One thing this book does not offer is a historical examination of witchcraft and the processes through which Benin developed its own unique characteristics (see Ranger 2007). While that would be a worthy task for a historian, my interest lies more in the ethnographic endeavor and the ways witchcraft ideas are currently marshaled in the quest to respond to life's challenges and opportunities. When possible, I refer to older ethnographic accounts of Benin, but their treatment of witchcraft and the occult is often superficial or nonexistent. Although there appear to be recent and dramatic changes in Beninese understandings of witchcraft, I do not mean to imply that witchcraft is something new. Linguistic cognates of *àzĕ* exist in neighboring languages (*adze* in Ewe and *aje* in Yoruba), demonstrating that the term and the category have old roots in the region.[6] Based on reports from elsewhere in Africa, it is clear that Benin is part of a broader pattern whereby witchcraft articulates with morality, kinship, health, development, and the state. While these features allow witchcraft to transcend the local and engage with globalizing trends and spiritual influences, this is an ethnography of a particular place that should not be considered identical to other parts of Africa.

In many ways, the study of witchcraft is really the study of the whole of a culture, since it touches on many other social fields in southern Benin, including notions of science and causality, family, religion, sexuality, wealth, jealousy, envy, political power, morality, health, and identity. Though I cannot hope to cover each of these issues with equal or comprehensive attention, this book will provide a sense of the important, even seminal, role of witchcraft and the occult in contemporary southern Beninese society. My goal is to weave together a number of threads, namely: (1) witchcraft is perceived as a science, a typically "African" science that inspires pride among residents of this postcolonial nation; (2) like technology, the occult can be applied to both destructive and productive ends, informing Beninese racial comparisons between Africans and foreign others; (3) discourses of witchcraft's good and evil sides reflect an abiding philosophical outlook about duality and cosmic balance; (4) Beninese people's belief in the convergence of science, witchcraft, and religion calls into question Western disciplinary distinctions and creates fertile ground for thinking about alternate realities; and (5) Beninese occult beliefs involve a universal notion of power in the world that includes science, technology, religion, and healing, opening the door for the appropriation of foreign religions and esoteric traditions.

chapter one

Àzĕ and Bŏ

Witchcraft and Sorcery in Benin

People in Benin speak frequently of malevolent individuals and the powers they harness to attack others. In the Fon language of southern Benin, there are two terms for these occult forces, *àzĕ* and *bŏ*, both of which are rendered in French as *la sorcellerie* ("witchcraft" or "sorcery" in English). Benin was a French colony until 1960, and French remains the official language, so most educated people use French terms interchangeably with indigenous ones.[1] As the single French term suggests, both Fon words generally denote mystical, malevolent abilities, but Beninese typically point out that the two phenomena are different. In fact, in some ways *àzĕ* and *bŏ* correspond to E. E. Evans-Pritchard's ([1937] 1976) account of the Azande distinction between witchcraft and sorcery. In this chapter, I relate Fon terms to Evans-Pritchard's conceptual dyad for defining the two varieties of magic and describe how people acquire and use these powers to kill, protect, and manipulate the world to their advantage. I discuss the recent rise in child witchcraft and the association of femininity with witchcraft to lay the groundwork for a deeper understanding of the social tensions and ambiguities surrounding the occult in Benin. This chapter also focuses on the negative functions of the occult, since stories of death and misfortune are the most usual topics of discussion. Although I take pains to convey how many informants differentiate between *àzĕ* and *bŏ*, I should stress that this distinction exists only on one level of discourse—the most public—and this was how I understood these two occult forces in my earlier fieldwork. A casual observer would perceive two separate but primarily malevolent practices, but as I explain in chapter 2, the occult cannot be reduced to its negative side, and many of the differences between *àzĕ* and *bŏ* unraveled following deeper questioning of healers, priests, and others who take an interest in these supernatural matters. In other words, we might think of the discourse regarding *àzĕ* and *bŏ* as existing in two different styles of speech, or registers. In the present chapter, I outline the ordinary, public register used to describe occult forces. People using this register are employing a default classification of *àzě* and *bŏ*, one that is common to ordinary people and others making standard comments about witchcraft and sorcery. Chapter 2 draws on another register that admits to ambiguity between *àzě* and *bŏ* and to the possibilities of benevolent witchcraft. We must be cautious about regarding one register as "correct." As I will show throughout this book, in all matters related to witchcraft, there are multiple and contradictory views among people, so we cannot declare a definitive or consensus understanding of witchcraft and its manifestations.

Àzě

Evans-Pritchard's ([1937] 1976) original distinction between witchcraft and sorcery among the Azande is a useful starting point for understanding the supernatural practices of *àzě* and *bŏ* in southern Benin. Like the Azande, many Beninese people say that there is a difference between involuntary psychic powers, on the one hand, and intentional magical actions, on the other. The basic Beninese conception of *àzě* as an internal, invisible, and involuntary power suggests that it is similar to Evans-Pritchard's definition of Azande witchcraft. And like Azande sorcery, *bŏ* are tangible magical formulae and objects. If we were required to find English equivalents for these two terms, *àzě* could be translated as "witchcraft," and *bŏ* could be translated as "sorcery," "magic," or "charm." But unlike Evans-Pritchard's witchcraft, *àzě* is not necessarily inherited, because it can be transmitted from an *àzètɔ́* (witch) to another individual (discussed below). As Victor Turner (1964) correctly established, Evans-Pritchard's distinction between witchcraft and sorcery does not apply precisely nor everywhere in Africa, but in the public register we do find some striking similarities between Beninese and Azande beliefs.

When first asked to define *àzě*, people generally described a mystical psychic ability, an invisible evil force. Others described *àzě* as "knowledge of the night," *les choses obscures* (hidden/obscure things), a "typically African" supernatural power, a limitless force, a science of the invisible, the ability to leave one's body, or an ultimate strength held in the stomach. The variety of characterizations is typical of the multifaceted and indeterminate nature of *àzě*, but most would agree that *àzě* is a divine power that inheres in people or other supernatural entities. As with Azande witchcraft, the dominant notion of *àzě* is negative, since it produces evil, death, and betrayal. People fear and despise *àzètɔ́* and frequently blame them for the deaths of loved ones or for bad luck and illness. *Àzètɔ́* can cause impotence in men and infertility in women, and they make people go insane or lose all their money. They can take the form of someone else and commit nefarious acts for which the other person is blamed. An *àzètɔ́* can turn into a bull in the middle of the road and cause the driver to have an accident. Many said that *àzě* involuntarily compels someone to harm, kill, or consume other people. Usually, *àzètɔ́* are said to attack family members, and an *àzètɔ́*'s own children are some of the most frequent targets. One man in Bohicon offered the following expression as a metaphor for *àzě* targeting family members: "Xɔ́nɔ̌ wè nɔ̌ ze zē bo e nɔ̌ hu ajakà" (It is the owner of the house who lifts the jar to kill the mouse; i.e., family members "own" each other and therefore control each other's life and death). Other expressions further illustrate this sentiment: "Mɛ e sɛ kpɔ mɛ, ye wè nɔ̌ wa nu xa mɛ" (Those who are close to you are the ones who do you harm); "Àzě nɔ̌ hu aliwáyitɔ ǎ" (*Àzě* does not kill strangers).

Most people affirm that a key motive for witches to kill is envy, like that directed at a brother who is more successful or at a cowife whose children are favored by their father. People said that ill will and rancor usually occur between individuals who know each other well; even if they are not family, they are likely to be friends or coworkers. Although inequality exists between strangers, it is the inequality between intimates that generates social tension (Geschiere 2013). This tension takes the form of envy and jealousy, which people assert lie at the heart of witchcraft fears and motives. Envy, the desire for what someone else possesses, reportedly drives poor people to employ witchcraft in an effort to bring down a wealthy sibling or friend. Jealousy is the fear that someone will take away what one already has, and this is the rationale for prosperous people to take supernatural precautions to protect against attack. While the rich are looking over their shoulder, their less fortunate friends suspect that the wealthy are likely to have used witchcraft to become rich in the first place. Although envy and jealousy can be differentiated in this way, Fon speakers tend to use a single term, *ùhwã́*, which conveys the general tension between those who possess something and those who do not. Therefore, the envy/jealousy dynamic associated with inequality is intimately connected to witchcraft motives, fears, and suspicions. Some suggested a slightly different understanding of inequality that does not manifest as either jealousy or envy. In this version, a witch could launch an attack against someone who stops helping her financially. An official in Abomey's court system provided just such an example. He told me about a man who moved to the United States and became wealthy and successful. On visits home, he would regularly give gifts of money to his aunt. During one such trip, the aunt's door was closed, so he passed by without making his usual gift. In front of the entire family, his aunt accused him of neglect and threatened him with a supernatural attack. Although her relatives tried to calm her, and she claimed that all was forgiven, from that moment on the man became confused and deranged. He eventually abandoned his life in America and returned to Benin before dying prematurely. This case demonstrates that curtailing one's generosity can engender as much resentment as outright hostility. This contributes to the notion that *àzètɔ́* can be fickle and unpredictable, often harming those who help other people and show them sympathy, in particular, members of one's own family. Indeed, the kinship-based conception of witchcraft was so strong that in my early fieldwork I was often reassured that my status as a foreigner meant that I had nothing to fear from witchcraft in Benin. For a number of years, people continued to accept my claims that, since I had no witches in my family, I must be invulnerable to witchcraft.

Despite the fact that the default conception of *àzě* locates the threat within families, some people acknowledged that *àzě* now extends beyond the family. Given that each family is presumed to contain at least one *àzètɔ́* and that *àzètɔ́* work in collaboration with each other, most people admit that anyone is a potential victim. Informants explained that an *àzètɔ́* with a grudge against a nonfamily member can contact another *àzètɔ́* in the victim's family, and this connection allows the aggressor to carry out his or her wishes. Much as Charles Piot (2010) has observed of witchcraft in neighboring Togo, there are widespread reports that *àzě* is changing, such that *àzètɔ́* can now attack unrelated people. Likewise, Peter Geschiere (2013) observes this trend occurring elsewhere on the continent, inspiring fear that witchcraft can now target anyone, not only kin.[2] Nevertheless, a healer in a village south of Abomey said, "A ma ko wa nu ɖe àzètɔ́ wa ɔ, e na ɖu we ǎ" (If you don't do anything to an *àzètɔ́*, s/he won't eat you), and most people acknowledge that *àzètɔ́* do not attack indiscriminately but rather target those who have wronged them or those of whom they are envious. An Abomey man offered an expression to illustrate this point: "E zu àzètɔ́ sĩ nɔ̃ yo me, e ko kpe bo e ɖa we ɖu" (It's enough for you to insult an *àzètɔ́*'s mother for her to cook and eat you). This reinforces the notion that *àzě* operates primarily within a community.

Despite claims that *àzě* is motivated by anger, jealousy, and envy, people also maintain that it compels people to kill, even against their will. Because *àzètɔ́* operate in groups, each member of the coven is required to take a turn in providing a victim (usually a relative) to be shared ("eaten") by the group. This is the most common explanation for why children would be the targets of *àzètɔ́*. Among family and friends, food sharing is a demonstration of connection, trust, friendship, and solidarity, and the communalism among *àzètɔ́* mimics this ethic of sharing. It is ironic that *àzètɔ́* live by these same social conventions, even when *àzě* represents the opposite values of animosity, deceit, and betrayal. At the same time, this fits with the notion of *àzètɔ́* inhabiting a parallel, opposite world governed by similar social rules, but with a perverse morality. Several informants noted that *àzètɔ́* are like thieves because they operate at night, they flout ordinary social conventions, and they maintain secrecy and solidarity within the group. People also spoke of the *àzě* society being an ordered hierarchy with different ranks, including a government with leaders, judges, and lawyers, just like the daytime world of ordinary society. The witches also have rules resembling the social obligations of the popular financial collectives (*tontine* in French, *gbě* in Fon), where each member must contribute his or her share at regular intervals or risk being punished (see Falen 2011). But in the case of the *àzètɔ́* society, a person must offer a human victim rather than money. There were conflicting reports of whether *àzètɔ́* are supposed to actually or metaphorically eat people. Some informants contended that *àzètɔ́* are cannibals who eat human flesh, but most said that *àzètɔ́* do not eat a person's body; instead, they mystically consume a person's life force or his or her soul, known as *sɛ́* in Fon.[3] They do this by magically transforming the victim's *sɛ́* into an animal that can be cooked and eaten. People said the victim takes the form of a fish, an agouti (a large bush rodent), a goat, a pig, a chicken, or some other comestible animal. The image of consumption is central to *àzètɔ́* activity. When describing attacks, people used the Fon word *ɖu* (to eat), as in "é nɔ̃ ɖu mɛ" (s/he eats someone; i.e., s/he attacks someone using *àzě*, s/he is an *àzètɔ́*). Eating is the ultimate metaphor for using or controlling people and resources. In Benin, as elsewhere in Africa, it is through the idiom of food and eating that people describe sex, gifts, and corruption (Bayart 1993). *Àzě* is also said to exist in the stomach; once you eat it, it resides permanently in your belly. Still others claimed ignorance of the nature of attacks, simply stating that witches kill by some invisible and mysterious power. *Àzètɔ́* are said to convene nocturnal meetings, during which they collectively feast on a victim. These meetings take place in the forest, often beneath or within large trees like the baobab and iroko.[4] While victims sleep in their beds, the witches' souls, whose bodies are also asleep, travel in the dreamworld to mystically capture their victims and take them to their meetings, where the victims' souls are transformed into animals, cooked, and eaten. Consuming a person's soul induces sickness or death in the victim, which can last for weeks or months, suggesting that consumption is a lengthy process.

At its essence, *àzě* is about transformation—of *àzètɔ́* themselves, of their victims, of the power of good and evil. *Àzètɔ́* can transform into other people, animals, or birds (especially owls). The Fon verb *hùzú* means "to change or transform," and this is the word used to describe one of the actions of *àzètɔ̀*: "E huzú xɛ̀" (s/he turned into a bird). *Àzètɔ̀* can fly or teleport instantaneously anywhere in the world. They engage in nocturnal travels, deadly attacks, shape-shifting, sapping of blood or life force, and their association with flying creatures has obvious analogues to the medieval European preoccupations with witches, vampires, and other mystical agents whose very nature impelled them to do horrible deeds.[5] The transformation of *àzètɔ̀* is also exhibited by good people becoming bad or corrupt, by a reversal or trade-off between good and evil. People regularly told me that the individual who uses occult power will suffer personally, for example, by having a shorter lifespan.[6] As did many informants, a female entertainer named Camille who performs in Cotonou and France pointed out that the witch society demands that its members sacrifice those dearest to them; they must either offer their own child or die themselves.[7] These negative results of using the occult suggest a law of limited good, whereby gains in one area are balanced by losses in another. This zero-sum game is a common theme in the moral economy of supernatural deeds in both African and New World magical systems (Austen 1993; Bowie [2000] 2006; Herskovits [1937] 1971). This demonstrates the reversal and opposition that accompany occult beliefs and actions, in addition to the way the occult obeys a cosmic moral balance, which some liken to the law of karma.

Many people claimed that *àzètɔ̀* are governed by a code that requires their secret acts to be revealed. On the brink of death, they confess to the number of people they killed in their lifetime, either involuntarily or as an attempt at obtaining absolution for their acts.[8] One Fon adage reflects this belief: "Nu ñàñã ɖe a wa ɖo gbɛ mɛ fi, a na ɖɔ̃ bi co bo na kú" (You'll have to tell all the bad things you've done in this life before you die). I have witnessed several *àzètɔ̀* confessions in different circumstances. In the town of Save in 1999 I was introduced to a presumed witch on her deathbed surrounded by dozens of people; she had just confessed to killing seven people in her family. I have also met people who confessed because they were converting to a new religion or after their witchcraft had been discovered. Whatever the circumstances of confession, the evil acts performed at night are occasionally brought to the light of day, creating another transformation/reversal, from *àzètɔ̀* who previously acted with impunity to humble and vulnerable people who have lost their power.

Bŏ

Unlike *àzĕ*, the term *bŏ* represents a voluntary, learned occult power, most closely resembling Azande sorcery (Evans-Pritchard [1937] 1976). When making an explicit distinction between *bŏ* and *àzě*, people often used the African French word for magical charm, *gri-gri*, to refer to *bŏ* but not to *àzě*.[9] Likewise, the French term *envoûtement* (spell or charm) and the verb's past participle (*envoûté*) refer to a *bŏ* victim's condition. The effects of *bŏ* may be either positive or negative, and the target may be a relative or an unrelated individual. While *àzě* is usually thought of as a psychic power without any specific physical location, *bŏ* connotes both the abstract notion of magic and concrete magical or medicinal objects. As Suzanne Preston Blier (1995) shows in her extensive examination of magical art and empowerment objects, *bŏ* are charms, amulets, or magical items and substances composed of leaves, minerals, and other natural ingredients.[10] Depending on the *bŏ*, incantations and animal blood may be used in the course of its production in order to imbue it with power.[11] Those who make *bŏ* include *botɔ* (sorcerers), *bokɔnɔ̃* (diviners), or other ritual specialists and religious leaders. The motivation for *bŏ* may arise out of intense longing, envy, or jealousy. An individual may use *bŏ* to make someone fall in love or lose his or her money. *Bŏ* may be used to bring rain for crops or stop the rain during an important ceremony (see Dah-Lokonon 1997). Some popular types of *bŏ* have common names referring to their effects. For example, *sanu sanu* (sell sell) and *yirɔ* (to call) are intended to attract clients to one's business. On the other hand, a *glŏ* (block) can form a barrier to protect someone from supernatural attacks (Le Herissé 1911, 148; Mayrargue 2002, 60; Maupoil 1943, 363; Quénum [1936] 1983, 78–79). A *flĩ* (remember) gives the user improved memory during school exams. Other *bŏ* may cause an enemy to have a fatal accident, or they may be worn like an amulet to protect someone from accidents.[12] Children can be seen wearing *bŏ* in the form of small leather-bound pouches tied around their waists, used to protect them from illness and especially from *àzě*. Many homes have a collection of charms hanging over the doorway or buried underground to protect the residents from theft, illness, or other dangers.

Though *bŏ* can certainly have serious and even lethal consequences, their existence has typically been more openly discussed than *àzě*. People might lightheartedly conjecture about *bŏ* and even make jokes about the magical properties of food and drink. In such cases, *bŏ* could refer to true magic, but it could also refer to more pseudomagical objects. For example, people speak of women preparing a dish called *mǎ tēnjǎ*, which contains so many delicious ingredients that men who eat it fall hopelessly in love with the cook (Falen 2011, 138). There is another dish called *bomiwɔ*, which people claim has magical properties, as suggested by the word *bŏ* at the beginning. The word blends *bŏ* with *amiwɔ*, referring to a corn paste (*wɔ*) that is seasoned with salt and

FIGURE 1. A man feeds cow's blood to a protective *bǒ* in his home. (Photograph by the author)

red palm oil (*ami*). *Bomiwɔ̃* is made magical by boiling a chicken whole rather than in parts and then using the water to make the corn *wɔ̃*. One of the most common products believed to possess extraordinary properties is *soɖabì* (palm liquor), especially when infused with various roots, seeds, and nuts. Most old men keep a bottle of their "medicine" on hand to offer liquid hospitality to their guests, but many also claim that it treats stomachaches, malaria, dysentery, and especially impotence. In a widespread joke, men refer to their *soɖabì* as Viagra.

In contrast to popular references to pseudomagic, most *bŏ* are regarded as legitimate magical formulae. Out of respect for people's private and powerful knowledge, I never sought or requested formulae, but people occasionally volunteered *bŏ* recipes, and I offer some examples here.[13]

- A man gave me the following formula for court cases: draw a *vɛvɛ* in front of a twin's shrine (a shrine where family members make offerings to their deceased twins, who are considered semi-divine; a *vɛvɛ* is a design made from corn flour mixed with red palm oil, usually drawn in front of a family's twin shrine).[14] He said that the *vɛvɛ* should then be collected and combined with palm nut shells inside a calabash, and then the calabash should be placed at an intersection. This *bŏ* will ensure a favorable decision against opponents in a legal ruling.
- An old man from the town of Djidja provided a recipe for preventing rain from spoiling a ceremony: collect two intact *klɔmã̀* leaves and a fifty-centimeter branch from a *fãtĩ́* tree. Make a slit in one end of the branch and place the two leaves within the fissure, with both leaves facing the same direction. Take some alcohol and blow it on the leaves, then say the name of the region where the rain should fall instead of the ceremony location. The branch should then be placed in a nearby tree to ward off rains for as long as you request. (It was this man whom Gaston hired to prevent the rains during the funeral ceremony I described in the introduction).
- As a telling example of the increasingly public nature of occult knowledge, I happened to overhear a radio show with a prominent healer who is invited regularly to comment over the airwaves. He offered a formula for a protective spell. The ingredients included three kinds of leaves, one kind of bird, and both kinds of owls (smooth head and tufted ears).[15] The leaves should be crushed together and mixed with the owls' and bird's blood, along with soap. He instructed the listeners to bathe with this soap daily to protect against *àzɛ̀tɔ́* attacks.
- A university professor named Maxime told me the ingredients of a *bŏ* that is supposed to bring good luck to someone experiencing hard times. It is

composed of seven dead chameleons, two kinds of leaves (*ahehe* and *zētītī*), a woman's pubic hair, perfume, and kaolin. These ingredients are combined and rubbed on one's head.

- Mouni, my adoptive mother in Abomey, told me there is a formula for saving someone from an ongoing *àzètɔ́* attack. Though she did not state the specific ingredients, she explained that the spell works by collecting certain leaves, pronouncing incantations, and then throwing the leaves in the road. Whoever treads on the leaves will attract the evil magic (and contract the illness), thereby liberating the original target. She explained that this magic is a type of *kuɖiɔ* (death exchange), one of the more common treatments used by healers (see chapter 5).

- An informant told me of a man's recipe for taking vengeance against his wife. The man had five wives, and the first wife became so enraged about her husband marrying additional women that she vowed to leave him. Her husband collected a number of ingredients, all items that had once been in contact with his wife: sand from her footprint, hair, nails, urine, and pubic hair.[16] He used these to cast a spell against her, and the day she left him, she became sick and developed a herniated vagina. After a year of visiting healers and hospitals to no effect, she eventually decided to return to her husband and ask him to lift the spell. Unfortunately, he confessed to her that there was no way to undo the spell.

For other recipes, people referred to simple *bŏ* consisting of a single ingredient, such as a leaf that can be chewed to produce a desired effect. In one case, a female healer invited me to eat a tiny yellow flower that had a simultaneously sweet and spicy taste, almost like mentholatum. She said that when you eat this flower, nobody can speak ill of you. Of course, leaves and flowers are often said to have an immediate and automatic effect, attributed to the "natural" properties of *amǎ* (leaves), which some informants distinguished from manufactured *bŏ*. For example, a hotel manager in Cotonou provided me with a recipe for calling down lightning. He said it consists of taking a certain leaf and placing a cricket on it. Then you should run away, because lightning will strike the leaf and destroy everything in its proximity. Although the recipe included an insect, he insisted that the effect derives from the power of leaves rather than either *bŏ* or *àzĕ*. The line between *bŏ* and *amǎ* is unclear, because many people say that *bŏ* are natural formulae based on *amǎ*.

One of my good friends, Claude, whom I first met in Abomey in 1996, related an account of his father's good fortune to illustrate the use of a good luck *bŏ*. In Claude's father's younger years, during the colonial era, he was a

FIGURE 2. A healer's protective *bŏ*, which he called a *kpè*. (Photograph by the author)

gifted carpenter but had trouble finding work. A French man happened to see some of his work, sought him out, and immediately offered him a job as manager of the French man's construction crew. One day, the carpenter realized that there was some leftover wood from one of the jobs, and he was preparing to take it himself, but the French supervisor caught him. The boss threatened to fire him and the whole crew, so the man consulted a healer for assistance. The healer made a *bŏ* and said the carpenter would never be fired. The healer told him to test the *bŏ*'s effectiveness by approaching his boss and asking when he would fire him. When he did this, the boss yelled at him to get back to work, and the matter was never mentioned again for the rest of his career in the same job.

Like *àzĕ*, *bŏ* sometimes come at a cost; while protective *bŏ* at first appear to be risk-free, using them to upset the natural order of things may be dangerous. If a woman uses *bŏ* to get filthy rich, to have unnaturally good luck, or to harm an enemy, there might be an equal dose of bad luck for the owner of the *bŏ* or her family. A man might use a *bŏ* to become an exceptionally successful entrepreneur, only to lose his child to illness. A woman might be able to procure the fidelity of a lover, only to lose all her money. As the rain-stopping *bŏ* mentioned above demonstrates, preventing rain in one place demands that it rain somewhere else. The *kuɖiɔ bŏ* works in the same way: a person can be saved from a supernatural attack, but only if someone takes his place. In a related metaphor, informants often expressed the idea that occult forces can rebound. A spell cast against an enemy can sometimes return against its creator (see also Blier 1995, 72). There is always a natural order of good luck and moral behavior; any unjustified violation comes with repercussions. Consequently, depending on the good or evil purposes of a *bŏ*, the word could be translated as "white magic," "black magic," "sorcery," or "good luck charm." In short, *bŏ* are the product of specialized knowledge and powers that can be wielded only by trained individuals, making them voluntarily acquired and intentionally used.

Differences between *Àzĕ* and *Bŏ*

When I asked people about the differences between *àzĕ* and *bŏ*, most responses in the public register reflected the belief that *àzĕ* involves an internal psychic power that allows one to achieve incredible feats—like transformation, flight, teleportation, shape-shifting, long-distance communication, or the appropriation of others' wealth—but it comes with an urge to kill people and a requirement to provide victims for the larger society of *àzètɔ*. *Bŏ*, on the other hand, are seen as natural phenomena because they use formulae with specific ingredients, usually including leaves, roots, seeds, and minerals, often in association with incantations or animal sacrifices. In short, *bŏ* are referred to as "natural" phenomena. Other distinctions include the following properties: *àzĕ* is invisible, while *bŏ* is visible; *àzĕ* works only at night, while *bŏ* can be used anytime; *bŏ* works in the physical world, but *àzĕ* operates in another dimension. *Bŏ* is frequently characterized as a weapon, even as a missile (see Aguessy 1992; Mayrargue 2002, 60). Many informants felt that *àzĕ* is necessarily evil, though *bŏ* can be used for either good or evil. Furthermore, *àzètɔ́* act in concert within a secret society, but those producing *bŏ* act independently. *Àzĕ* is usually portrayed as more powerful, higher, or more advanced than *bŏ* (see Quénum [1936] 1983, 82). An elderly Abomey man said, "Bo lɛ bi xósu wɛ̀ ñi àzĕ" (*Àzĕ* is king of all *bŏ*). Finally, many people claimed that *bŏ* are possessed largely by men, whereas *àzĕ* is dominated by women. However, a number of interviewees claimed they were unsure about the differences between the two forces. While most believed *àzĕ* to be unequivocally evil, in contrast to *bŏ*'s ambivalent nature, on further questioning, the good and bad dichotomy often broke down. These contradictions point to a number of important ambiguities, which are developed in the next chapter.

There are also marked differences in the ways people acquire the powers of *àzĕ* and *bŏ*. As noted, *bŏ* is a learned skill, and mastering its uses is the culmination of a long process of studying plants and minerals and how their natural powers can be enhanced with the aid of incantations and animal sacrifice. These skills are usually passed on from a ritual specialist to a child or apprentice. Vodun priests (*vodǔnɔ̀*), healers (*àzɔ̃gblétɔ́*), and diviners (*bokɔ́nɔ̀*) may all possess this knowledge. Each profession requires a lengthy and costly series of initiations accompanied by ritual learning. *Bokɔ́nɔ̀* receive a coveted education in the Fá divination system, and since the divine entity of Fá is the source of all spiritual knowledge, *bokɔ́nɔ̀* are respected religious authorities to whom people turn for information and assistance (see Maupoil 1943). While a *bokɔ́nɔ̀*'s primary responsibility is to perform Fá divination, everyone understands that the information obtained in consulting Fá offers an opportunity to shape the outcome of one's life. To influence the deities on behalf of a client, *bokɔ́nɔ̀* prescribe animal sacrifices or offerings composed of ritual ingredients. Most *bokɔ́nɔ̀* also offer the ancillary service of manufacturing *bŏ*. Using their knowledge of plants, animals, and the deities, they can make charms worn on one's body or placed in one's home for protection or good luck.

The other ritual specialists well known for making *bŏ* are healers, or *àzɔ̃gblétɔ́* (destroyers of illness). These individuals undergo a long training period during which they learn the power of plants to treat illness. Typically, they prescribe infusions with particular leaves to treat ordinary physical conditions like stomachaches, headaches, diarrhea, impotence, and malaria, though their repertoire can be extensive (see chapter 5). The use of leaves (*amǎ*) is emblematic of the connection between nature and healing, and other names for healers include *amǎɖatɔ́* (preparer of leaves) and *amǎwatɔ́* (maker of leaves). One Fon word for medicine or medicinal infusion is *amasì* (leaf water), demonstrating the central role of nature and leaves in the healing arts. Like traditional medicines, *bǒ* are composed of leaves and other natural ingredients, blurring the lines between medicine and magic (Maupoil 1943, 143).[17] It is this connection between medicine and magic, along with the fact that physical illness is often interpreted as the manifestation of a supernatural attack or imbalance, that qualifies healers to make *bǒ*.

The training protocol of *vodǔnɔ̀* priests focuses on how to worship a deity (*vodǔ*), which consists of learning what foods, animals, rhythms, and dances the *vodǔ* likes or dislikes and how to call the *vodǔ* to possess the body of its adepts. *Vodǔnɔ̀* serve as troupe leaders by planning ceremonies and negotiating the terms with potential sponsors. Their position as religious authorities and intermediaries between people and deities makes a basic knowledge of Fá divination essential to their job. And because deities are responsible for some illness, or at least are capable of combatting illness, people appeal to *vodǔnɔ̀* for healing assistance. Though not all *vodǔnɔ̀* receive advanced Fá initiation or specialized training in healing, they are called upon to serve people in a variety of functions, including the manufacture of *bǒ*.

It should be clear that the distinctions between these ritual specialists are superficial, as they frequently perform similar functions by interpreting natural and supernatural discord and prescribing solutions to rectify it. And it is common for all three roles of healer, priest, and diviner to exist within a single individual, whether or not the person received formal training in all areas. No matter what title he or she may prefer to use, an individual who uses the power of *bǒ* could be referred to as a *boɖatɔ́*, *bowatɔ́*, or *botɔ́* (preparer, maker, or master of *bǒ*); but such terms are somewhat pejorative, and I have never heard them used in the presence of these ritual specialists.[18]

In contrast to the voluntary acquisition of *bǒ*, becoming an *àzètɔ́* is usually described as involuntary.[19] Though a couple of interviewees said that one can be born with *àzě*, most held that one becomes an *àzètɔ́* during the course of one's life. For example, an *àzètɔ́* might secretly slip a type of witchcraft poison into one's food, and one would then unwittingly become an *àzètɔ́*. A witch can place a piece of human flesh in a target's sauce, and once the target eats it, she or he experiences an irrepressible appetite to consume human beings.

A couple of informants stated that human flesh is secretly sold in the market by *àzètɔ́* who work as meat vendors, while others said that witchcraft poison can be disguised as candy or cookies that child witches share with classmates in order to initiate new members. The candy is composed of human blood, and if the treat is not consumed, it reverts to the state of blood. *Àzĕ* can also be transmitted by feeding someone a specially treated kola nut; after consuming the nut, the person will unavoidably be drawn to the nocturnal *àzètɔ́* meetings. People warn that hanging out with diviners, healers, or others suspected of witchcraft puts a person in danger; being friends with such individuals may make that person want to transfer witchcraft through the sharing of treated foods. Camille told me that her best friend acquired *àzĕ* and tried on several occasions to give it to her. But Camille said she is protected with the ability to detect and avoid such attempts. Their friendship has now gone cold, but Camille added that it is forbidden to talk about it, so neither of them discusses their supernatural jousting, even though they each know that the other knows. Harboring envy or evil thoughts and discussing them with *àzètɔ́* friends may prompt them to give you *àzĕ* so that you can take action against your rivals. *Àzĕ* is also transmitted in a more mystical way: since an *àzètɔ́*'s spirit travels at night while her body sleeps, she can visit others in the dream-world, enticing their spirits to follow her to the meeting site; there the unsuspecting initiate is fed a piece of cooked meat (transformed human flesh). If she consumes the meat, she seals her fate and will later awake to discover that she is an *àzètɔ́*. A minority of informants asserted that *àzĕ* is inherited, often by a daughter from her mother, or that an *àzètɔ́* must transmit her power to someone else before dying.[20] Since being a witch is associated with evil and killing, it is understandable that it would appear involuntary, like an illness or an evil spirit that takes control of one's body. This is consistent with the way someone is treated after confessing to being an *àzètɔ́*. She is treated either by a healer who tries to remove the evil force or by a Christian pastor or priest who performs an exorcism. Despite claims of involuntary acquisition, as I explain in chapter 2, some informants said that *àzĕ* cannot be acquired without one's consent, contending that *àzĕ* is sought out, purchased, or otherwise acquired intentionally. The voluntary *àzĕ* is often portrayed as a benevolent or healing variety of witchcraft.

Child Witches

As seen in other African countries, one prominent and recent feature of contemporary Beninese witchcraft is the rise of child witches. Child witches are not totally evil; instead, they are unpredictable and irresponsible, both qualities that render *àzĕ* dangerous and dynamic. When I asked people whether the occult is changing, the most frequent (though not universal) response was that children are now using *àzĕ*. In the past, children were seen as the targets of elderly *àzètɔ́*, but when children become witches themselves, it arouses considerable anxiety among people, since children are regarded as incapable of exercising reason in the use of this power. Some informants said that *àzĕ* was formerly a force for justice and social control wielded by mature and reasonable individuals, a perspective that echoes functionalist interpretations of the mid-twentieth century (Middleton and Winter 1963b; Nadel 1952). Children were traditionally dependent on their elders for protection and access to land, but today the youth rely more on education and employment, which give them advantages over their rural elders and often take them out of the sphere of family influence. Like other contemporary theorists, I have observed that this age inversion of witches may be connected to the drastic social, economic, and demographic changes that have begun splitting up extended families, disempowering the elderly, overturning the gerontocracy, promoting new professional skills in a market economy, and creating financial burdens on younger generations who are no longer willing or able to look after their parents and grandparents (de Boeck 2005). These tensions also result in an urban/rural divide, as wealthy individuals increasingly resist returning to their home villages, worried of being inundated with financial requests from envious kin. As documented by Marcy Hessling O'Neil (2012), these tensions emerge in university students' discourses about the dangers of kin who may use witchcraft to bring down those educated urbanites who are presumed to hide their success from their families back home. These circumstances are part of a broader trend undermining village communalism in favor of individualism and contributing to a loss of respect for the elderly and their ways of resolving disputes (see Marie 1997; van Binsbergen 2001).

A common theme in my informants' testimony was unruly schoolchildren who use *àzĕ* indiscriminately and without remorse. A teacher told me he can identify a child *àzètɔ́* by the feeling he gets in his arm after spanking the disobedient student. He said that children who possess *àzĕ* feel nothing, but he himself feels pain in his arm for a long time afterward. I heard another story of schoolchildren in Porto-Novo who experienced an epidemic of falling down, and they discovered that there was an *àzètɔ́* in their midst. Children are suspected of bringing a specially treated *gari* (granulated manioc) to school and sharing it with their classmates to transform them into *àzètɔ́*. One illustration of the economic motives of witchcraft is the case of a girl who reportedly confessed to a social worker that she used *àzĕ* to acquire the latest beauty products; she then sold them and shared the profits with the woman who gave her *àzě*. Child witches reportedly can look at someone's belly and see what they ate or view people's intestines and heart. These accounts of looking inside the body point to the similarities between witchcraft and medical diagnostic tools, particularly the X-ray, which comes as no surprise, given the conceptual convergence between healing, science, and the occult (see chapter 2).

When I asked people why children have begun acquiring *àzě* more than before, I received a variety of responses. Some felt that purveyors of malevolent occult forces are under attack, so they seek new and younger recruits, even infants, in order to maintain their numbers. According to this line of thinking, in the old days, elderly people knew how to keep secrets, but children are impulsive and lack discretion, so knowledge of the occult has spread among the general population. The spread of witchcraft is also linked to the desire for status, since *àzètɔ́* transmit their power to children as a way of expanding their networks and claiming a higher position in the witchcraft hierarchy. Much like the way pyramid marketing schemes function, a witch achieves promotion by inducting subordinate members. In general, recent changes in *àzě* are analogous to an arms race, with people referring to these changes as *évolution*. People explained matter-of-factly that things are always changing and improving, so the same must be true for *àzě* as it adjusts to new circumstances and new strategies of opposition. Beninese use *évolution* or *évolué* in referring to sophistication, progress, or development, which also conveys the notion that *àzě* is tied to Beninese understandings of development (see chapter 2). Whatever people's explanations, it is clear that *àzě* is dynamic and continues to transform in profound ways, and the growing prevalence of child witches is but one example of the dynamic mutation of which *àzě* is capable.

Women and Men, Witches and Healers

In discussing children's *àzě*, many informants subtly marked the gender of child witches as female. Although there were stories of boys who reportedly killed people, many referred to child witches as girls. Men especially voiced distress that seemingly innocent adolescent girls, even those who may enter romantic relationships with young men, could become ruthless, selfish, and manipulative *àzètɔ́*. However, gender is most conspicuously marked as female for adult *àzètɔ́*. Both women and men overwhelmingly stated that female *àzètɔ́* far outnumber their male counterparts, with many people estimating that as many as 99 percent of *àzètɔ́* are female (see Blier 1995, 33), often young girls of eight or nine years old, but especially old and impoverished women (see also Kahn 2011; Kohnert 1996). In all the cases of confessions that I witnessed, and for nearly all of the accusations and suspicions I heard about, the presumed witch was female. Naturally, the public outing of suspected female witches does not preclude the existence of male àzètɔ́. In fact, one court official admitted the possibility that men are more involved than people know but added that if men are complicit, they simply are not caught.[21]

Despite a few uncertainties, most people agreed that in terms of sheer numbers of àzètɔ́, women dominate men, and the symbolic association of femininity with àzě is indisputable (see also Apter 1991; Brain 1982; Jean Comaroff and John Comaroff 1999; John Comaroff and Jean Comaroff 2004; Drewal and Drewal 1983; Matory 1994). To explain this gender imbalance, a group of village healers told me that the very first àzètɔ́ was a woman. This fits a widespread and essentialized view of women's role in the occult, with àzě characterized as "women's science." People repeatedly told me that male àzètɔ́ are the butchers (akpakpojinotɔ́) at their nocturnal meetings, but only female àzètɔ́ actually eat the meat. The means of acquiring àzě are correspondingly different between the genders: women acquire evil power through food (suddenly and involuntarily), while male healers obtain benevolent àzě through study and initiation (gradually and intentionally). People's responses suggested that they see one form of àzě as a quintessentially evil and female power that must be held in check by the benign male power possessed by healers. Unsurprisingly, nearly all healers whom I met or heard about were male. In 2008 I attended a meeting of a village healers' association where only one of the dozen healers present was female, and in my only interview with a female healer, she admitted that there are very few woman healers (see figure 3). There is a clear gendered dichotomy connected to the good/bad tension discussed above, such that women are associated with destructive and evil occult forces, while male occult powers are portrayed as either resistant to evil temptations or possessing a version of àzě that can combat the malevolent kind (see Goody 1970). In other words, in the supernatural battle between good and evil, witches are unmistakably female, and healers are unmistakably male.

Some informants made the connection between women and àzě more exclusive by claiming that men's talents lay less in àzě than in bŏ. As one man put it, "Les hommes s'intéressent plus au bŏ qu'à la sorcellerie" (Men are more interested in bŏ than in àzě) (see Blier 1995, 372n32). There is a perceived gendered hierarchy among àzètɔ́, with the higher ranks and leadership occupied by women (Falen 2011; see also Augé 1976).[22] Several people said that a single woman governs the whole society, claiming that her name is Mĭnɔ̃nà̃.

FIGURE 3. One of the few female healers, in Bohicon. (Photograph by the author)

Informants repeatedly translated Mĭnɔ̃nằ as "our mothers," despite the fact that this is an awkward and perhaps ungrammatical rendering.[23] Mĭnɔ̃nằ was also translated as "Queen Mother," "vagina," "*àzètɔ́*," or "*àzĕ* itself."[24] A retired man in Abomey told me that he used to know who the leader was—a woman with only one breast who lived in Abomey-Calavi (outside of Cotonou)—but he no longer knew who the current leader was. I heard of another man who met the *àzètɔ́* leader; she was seated, naked, and when he looked at her vagina, it was huge, like a village one could walk into. Though some say the witch leader is a woman named Mĭnɔ̃nằ, Mĭnɔ̃nằ is also the name of a *vodũ* (a deity), and, not surprisingly, she is a female deity usually described as the patron of female sexuality and motherhood, as well as of *àzĕ* (see chapter 4). Whether Mĭnɔ̃nằ refers to women leaders, mothers, witches, or a *vodũ*, the term clearly embodies a concentration of feminine power and represents a challenge to the assumption of male dominance.

Many informants claimed that women possess exceptionally strong occult power, and as the preceding comment about the *àzètɔ́* queen suggests, it is often an intimidating and crudely sexual power. Over and over, I heard informants refer to women as stronger and more dangerous than men, with frequent mention of genitalia, sexuality, and reproduction. Recall from the earlier section that one of the ingredients for a *bŏ* was a woman's pubic hair (the man providing me with the recipe told me that we needed to take precautions merely to discuss pubic hair: we had to remove our shoes and eat a small piece of *atákũ*—Guinea pepper—holding it in our left hand).[25] *Àzĕ* is explicitly linked to women's sexuality and reproduction, and the vagina is often described as a source of supernatural power or even as the entity that consumes a victim's soul. One informant said that before having sex, a man must kneel down in front of the woman—a common gesture of respect and subordination.

Because reproduction is the creation of life, it is a supernatural act that imbues women with power and garners respect. Women can not only create life, but some said they can heal illness and accomplish other miraculous acts by virtue of their sexuality. For example, I heard a story of a child who broke his leg. After the accident, a woman took the cloth she used to cover her vagina and put it on the child's leg, and within thirty days, he was healed.[26] Maxime, a university professor, once spontaneously told me that women have a maternal power, found in their ability to console children, to nurse them, and even to know what is wrong with them by the way they cry. He said that mothers teach their children how to drink, how to walk, and everything they need to survive. He has great respect for women's superior power, and sometimes he tells his students that women have a higher status than men. Others viewed women's power as more discreet, saying that even though people portray Beninese women as subordinate and disempowered, they have important and powerful roles to play behind the scenes.[27] For example, Benin's precolonial kingdom of Dahomey created an important role for the monarch's female counterpart (the queen mother) (see Bay 1998). In the nineteenth century, King Guezo's mother reportedly had her own seat beside her son, and she exercised authority alongside him. One man stated that any *vodŭ̃nɔ̃* (priest) has a female assistant to help him manage the deity's shrine and that the pope in Rome has a hidden room where a nun stays and gives orders just as important as the pope's. Camille said she is convinced of her own superiority and therefore does not bother to seek gender equality. She asserted that male fear and awe of women's vitality and strength are what drive men's sexist behaviors. She acknowledged that women's essence is *àzĕ* because they give life, adding that menstruating women are ten times more powerful than menopausal women (or men) because reproductive women can expel blood every month without harm. Though it is rare for women to express such arguments, it is not uncommon for men to demonstrate insecurity, fear, and admiration of women (Falen 2011). Similar insecurities have been reported among men in other parts of the world where machismo attitudes prevail (Gilmore 1990; Herdt 1982; Kimmel 2000, 75), and James Brain (1982) suggests that men's envy is one underlying reason for the disproportionate numbers of witchcraft accusations against women.

Although women's reproduction and supernatural abilities earn them respect and admiration, they are also regarded as dangerous. Much of the fear and apprehension surrounding women's abilities is based not only on their powers over reproduction, life, and death but also on the belief in their inherently volatile character. Over and over, informants reported that one reason women are so closely tied to *àzĕ* is because they are naturally more selfish and impulsive, inclined to do evil. A Cotonou mechanic said, "Ñɔnu nɔ yaŭ wa nu ñãñã" (Women are quick to do bad things). He illustrated women's nature with a biblical reference to Eve taking the forbidden fruit. This propensity for evil is said to make women use *àzĕ* for malevolent and destructive purposes. People held that women lack men's wisdom, calm, and patience; women are quick to anger, they are impetuous, and they possess a vengeful and envious nature; they will use *àzĕ* to seduce and control men, block their success, and kill their children. As I heard time and again, this type of selfish, vengeful, and destructive behavior is the essence of the evil variety of *àzĕ*, and because these characteristics are associated with women and femininity, *àzĕ* itself is marked as feminine. An Abomey retiree summed up this view by saying that a woman is "plus méchante que l'homme. La créature féminine pardonne moins vite que le gendre masculin" (meaner than man. The female creature is less forgiving than the masculine gender). He added that women's nastiness is an abomination and that a woman has no qualms about harming someone or betraying her husband. Regarding women's use of *àzĕ*, he stated, "La femme qui est prédisposée au mal est plus à l'aise dans le milieu" (Women who are predisposed toward evil are more comfortable in the [witchcraft] setting).

Other people attributed women's superior command of *àzĕ* to the fact that they are more ambitious and power hungry than men, always in search of protection and control, going from diviner to diviner in search of success. This was the explanation given by a single mother I know who was poor and had lost both her mother and husband to witchcraft the previous year. She explained that desperation and poverty can lead women to seek the assistance of diviners. However, since associating too freely with diviners and other mystical specialists often leads to contracting *àzĕ*, she said that many of these women unwittingly become witches and are compelled to do evil. While most women's responses resembled those of men who placed the responsibility of destructive *àzĕ* on women and their envious and vengeful nature, this informant was the only one who offered a social critique of gender inequality that almost makes room for a sympathetic view of female witches.

The information reported here demonstrates people's perception of a powerful connection between women and *àzĕ*. Though women generally share this perception, the connection seems to rest primarily on men's fear of women and their admiration of women's sexuality and reproduction. The charged relationship between sexuality and the sacred is well known throughout West Africa, since many religions impose menstrual taboos on women. In the Vodun religion of Benin, menstruating women are forbidden to enter shrines and are theoretically denied access to the occupation of diviner. Some explanations are that female diviners would be too strong and dangerous or that the taboos are intended to protect women, since the *vodũ* would cause them to become sick. On the other hand, a religious artist explained the taboo by saying that reproductive-age women who enter the diviner's sacred forest would find their menstruations suspended and be unable to conceive. However, he added that women are already so powerful that men are afraid of giving them additional abilities that they would not be wise enough to use.[28] Like many male informants, these men depicted women as potential adversaries, and though women and men can enjoy cooperative, friendly, and even loving relationships, there is widespread mistrust and apprehension between the genders, particularly involving sex and money (Falen 2011).

While I stop short of saying that women's connection to *àzĕ* represents gender antagonism (because Beninese are unlikely to see it in these terms), there is a clear resonance between the gender imagery of *àzĕ* and the ambivalence over men's fear and respect for women. And despite the structural advantages that men enjoy in Beninese society, women have considerable informal influence, as asserted by both male and female informants. In a society where men dominate publicly but retain strong anxiety about women's powers, the capacity of *àzĕ* for reversal means that nothing is taken for granted.[29] In a world with *àzĕ*, the blink of an eye can be all that separates friends from enemies, life from death, the poor from the rich, and women from domination.[30] Nowhere is this clearer than in the claims that the witch society is governed by a female leader or by the female deity Mĭnɔ̃nằ. And as a Cotonou healer told me, though men may specialize in *bŏ*, *àzĕ* is far stronger, so *bŏ* cannot stand up against the energy of female sexuality. What my informants make clear is that *àzĕ* is about envy, jealousy, sexuality, and unlimited power. This power is portrayed as unequally shared between women and men. Yet, true to form, *àzĕ* continues to reverse and to elude simple definitions, because although it is seen as an unbounded female power, those who are most often accused are young girls and poor old women—some of the least powerful members of society. This is one reason that human rights activists condemn witchcraft beliefs and accusations, arguing that powerless individuals are scapegoats, transformed into whipping posts for people's envy, fear, and frustration. One feminist reading suggests that the association of witchcraft with women demonstrates men's envy of women's powers over reproduction and the occult. However, another reading is that men are attempting to protect their privilege and that their jealousy and fear over women's threat to undermine the status quo explain men's dominance of the healing occupation and motivate their accusations against female witches.

The Limitless Power of *Àzĕ*

Though *bŏ* clearly deserves attention, and some people said it is more powerful than *àzĕ*, there is something extraordinary about *àzĕ* that elevates it by comparison to *bŏ*. It is *àzĕ* that surpasses, that reaches into the invisible world, and that evokes a sense of wonder and awe. *Àzĕ* is synonymous with transformation, reversal, imagination, darkness, the hidden, the surreal, the supernatural, and unlimited power. And just when it seems *àzĕ* might be knowable, it changes and multiplies. I heard widely conflicting reports of *àzĕ*'s different forms. Some said there are 3 kinds of *àzĕ*, or 7, while others claimed there are 41, 241, 246, 277, or even more varieties. Ultimately, *àzĕ* is impossible to define with any precision, and Geschiere (2013) cautions that trying to define or delimit witchcraft may even erase its most salient qualities: its indeterminacy and uncertainty. Indeed, it is perhaps its flexibility and fluidity that account for witchcraft's persistence and viability. In Geschiere's words, "Witchcraft is a preeminent example of a phenomenon whose very strength is that it defies all classification and distinction. The diffuseness of the discourse seems to be the secret of its power" (2013, 10).

One of the more awe-inspiring features of *àzĕ* is its capacity for flight. People frequently said that *àzètɔ́* take the form of birds or owls—particularly birds of the night—and the association is so commonplace that birds have become a metaphor for *àzĕ* (Blier 1995, 227). Nighttime birds and owls are often called *àzè-xè* (witchcraft bird), and the expression "e ɖo xè" (s/he has a bird) is an idiom meaning someone is an *àzètɔ́* (Henry 2008b).[31] There is perhaps something magical, impossible, and even supernatural about flight that captures the imagination of Africans and Westerners alike. It animates many Western stories of witches and superheroes. (Flight is one quality that transformed Superman from an ordinary to an extraordinary individual. In Benin, Superman would undoubtedly be viewed as an *àzètɔ́*.) Though it may not be a universal dream, flight has long been a dream in Western society, finally realized in the invention of airplanes. Perhaps this achievement is what makes flying central to Africans' view that airplanes and technology are white people's witchcraft (Piot 2010). Although people are repulsed by *àzètɔ́*, fearful of the dangers they pose, there is often a hint of admiration and envy in people's descriptions of witches' fantastic abilities. A Cotonou healer and an Abomey journalist both said that possessing supernatural power makes one a superman. *Àzètɔ́* are like real-life superheroes and supervillains, battling it out in dreams, the supernatural nocturnal world. The *àzètɔ́*'s capacity for flight, for magical transformation, for becoming invisible, for unsurpassed power, and, as one informant said, for "unlimited possibilities" allows one to approach the status of divinity, to become a god. No wonder so many people spontaneously confided in me that they wished they possessed *àzĕ*. *Àzĕ*'s power is related to a more general notion of power, known as *acè* in Fon. *Acè* is not physical strength but rather a personal attribute that gives one confidence, intelligence, the ability to persuade or control others, and most of all a spiritual strength and resistance. Important religious leaders, politicians, and family elders typically possess *acè*, and frequently one source of their power is supernatural. Undergoing religious initiation, learning recipes for *bŏ*, and installing protective deities in one's home are types of *acè*, but *àzĕ* would be the pinnacle of this personal supernatural power and protection. Having *àzĕ* means complete autonomy and the ability to fulfill all of one's dreams, but people recognize that absolute power corrupts absolutely, and so, as they do with superheroes, they suspect that well-meaning people with *àzě* could be turned to the dark side. The turning and reversal of betrayal is yet another example of the ambiguous and transformative capacity of *àzě*. Because *àzě* gives one supernatural abilities like shape-shifting, teleportation, and control over life and death, people admit that it might be tempting to use *àzě* to attack rivals, to get rich, or to perform fantastic feats for pleasure. But, like making a deal with the devil, informants explained that having *àzě* comes with a price to yourself or your loved ones. With the good, there is always the bad, and their balance in the moral economy of the occult is a topic taken up in greater depth in the next chapter.

chapter two

Black and White

WITCHCRAFT, SCIENCE, AND IDENTITY

While my previous research uncovered the standard register distinguishing between *àzĕ* and *bŏ*, my more recent fieldwork has permitted me to learn a new register about the occult, one that blurs distinctions between *àzĕ* and *bŏ*, good and evil. The data I report in the present chapter focus on ideas emerging especially from religious leaders but now also spreading to the wider population as occult discourses become more public. The growing ambivalence and convergence of *àzĕ* and *bŏ* draw up Beninese views of good and evil, science and magic, African and European, and tradition and modernity. While *àzĕ* previously appeared to me as a solely negative phenomenon, and this is still common within the standard register, today some people openly attach potentially benevolent meanings to its uses, bringing it, in their eyes, into the realm of technology and development. These changes prompt questions regarding the universal applicability of Western and anthropological definitions of witchcraft, sorcery, and science. In this chapter, I address similarities between *àzĕ* and *bŏ*, their positive and negative features, and the significance of the occult for the Beninese sense of identity and relationship to foreign others in Europe and North America.

The Convergence of Occult Powers

In spite of the widespread fear of the occult and of the relatively neat distinctions reported in the preceding chapter that seemingly correspond to E. E. Evans-Pritchard's ([1937] 1976) definitions of Azande witchcraft and sorcery, other discourses about the occult demonstrate that *àzĕ* and *bŏ* may not be so different. As noted, despite the generally negative view of the occult, *bŏ* have always contained the potential for good and bad actions, and this has not changed since my 1998–2000 research. But when I returned to Benin in 2006, I noticed that people spoke of *àzĕ* as having more public acceptance and more positive uses. Some still reported that possessing *àzě* compels one to kill, either involuntarily or out of obligation to the witch society, making "good *àzě*" an oxymoron, but a growing number of people claimed that *àzě* can be directed toward productive ends, attributing to it more voluntary qualities similar to *bǒ* (see also Austen 1993; Bongmba 1998; Fisiy and Geschiere 2001; Geschiere 1997, 2000; Goody 1970; Moore and Sanders 2001; Rasmussen 2001).

In order to understand the convergence of *àzě* and *bǒ*, we must examine the recent spread of notions of benevolent *àzě* in Benin. According to some informants, the potential for good *àzě* has always existed, but media attention and popular interest have made both positive and negative occult forces more common topics of conversation.[1] Whereas *àzě* was previously a secret and taboo phenomenon, I found that some people spoke openly about it. My friend Gaston speculated that attention to witchcraft among Christians and adherents of the deity Trǒ accounts for the rise in witchcraft discourses, and his argument is supported by recent research. Scholars of African Christianity have suggested that Pentecostalism in particular may be a significant reason for the persistence and proliferation of witchcraft discourses (see chapter 4; Marshall-Fratani 1998; Meyer 1999; Newell 2007). As Peter Geschiere (1997, 217; 1998, 811; 2000) has noted in Cameroon and Charles Piot (2010) has noted in Togo, the occult has gone public, and it may be the public appropriation of *àzě* that empowers people to gain control over this force and attempt to put it toward positive uses. In the past, if one were to have demonstrated knowledge of *àzě*, it might have aroused suspicions of being a murdering *àzètɔ́*. This is less so today, since many people now profess knowledge and control of *àzě*, particularly traditional healers. After hearing of benevolent *àzě*, I wanted to learn more about what good outcomes are possible. Some of my Beninese friends like Gaston had also been wondering how the occult can be used for good, and those friends accompanying me to interview religious leaders frequently asked our interlocutors this very question on their own initiative. When responding to inquiries about the distinction between positive and negative uses of witchcraft, people often spoke of *àzě wiwi* (black *àzě*), and *àzě wewé* (white *àzě*), which are translated in French as *sorcellerie / magie noire* and *sorcellerie / magie blanche*, the white variety representing benevolent powers and the black variety representing the evil, destructive side.[2]

Though many people acknowledged the existence of both black and white forms of magic, these two varieties were not believed to be capable of performing the same feats, nor were they equivalent in their properties or prevalence. While evil *àzě* was universally recognized to cause misfortune, bad luck, illness, and death, good *àzě* was said to operate in the domains of good luck, spiritual protection, professional success, wealth, and health. And sometimes people said it holds the potential for broader society-wide benefits resembling the goals of international development. Many added that the difference between the two varieties is that negative àzĕ forces people to eat and kill their family and friends, while the positive variety does not; in fact, it is through good àzĕ that people seek protection from the malevolent form. Those accepting the existence of good àzĕ frequently acknowledged that benign witchcraft is extremely rare; almost nobody makes use of the positive potential. They asserted that àzètɔ́ are either corrupted by power or motivated by envy, greed, and ill-will more than they are by benevolence. There is also a prevalent claim that positive àzĕ, in contrast to the negative kind, is voluntarily acquired through a type of initiation. And like other spiritual initiations in Benin, that involving àzĕ involves a financial expense. It is nearly universally believed that positive àzĕ is exorbitantly and prohibitively expensive, costing anywhere from 200,000 to 5 million FCFA ($400 to $10,000), while the negative variety can be obtained for as little as 2,000 FCFA ($4), or even for free.[3] For many, this is a simple economic explanation for why there is so much more evil than good in the world. Yet another factor in the high price of good àzĕ is that traditional healers use the good form in their work, so in order to protect their business, they charge high prices to transmit this coveted knowledge.

The narrowest conception of good àzĕ generally consists of satisfying individual desires for wealth or protection, sometimes extending to the rest of one's family. Informants stated that white witchcraft can allow you to obtain a good job or to manipulate people and events for your benefit. For example, David, whose father's funeral I discussed in the introduction, related an account of ambivalent mystical power. David's father, the household head (Daǎ), had a friend who had embezzled money from his place of employment. The friend told David's father that his employers had discovered him and were uncovering documents that would certainly lead to him being fired. The fearful man sought assistance from the Daǎ to avoid being held accountable for the theft. The Daǎ accompanied his friend to visit a specialist in a distant village. The specialist asked his two clients to pile up a mound of sand while they told him the problem. Then he climbed atop the sand pile, and they watched him turn into a whirlwind and disappear. A few minutes later, he returned with the incriminating files in his hand. He tore them up and assured the men that the matter was settled. According to David, the company's auditors never discovered any wrongdoing. This story represents a positive outcome for the man who had stolen, so in this respect, selfishly motivated àzĕ (or bǒ) can bring good fortune. But as with so many examples of manipulative magic, it is harder to state unequivocally that this leads to a benevolent outcome, since it depends on one's perspective. The man's employer would be displeased that the thief got away with his crime. Recall from chapter 1 that in a zero-sum game, or a scenario of "limited good," helping yourself comes at another's expense (Foster 1965), accumulating wealth makes somebody else poor, and feasting on someone's soul causes the victim to wither and die, so there are no winners without losers.

Because of the perennial give-and-take between benevolence and malevolence, most people accept that good and evil are incontrovertible facts of life. Both *bŏ* and *àzĕ* demonstrate the extremes of good and evil, the joy and danger of human actions and desires. But they also imply a balance of opposing forces. Frequently, my informants were explicit about the balance of good and evil and acknowledged the ambivalence associated with using *àzĕ*. People regularly told me that healers' power to protect others from supernatural attack automatically means they also possess the ability to kill (see also Geschiere 2000, 2013; Herskovits [1938] 1967, 2:285). One man suggested that part of the ceremony for initiation into the *àzĕ* society involves consuming some food that gets temporarily stuck in the throat. The initiator asks what child you will sacrifice to the society, and only after naming the victim will the food descend into the stomach. This implies that an initiate interested in benevolent magic must still participate in evil acts. As scholars have observed in magico-religious thought from Africa to indigenous Amazonia, the Caribbean, and Afro-Brazilian religions, good and bad are not so easily distinguished, because although there is a constant struggle between them, they are often part and parcel of one another (Hayes 2011; Herskovits [1937] 1971; [1938] 1967, 2:285; Kapferer 1997; Parés 2013; Whitehead and Wright 2004). Geschiere observes that his Cameroonian informants view the occult "as an integral part of the social order: it may be an extremely evil force, yet if channeled correctly it can also bring riches, luck, and power" (2006, 224). Similarly, Harry West (2005) describes the supernatural struggles between Mozambican sorcerers of destruction and sorcerers of construction (healers), who in reality are not necessarily different people (see chapter 5).

In Benin too, destruction and protection go hand in hand. My friend Claude in Abomey told me that his father was given the power to cure epilepsy, but along with that, he acquired the ability to infect someone with the same illness. Rather than think of humans as exclusively good or evil, Beninese appreciate that everyone is capable of both; nobody is completely good or bad, and someone's true nature is unknowable, since people are secretive. A healer with whom someone trusts his or her life may be perceived as a treacherous killer by another. Diviners and healers described energy in terms of duality, similar to positive and negative electrical poles. A shopkeeper at an electronics store said that God created both good and bad, that he is both God and the devil at once, while a healer and Trɔ̃ priest said of the occult, "Zã kpɔ́ɖɔ́ keze kpó wè" (It's like night and day). According to these types of testimony, the world needs evil in order to recognize the good; they complement and depend on each other, bringing the counterpart into relief and ensuring a cosmological balance. The role of opposites and alterity is also important when performing occult rituals. For example, the left hand is less frequently used for ordinary activities and therefore is more appropriate when dealing with the other, invisible world (see Blier 1995, 164). Similarly, burial cloth must be torn before being placed in a coffin, because this is the opposite of what we think of as acceptable clothing in this world. For many, spiritual matters evoke images of reversal and opposition, the balance of left and right, day and night, good and bad.

Paul Mercier (1954) observed that the dualism of the female and male creator gods, Mǎwǔ and Lisá, and the supernatural creation of twin births represent the emphasis on cosmological equilibrium. He further noted that the supernatural is part of a broader dualism in the Fon ontology, which recognizes dyads in the precolonial political leadership—in the form of ministers and their doubles, as well as ministers and their female counterparts (see chapter 1).[4] Marc Monsia (2003) contends that dualism is a constant in Fon philosophy, including positive/negative and masculine/feminine, and he illustrates this dualism with the expression "Gbɛ mɛ nu bi webɔ-webɔ wè" (In life, everything comes in pairs). Eastern religious traditions have a similar reliance on duality and the inclusion of good and evil as two aspects of a single reality (Capra 1975; Tambiah 1990), and, as we will see in chapter 5, Eastern religions have become increasingly popular models for my informants' understanding of the occult.

For some people, the balance of opposing forces implies an inherent sense of justice in the occult similar to the law of karma. While misfortune can bring misery to someone, people assert that victims may deserve what they get because they are likely guilty of things that nobody knows about. My friend Chams told me that ordinary people may be hiding terrible wrongdoing, and he gave the example of a man he knew with three attractive daughters. The man was unusually strict and did not allow his daughters to be visited by the numerous boys who attempted to court them. After the girls achieved adulthood, one of them revealed the secret that their father had deflowered each of them and had prevented other romantic overtures in order to keep his daughters for himself. Though the father did not meet with any supernatural calamity, Chams used the story to illustrate the hidden and ambiguous nature of right and wrong. From the outside, the father appeared to be firm but righteous in protecting his daughters' virtue, but in the end he was found to be treacherous, deceitful, and sexually abusive. If people cannot know who is good and who is bad, then they may feel justified in relying on a supernatural arbiter.

Others made the argument that a group of àzètɔ́ actually sit in judgment over their victims. My entertainer informant Camille stated that in former times àzètɔ́ would employ their power at night to resolve societal problems that could not be fixed during the day. She emphasized that supernatural power was held by kings and other elderly and responsible individuals whose job it was to ensure that people showed each other proper respect.[5] Wade Davis (1985) claims to have uncovered the same ideals of justice and social regulation in Haiti, where people are said to be poisoned, killed, or transformed into zombies by a jury composed of members of a secret religious order.[6] Some regard àzètɔ́ as judges who sentence people to death; whether or not someone is guilty of a specific crime, all witchcraft killings represent the will of God and therefore are enacting cosmic justice. In other words, sometimes people must die to conform to the will of the universe, so even an àzètɔ́ who kills out of malevolent or selfish motives is an instrument of higher justice. According to this thinking, society needs unsavory elements to function properly, such that thieves, prostitutes, and witches keep people humble. Of course, those who lose loved ones at the hands of àzètɔ́ are unlikely to accept that the killing was justified, and this is an important reminder that there are multiple visions for the good and bad aspects of the occult, which is always contested, always ambiguous. The preceding testimony suggests a deeply postmodern sensibility in the way Beninese understand good and bad, right and wrong, truth and falsehood. They recognize that one can never know exactly what someone else is thinking or whether someone has entirely benevolent intentions. Even among friends and family, there is always jealousy and envy; danger is lurking everywhere.

Despite àzě's ambivalence, some people contend that it can perform legitimately good acts without a loser. Geschiere (2000, 2006) has found a similar claim among Cameroonians who want to use the occult for productive purposes, and West (2005) notes that Mozambican healers are believed to use positive occult forces to combat the evil ones. In Benin, too, an example of good àzě is its use in fending off witches' supernatural attacks. This is the type of magic that healers use to save people from the predation of àzètɔ́. But some go further, suggesting that *àzĕ wewé* (white *àzĕ*) can also enable miraculous cures for a broken leg, sickle cell disease, malaria, cancer, reproductive sterility, or AIDS. A longtime friend named Hervé maintains hope for the potential benevolent uses of *àzĕ*. Hervé is an educated single man who works in the local agricultural development office. He has an outgoing personality and takes an interest in exchanging ideas with foreigners, so he had always been open to talking to me, even about sensitive topics like witchcraft. As it happened, he was himself interested in *àzĕ* and had undertaken his own research to understand (and possibly harness) its power, so when he learned of my research objectives he immediately offered to provide me with information. He related a story of his heart condition, which was diagnosed by medical doctors who were unable to treat him. However, he told me his girlfriend was an *àzètɔ́*, and she supernaturally restored him to health and astonished his doctors. He also asserted that *àzĕ* could be used for other humanitarian purposes like disabling landmines and safely landing a plane whose engines had failed. Cyrille, a friend of Hervé's who is a healer south of Abomey, told me that one potentially positive use for *àzĕ* would be to locate precious materials like buried gold. Cyrille argued that this type of activity, in contrast to the zero-sum game, would have no victim. Indeed, a number of informants referred to alchemy in their desire to use *àzĕ* to help people make money without producing any losers, a feature Andrew Apter (2005) has also noted in Nigeria.[7] These discourses begin to blend ideas of magic with development, as many people see development's mission as creating wealth (see Fisiy and Geschiere 2001). Not everyone agreed that *àzĕ* can be applied to development, but a number of informants used language similar to that of international development, talking about the potential of *àzĕ* for helping humanity, bringing peace and harmony, and promoting socioeconomic progress. For example, agriculture could be improved by using *àzĕ* to bring regular rains to farmlands, and one Abomey healer admitted that he already does this for his own crops. Others saw *àzĕ*'s power of teleportation and telepathy as a wonderful technology to allow people to travel and communicate cheaply and quickly.

These comments suggest that at least one of *àzĕ*'s dimensions resembles the promises of Western development organizations and nongovernmental organizations (NGOs) in seeking better health care and more productive agriculture, as well as other elements associated with economic development, such as international travel and communication, and financial success for all. As others have noted, Western-inspired development efforts have largely failed to bring financial independence to Benin and other African countries, which

makes the search for indigenous sources of development ever more compelling (Apter 1993; Bastian 2001; J. Smith 2008). In 2008 I visited a Cotonou
diviner who also runs a spiritual training school, and I was impressed by how
explicitly he evoked the notion of an indigenous model of development.
While in the waiting area with a handful of his clients, I perused some of the
literature and posters adorning the wall. One poster spoke about the diviner's
mission to reveal secrets formerly known only to kings and the highest levels
of religious initiates in order to benefit all society. The poster read, "Notre
volonté de mettre la culture au service du développement nous oblige à mettre
cette connaissance au service du grand public" (Our desire to put culture to
work for development requires us to make this knowledge available to the
entire public). One type of secret knowledge he offers takes the form of a ring
worn for prestige and prosperity, for which he charges 5,000 FCFA ($10).
Since development projects are viewed with a great deal of awe, frustration,
envy, and resentment, they also embody many themes drawn up by the term
àzě. Indeed, most people want to be involved in NGOs for the financial benefits they promise their employees, yet those excluded from development
projects routinely lament the closed nature of these positions, the perceived
decadence of Western workers, the inexplicable disappearance of vast sums
of aid money without visible results for the community, and the sustained
economic dependence that external projects create. Development projects
represent the disappearance of money, perceived betrayal, inequality, and
shameless exploitation—the very same qualities associated with àzě.

As might be predicted, the ability to use àzě for either negative or positive
purposes implies that people would have voluntary control over its powers.
Informants repeatedly told me that those possessing supernatural powers
have a choice whether or not to eat people. In this conception, people themselves determine whether àzě is used for good or evil. Those promoting the
existence of benevolent witchcraft stated that àzě is not inherently evil; rather,
it represents a neutral force, like a tool. The knife was a common metaphor
for the ambivalence of magical powers. The knife is neither good nor evil, but
it can perform both good and evil tasks; a knife has two sides, one that cuts
and another that does not. People described natural gas and atomic energy as
analogous; both sources of power are helpful tools, yet they can both explode
and bring tremendous destruction. Healers claimed that people's ignorance
unfairly tarnishes àzě; they held that the person, not the method, is responsible for good and bad supernatural acts. These sentiments suggest that for
many people, àzě's voluntary qualities share a great deal with its supernatural
cousin, bǒ.

Aside from the similarities in terms of good and evil and in terms of voluntary control, another way in which the occult forces converge is in their methods of operation. Time and again, informants would say that *àzě* and *bǒ* work differently, but on deeper probing, informants often contradicted themselves, with statements such as *àzě* uses *bǒ*, *àzě* is the boss of *bǒ*, and *àzě* is the teacher and *bǒ* is the pupil; the two forces complement one another.[8] This ambiguity over the distinction between *àzě* and *bǒ* was expressed across the board, and sometimes people admitted that they were confused. Though I experienced this similarity between *àzě* and *bǒ* as a recent phenomenon, Melville Herskovits ([1938] 1967, 2:287) reported in the 1930s that makers of *bǒ* could transform into bats and other animals, an ability usually associated with *àzě*. Therefore, it is possible that the ambiguity over these occult forces has a much longer history.

Although some informants echoed the standard register about *àzě* being an invisible psychic force and *bǒ* being a visible intentional act, many of them also qualified their answers by saying that *àzě* is a more advanced form of *bǒ*. They contended that *àzě* and *bǒ* are in the same family because they both employ leaves, recipes, formulae, and the forces of nature. Numerous people stated that mastering *bǒ* is equivalent to possessing *àzě* or that the advanced initiate of *bǒ* will almost surely be given *àzě*. *Àzě* is often regarded as the pinnacle or culmination of training in the art of *bǒ*. And while *bǒ* have always been learned through a long initiation process, I started to hear about a similar process for acquiring the power of *àzě*. This testimony is markedly different from claims that *àzě* is acquired instantly and involuntarily by accidentally eating something or through mystical kidnapping. In fact, some assert that *àzě* involves a series of initiatory stages accompanied by the learning of a sacred language, with gatekeeper specialists monitoring the secret society and providing authorization before admitting new members. I have met people who spent time investigating the benevolent form of *àzě*, some of whom said that the *àzètó* society specialists conduct an assessment of every candidate before offering the full power. One part of this evaluation involves a projection of the next three years of the candidate's life. If great misfortune is predicted for the candidate (such as losing a job or having a spouse or family member die), the specialists will refuse to admit him to the society for fear that he will blame his bad luck on his initiation. If their projection shows nothing alarming, then they will agree to sell *àzě*, which everyone admits comes at such a cost that most people cannot afford it. One elderly man in Cotonou admitted to possessing *àzě*, explaining that the society had first given him the recipes for destructive *bǒ* and then studied him for seven years to make sure he was honorable before offering him *àzě*. Several others revealed that they had begun some of the early stages in the initiation, one remarking that he had achieved the level that allows him to travel mystically at night but noting that he is not a full member.

Many people, as well as the healers who claim to possess *àzě*, said that witchcraft can be manufactured using natural products. They referred not only to achieving specific goals through such recipes but also to the power of *àzě* itself being acquired in this manner. Reportedly, one can combine certain plants and minerals to become an *àzètɔ́* or possibly merely to hold the power of *àzě* temporarily.[9] An old villager gave me a recipe allowing one to travel at night during one's sleep, assuring me that if I followed this formula, all the *àzètɔ́* in the community would come visit me in their nocturnal outings and tell me where they plan to go.[10] Multiple people said there are special leaves that, when applied to the eyes, allow one to see all the *àzètɔ́* in the area. Hervé told me that in his own research with ritual specialists, he acquired the recipe for *àzě*, which involves combining a set of ingredients in a special variety of calabash, known as the *àzě-ká* (*àzě* calabash) or *ká gohǔ* (bumpy calabash), recognizable for being smaller than ordinary calabashes and characterized by bumps on the exterior (see figure 4). He provided the recipe but swore me to secrecy, claiming that his life would be in danger if members of the society learned that he had divulged their secrets. If there is actually a recipe for *àzě*, this would imply that *àzě* is created by using a *bǒ* or that *àzě* is actually a *bǒ*. This calls into question both the distinction between the two forces and the perception of which one is more powerful. Though nearly everyone says that *àzě* is stronger, this ambiguous testimony would mean that *àzě* is merely a facade and that the true power lies with *bǒ*. While the convergence between these terms is a complex process emanating from local conditions and desires, it is also possible that Beninese views are influenced by the fact that both phenomena come under the umbrella of the French word *la sorcellerie*.[11] Both *àzètɔ́* and *botɔ́* are translated as *sorcier* (sorcerer). As other scholars have noted, the European terminology for occult powers creates confusion among scholars, but it can also have an effect on African people's own conceptions, since European terms are often used by Africans themselves to describe these phenomena (Middleton and Winter 1963a, 2–3; Pels 1998; Piot 2010).

In sum, the ideas reported here suggest that *àzě* increasingly resembles its supernatural cousin *bǒ*, which has always been seen as a personal tool subject to the whims of its user. As noted, many people argue that *àzě* and *bǒ* are part of a larger moral universe that involves the cosmological equilibrium of good and evil (Geschiere 2006). And if good and evil are present in every person

FIGURE 4. *Ká gohŭ* (bumpy calabash, *left*), used to make an *àzĕ-ka*. For sale in Abomey's market. (Photograph by the author)

and in every power, then it stands to reason that *àzĕ* could be expanded to encompass positive qualities. The metaphor of guns and bombs for the potential of good and evil is even more relevant to our discussion of technology because Europeans and Americans use guns and bombs in the same way that Africans use the occult.

African Science and White People's Witchcraft

As suggested by the metaphor of white people's weapons, the ability to use *àzĕ* voluntarily for either productive or destructive purposes prompts people to compare it to Western science and technology. Like people in other parts of Africa, Beninese equate Western technological inventions with African mystical powers, giving rise to informants' explicit analogies between "white people's witchcraft" and "African science" (see also Akrong 2007; Ashforth 2005; Ellis 2001). In this section I recount informants' testimony to outline the ways Beninese people talk about science, technology, and the occult and how these views reflect their understandings of contemporary and historical white and black identities and relationships.

African Science

During interviews, rural and urban women and men repeatedly defined the occult as a "science," and some informants used the French term *chimie* (chemistry) or referred to compositions, formulae, and the attributes of elements found in nature. Occult powers derive from natural properties of the flora and fauna, and one man offered the example of sulfur and water producing fire as a simple law of nature similar to those found in African occult powers. Some expanded the scientific classification of mystical forces to include the Fá divination system, whose taboos, predictions, and recommendations many people argued could be scientifically verified through experimentation. Some went a step further to say that Fá, *bŏ*, *àzĕ*, and the actions of Vodun deities are all science. This collection of statements is not intended as evidence that people perceive science and the occult as identical; many acknowledged a difference in either their results, methods, or strength. Hervé explained that science and *àzĕ* are different in that science needs a needle to inject something into someone, but *àzĕ* can do it from afar. He also said that *àzĕ* can ruin or fix the things that science makes, but science cannot interfere with *àzĕ*, because *àzĕ* is stronger. Instead of calling *àzĕ* by the name *sorcellerie*, he prefers the more positive term *science noire* (black science, or science of blacks). Although he distinguished between these two forms of science, his statement represents a widespread view that African occult forces are a scientific phenomenon.

People sometimes included *bŏ* among the African sciences, and the examples provided about chemical formulae would certainly include *bŏ*. *Bŏ*'s use of leaves and other natural ingredients also places it in a category similar to that of a drug or, in the case of malevolent *bŏ*, to that of a poison. Indeed, people were often unclear as to the difference between somebody being poisoned and being the target of an evil spell. In reference to the introduction of the smallpox vaccine during colonial times, Herskovits noted, "To explain this acceptance of vaccination, it may merely be stated that European vaccine is envisaged as a kind of new magic charm given to the White man" ([1938] 1967, 2:139). A *gri-gri* (*bŏ*) is routinely described as an "African medicine." Furthermore, since healers use plant products to make medicine known as *amasĩ* (leaf water, infusion / wet medicine) and *atíkĕ̀* (tree powder, pills / dry medicine)— both of which terms also apply to Western pharmaceuticals—there is an obvious connection between local notions of biomedicine, magic, and traditional healing. Moreover, although people generally acknowledge germ theory, illness is often diagnosed as having a supernatural origin. A healer's role, then, is one that necessarily bridges the natural and spiritual worlds.

Another sign of the converging domains of biomedicine and traditional healing is the growing collaboration between medical centers and traditional healers not only in Benin but elsewhere (Kiniffo 1997; West 2005). I once stumbled upon a meeting between healers and local government officials at a district capital. The objective was to determine how healers and the medical center can work together to handle illnesses that biomedicine cannot diagnose. My friend Simon was with me at the time, and he added that this type of cooperation is important because we live in a world of witchcraft. In fact, a healer known as Daă (honorific title) Adegbenon told me that it is common for Beninese doctors to refer patients to healers when medicine has no answers for their problems. In his estimation, 50 percent of hospital patients suffer from *àzě* attacks. He himself said that he partners with the local health ministry to promote pharmacopeia and herbal medicines. I know of at least two healers who claim to have developed cures for AIDS, and one of them is known throughout the country and was reported to have successfully tested the treatment in three patients. The other healer, a friend of Hervé's, said he wants to transform his discovery into a pill and to combine it with a scientific approach.[12] These are some of the ways that the occult converges with notions of science, sometimes with the explicit intent to approximate or appropriate Western concepts.

Although *bŏ* are among the Beninese sciences, *àzě* was compared to science and technology in more intriguing ways than *bŏ*. In the case of medicine, perhaps the association between *àzě* and science results from the belief that *àzě* is stronger than *bŏ* or from the fact that most people see traditional healers as supernatural warriors, who must already have *àzě* in order to perform their curing/protective services. The other reason that *àzě* has a more profound connection to science is because so much of what *àzètɔ́* do resembles technological achievements such as flight and instantaneous communication. Moreover, people repeatedly referred to *àzě*'s powers as electrical currents, vibrations, waves, and signals, like those used in cell phone technology, and they compared these to the components of a person's soul (the *yè*, a shadow or aura).[13] A telecommunications technician located the source of magical power in vibrations and frequencies before drawing an analogy between mystical power and Einstein's $E = mc^2$ equation. As noted earlier, many people see the change and evolution of *àzě* in the same way that recent scientific advances now permit people to send rockets to Mars.[14] While I was speaking with Camille, my audio recorder malfunctioned, and she took the opportunity to draw the comparison between supernatural abilities and the device sitting on the table. She said that if we were inclined to believe in *àzě*, then we might say that it was responsible for disabling the recorder, because both operate through magnetic waves.[15]

As previously mentioned, some informants described supernatural technology through analogies to knives, guns, atomic energy, and bombs. These comparisons not only represent the ambivalence of positive and negative occult purposes but also emphasize the comparisons to weapons technology. In fact, as noted in chapter 1, aggressive *bŏ* are considered "missiles" (see also Aguessy 1992, 124–25). Another well-known occult weapon is named *cakatú*, often referred to as a mystical gun (Constantin and Coulon 1997, 154). But the *cakatú* is not merely a technological metaphor, because people claim that it performs the same functions as a firearm. While I was talking to an old healer and a young man named Olivier in Cotonou, Olivier told me how the old man treated him for a supernatural ailment. The source of the ailment was a mystical weapon that fired things into Olivier's body (see Kiniffo 1997). During our conversation, the old healer picked up a jar containing the objects retrieved from Olivier's body. Among the objects he identified were tomato seeds, hot pepper seeds, *azefĕ*, and *azenukŭ* (these last were described as a tree and a seed that people said are used in combatting *àzĕ*).

Occult Knowledge

One of the features that science shares with the occult is the belief in the advancement of knowledge. People frequently told me that *àzĕ* amounts to knowledge or wisdom. One man called it a "connaissance de tout" (knowledge of everything), and others said that *àzètɔ* are "des gens extra-lucides" (exceptionally aware/intelligent/clairvoyant people), or superintelligent.[16] Camille called this supernatural knowledge *nyctosophie* (knowledge of the night) (see Creppy 1988).[17] Other informants expressed the view that *àzĕ* comes after long and focused research. The notion of *àzĕ* being the product of a learning process was discussed above, but in the context of science and technology, some people suggested that acquiring *àzĕ* could be an individual research mission rather than an initiation into a secret society. In fact, a number of informants admitted that they were interested in *àzĕ* and were engaged in their own private research to learn more. They disclosed their own desire to become *àzètɔ*, and a noteworthy characteristic of these individuals is that they are often educated members of the urban sophisticated class rather than the older peasants who seemed to control knowledge of the occult a generation ago (see Geschiere 2006). I have heard reports that some of Benin's university students are interested in researching the occult and preserving the disappearing traditional knowledge.

Another aspect of this developing interest in witchcraft is that many young, educated people expressed a desire to mainstream occult knowledge. They said they want the occult to be studied systematically like a science. They hoped witchcraft, like science, can be shared with the world and applied in the service of humanity. Maxime, the university professor, told me he wants to popularize the knowledge of *àzĕ*, and others said that they wanted to start an educational program or school to teach people how to use *àzĕ* for good, making it similar to science and technology (see Bond 2001). Such wishes were expressed by Beninese academics at a 1987 conference in Benin (Dah-Lokonon 1997). Interestingly, schools of Fá have recently emerged, teaching people the art and science of divination, which was once only revealed through secret apprenticeship with diviners. The thrust of these changes is an emerging aspiration to institutionalize and popularize spiritual and occult knowledge. Whereas the prevailing notion of *àzĕ* as a secret society persists, some people contend that *àzĕ* no longer needs to be acquired on a private, individual basis. Instead, they feel this knowledge should be available to the masses and even taught in special occult schools. These changes contribute to the sense that the occult resembles Western science and technology and that it can be applied to positive purposes.

White People's Witchcraft

While informants regularly equated occult forces with science and technology, they also insisted that white people's technology was a form of witchcraft (see also Niehaus 2001; Piot 2010). The Fon word for European, white person, or any non-African is *yovó*, and technology was often referred to as *yovó àzĕ*.[18] People repeatedly told me that *yovó àzĕ* includes the creation of airplanes, automobiles, cell phones, and computers. A minority of people either denied this classification or claimed ignorance of white people's witchcraft. In one case, a Cotonou artist and businessman named Rodrigue said that he laughs when people talk about technology being *àzĕ*, claiming that he is disgusted by "l'ignorance des Africains." Some people said *yovó* do not have *àzĕ*, have less *àzĕ*, or have a different kind of *àzĕ*.[19] One of the key differences is that *àzĕ* is secret and unknowable in its entirety, whereas science is documented. At the same time, a few informants said that *yovó* actually do have a similar *àzĕ*. My friend Claude told me the story of a *yovó* tourist in Abomcy who was attending a sporting match with her daughter. The girl fainted during the match, and the people brought her to a healer in a nearby village. He diagnosed the girl's condition as an *àzĕ* attack emanating from her own mother, who later confessed to the accusation. Other people said that *yovó* come to

Benin specifically to acquire àzĕ, and there are a number of stories circulating about foreigners who initiate into the àzĕ society to acquire occult power. One yovó woman came to Benin to initiate into both Fá and àzĕ, and now she works alongside her Beninese mentor to cure mental illness. She lives in Europe but works regularly in Abomey. Although I never met this woman, she is widely known, I was told, because there was a show about her on television.

Despite some people's claims that yovó either do not have àzĕ or have Beninese àzĕ, the majority of people reported that yovó definitely have their own form of àzĕ. As one healer and vodŭnɔ̃ told me, "Yovó ɖàzĕ taŭ!" (Yovó have strong/pervasive àzĕ). The distinct type of àzĕ that people call "white people's witchcraft" is science and technology. When I asked interviewees whether white people have witchcraft, they would invariably point to a cell phone, my camera, or my audio recorder sitting beside us and say something like "of course, here's your àzĕ!" Cell phones and televisions are compared to àzĕ because they use specialized knowledge to send images and messages via invisible waves and signals. When my friend Claude accompanied me to an ATM machine in Bohicon, he spontaneously remarked in amazement, "Voilà la sorcellerie des blancs!" (Now there's white people's witchcraft!). People also compared àzĕ to yovó people's invention of remote control surgery, genetically modified organisms, airplanes, refrigerators, and other Western inventions, all pointing to the same discursive comparison between Western science and African witchcraft.

Black and White

Equating African occult forces with Western science and technology has obvious implications for people's understanding of what it means to be African or European. The discourse on white people's witchcraft and African science carries a strong message about the relative morality of whites and blacks. In discussing different applications of these two forms of knowledge, informants consistently made explicit statements about Africans' selfish and vengeful magic, in contrast to white people's productive and altruistic occult power. People voiced clichés of malicious Africans and benevolent whites, telling me that even though àzĕ has the potential to do good, Africans are incapable of using it this way. They contended that Africans either cannot or will not use àzĕ to develop inventions like cell phones and airplanes. People portrayed Africans as inherently selfish, mistrustful, greedy, and destructive, and some suggested that Beninese or Fon people have an even greater proclivity for evil. Hervé told me, "C'est l'Africain qui a cette idée de tuer son prochain" (It's the African who has this idea to kill his neighbor), and then added, "Le Dahomey

est encore pire" (Dahomey [Benin] is even worse). He described this negative instinct as *la pensée africaine* (the African way of thinking). If whites
can use *àzě* to accomplish beneficial things, people overwhelmingly said that
Africans mainly use it to kill and destroy (see Meyer 1999, 227n4). People held
that witches are only interested in eating people and that Africans think doing
harm is a good thing, whereas white people are smart because they travel
by plane or car. People spoke of the "African mentality," whereby Africans
prefer to bring others down rather than lift everyone up. An Abomey businessman summed it up by saying that *àzě* produces what people imagine and
desire, and in Benin people imagine misfortune, but *yovó* imagine progress
and industry. All these criticisms echo the refrain that Africans are inherently
greedy and envious (this is, of course, the principal motivation for negative
àzě). People repeatedly talked about Africans' and Beninese people's unwill-
ingness to share secrets and power as a reason for the prevalence of evil *àzě*.
According to these views, *àzě* exists because of Africans' selfishness and lack
of solidarity, and this prevents the country's development. As the story goes,
people are afraid to share their power with their brother for fear that he would
use it against them, and old people are willing to die with their occult secrets
rather than pass them on to others.

Yovó were consistently portrayed as using their technological inventions
to develop productive businesses or to improve communication and trans-
portation—in short, people said *yovó* use *àzě* to help humanity. Others spoke
of *yovó* using the occult as a form of research to "modernize" or "develop"
the world. An elderly man put it this way: "Les blancs sont des chercheurs qui
démocratisent leurs découvertes. . . . Les blancs sont des sorciers plus posi-
tifs . . . qui libèrent l'homme" (Whites are researchers who democratize their
discoveries. . . . Whites are more positive witches . . . who liberate humanity).
A Cotonou woman talked about *yovó* using *àzě* to modernize the world in the
following terms:

C'est ça que nous appelons la sorcellerie blanche, et ça fait évoluer le monde.
Ça ne détruit pas. Mais chez nous en Afrique, plus précisément au Bénin, . . .
ils ont le pouvoir de détruire. . . . Ils n'ont pas vu le bon côté . . . alors que le
blanc, lui, quand il fait ses recherches, . . . ça développe le monde. . . . Mais
chez nous, la technique destructive, c'est ça que nous utilisons ici.

[That's what we call white witchcraft, and it brings progress to the world. It
doesn't destroy. But here in Africa, especially in Benin, . . . they have destructive power. . . . They haven't seen the good side, . . . whereas the white person,

when he conducts his research, it brings development to the world. . . . But
here we use the destructive technique.]

These essentialist portraits also suggest profound cultural and intellectual
differences between whites and Africans, positing the existence of two incompatible civilizations—an inherently "scientific" Europe, on the one hand, and
an inherently "religious" Africa, on the other. A Cotonou woman opined that
àzĕ thrives in Africa because there are forests, darkness, and beliefs. Others
portrayed Africa as backward and primitive, in need of European assistance.
An Abomey barber mentioned that the French invention of the *paratonnerre*
(lightning rod) saves people from lightning, and so Africans need the French
to invent a *parasorcellerie* (witchcraft protection).[20] Within these comparisons we can detect a depressingly negative attitude about an inferior, dependent, and recklessly superstitious Africa that seems to echo many of the racist
European precolonial and colonial images of primitivism.

In outings with my friend Gaston, he was a frequent purveyor of the view
that whites are more advanced. He regularly praised white people's morality,
as well as their technological and social inventions. On more than one occasion, he told me that he teaches his middle school students to respect white
people for their achievements and progress. Although his attitude could have
been merely an overly ebullient attempt at hospitality toward me, it has never
wavered in the years that I have known him, in spite of my efforts to discourage his hierarchical comparisons of whites and Africans. During one such
conversation, I pointed out that he himself champions the idea that whites
and blacks share the same red blood and have a common humanity. He
admitted the contradiction but insisted that Beninese need to recognize that
inventions like airplanes allow white people to do amazing things. It is tempting to interpret such statements as a simple product of envy and internalized
racism, as a sad example of people losing pride in their indigenous customs
and desperately seeking to mimic the behavior of their former colonizers.
These are troubling issues that arise in other postcolonial settings where technology and wealth are symbolically linked to racial identity and morality. For
example, Ira Bashkow (2006) offers an exceptionally rich account of how
the Orokaiva of Papua New Guinea deploy discourses about "whitemen" and
luxury "cargo" in defining morality and racial identity. But Bashkow insists
that these discourses are locally produced rather than imposed from abroad,
and they carry local meanings. He argues that reference to the wealthy "other"
is not merely a message of despair and self-hate; instead, it is a way that local
people make sense of their own world and offer both positive and negative

evaluations of people's behavior.[21] Orokaiva admire foreign commodities and the seemingly carefree lifestyle of whites, but their comparisons also signal the incomprehensible antisocial behavior of whites who refuse to share their goods and who avoid entering into reciprocal exchange relationships. These discourses do more than attest to Orokaiva envy over foreigners' material goods, and they are far from an endorsement of white people's way of life. They are instead a means by which locals can comment on and critique their neighbors' behaviors through reference to whites. In Papua New Guinea and Benin, acting white is not necessarily a compliment, since it refers to behavior that is selfish and arrogant. For example, Beninese criticize each other when they enact European behaviors such as refusing to eat local foods, using utensils rather than hands, refusing to share their wealth, and avoiding solidarity with family and friends.

I follow Bashkow in opposing the interpretation of internalized racism because it casts Africans in a negative light and robs them of their agency. Although occasionally informants appear to engage in self-flagellation regarding African selfishness, cruelty, and underdevelopment, a full accounting of the discourse suggests that their views do more than express dissatisfaction with the self. Beninese conceptions of the relationship between white and black peoples and their witchcraft also demonstrate a critique of the West's failed development policies. Piot has observed this mentality in Togolese stories of the occult, and it is worth quoting him at length:

Increasingly ... Europeans are now beginning to appear in these stories, and this despite the fact that the long-dominant [local] narrative about Europeans has been that they do not engage in witchcraft. Europeans have special (mystical) powers, villagers assert, powers they use for good—to produce the technology for which they are known—while Africans, lacking the means to produce such things, use their power to kill. I initially read this as a false consciousness narrative—of locals having internalized a demonizing/neocolonial story about Africa. But when the canton chief repeated it in 2005, I understood it differently—as a vernacular theorization of African underdevelopment. Namely, it asserts that Africans, like Europeans, are endowed with strong powers but lack the means (infrastructure, money) to bring about their own development. Seen in this light, it is a story that bears resemblance to Euro-American scholarly critiques of global inequality—which connect wealth in Europe to its absence (cultures of death, necropolitics) in Africa—while nevertheless differing in its insistence on an agentive Africa, that, denied wealth creation, exercises its agency in the only way available to it. (2010, 125)

In a similar vein, James Howard Smith (2008), writing about witchcraft and development in Kenya, sees in witchcraft discourses a political critique of government corruption and of the exploitative policy of the International Monetary Fund (IMF). These accounts present a view of witchcraft as a form of agency whereby oppressed people can express their frustrations with the status quo. As with the Orokaiva discourse, the meanings of Beninese stories about African and European witchcraft are just as much about the inexplicable wealth and unfair privileges enjoyed by white people at the expense of Africans.

Pride and the Postcolony

The approaches of Piot and Smith identify the occult as a form of critique or rejection of Western development models (cf. Austen 1993), but they suggest that witchcraft discourse reflects a belief that Africans are unable to create their own development. Smith contends that witchcraft is a metaphor for "despair, inadequacy, and lost control" (2008, 116). My Beninese informants also exhibit a degree of frustrated critique, but I believe that the agency behind the frustration expressed in the white/African divide is found not just in the critique but also in the endorsement of indigenous models of knowledge that people think could be used to do something about their own development (see Bond 2001; Moore and Sanders 2001; Sahlins 1999). In fact, the critical discourse is often accompanied by expressions of pride in Beninese occult powers. Though these voices are not overpowering, they occur frequently enough, despite the fact that my identity as a white foreigner could have discouraged some people from stating these opinions. A healer in Djidja even asked my pardon for criticizing hospital medicine because, he said, biomedicine was invented by white people. But he went on to recount a story of the pregnancy of his wife, for whom the doctors prescribed a number of medicines costing 12,000 FCFA ($6). The healer said he was wary of so many medicines, so he consulted Fá about each one, after which he learned that only two of the medicines were approved by the oracle. The doctors warned him that his wife should take all of the medications or the child would be born malformed. He refused to comply and proudly declared that the child was born completely normal. Similarly, a hotel manager told me a story about a woman who went to a medical center because she thought she was pregnant. The sonogram showed nothing, so she went to a religious specialist, who performed a type of divination using a mirror (my informant claimed it uses àzě).[22] The diviner diagnosed her as being four months pregnant. He told her to take a certain product for seven days and then go back to the hospital.

When a new sonogram was performed, the results were consistent with the divination. According to my informant, the exasperated white female doctor was so surprised that she told the woman not to give birth in her hospital, saying that only in Africa do such bizarre things happen.

Other people expressed displeasure with the West's manipulative business tactics. Hervé, who claims his friend Cyrille has a cure for AIDS, told me that Cyrille is afraid to go public with his discovery because he fears that white people would kill him, since his cure would threaten their drug business. Likewise, Philibert Dossou-Yovo, a nationally known healer in Porto-Novo, rebuffed my attempts to meet with him probably due to his distrust of whites. He has appeared on television and radio, publicly claiming to have a cure for AIDS, so I was eager to meet him and learn about his view of medical and supernatural conditions. I was able to talk to his secretary, who told me that her employer is skeptical of foreigners because he met with Western pharmaceutical representatives about his cure, but they were secretly videotaping their meeting in order to steal his formula. A common viewpoint among ordinary people follows the sentiment that Westerners are interested in money and are willing to get it at the expense of Africans. Many are convinced that a cure for AIDS has already been discovered in Europe or America but that the West has no interest in releasing it because there is too much money to be made in the sale of drugs and condoms and in international health programs. My friend David asserted that he never uses condoms because he suspects that Western nations intentionally distribute condoms contaminated with AIDS as a way of spreading the virus and promoting increased condom and pharmaceutical sales. Such comments and conspiracy theories are common in Africa (Rödlach 2006), and they demonstrate a widely held belief that whites engage in exploitative and predatory business practices in order to accumulate wealth (Bayart 1993). Paradoxically, though whites are believed to use the occult altruistically, their commercial activities are portrayed as anything but benevolent.[23]

But amid the outrage, there is a sense of pride in Beninese and African abilities to use magic and other "traditional" methods to surpass Western capability. As many people have told me, doctors occasionally concede their inability to treat someone and therefore recommend that patients either seek answers "in tradition" or, as Paulin Hountondji observes, "go back to the village" (2002, 23; see also Ahyi 1997). The walls between healers and doctors are beginning to crumble, but, as noted earlier, there are long-established divisions between the domains, and people still feel that modern medicine is not always right and not always respectful of African ways of knowing. My informants often used the terms "traditional" and "modern" to refer to African and Western approaches, and although this reinforces misleading stereotypes that have been critiqued in social science scholarship, these categories are often meaningful to native peoples (Ferguson 1999).

Apart from the medical critiques, people offered other statements that emphasized African powers and resistance to Western intervention. I once stopped in a Cotonou drinking establishment, where two men sitting at an outdoor table on the sandy ground quickly began a conversation with me about race and the occult. One of the men held that whites do not want blacks to get ahead, claiming that this is why whites colonized Africa. He expressed admiration for the last precolonial king, Béhanzin, who resisted the French army before finally surrendering. My informant spoke nostalgically about Béhanzin's mastery of the occult, saying he was a great *sorcier* who used the occult to evade capture by the French between 1890 and 1892 before being taken prisoner. Even when the deposed monarch was deprived of food in captivity, he amazed his jailors by magically procuring full plates of food. My interlocutor continued, saying that while exiled in Algeria, Béhanzin could

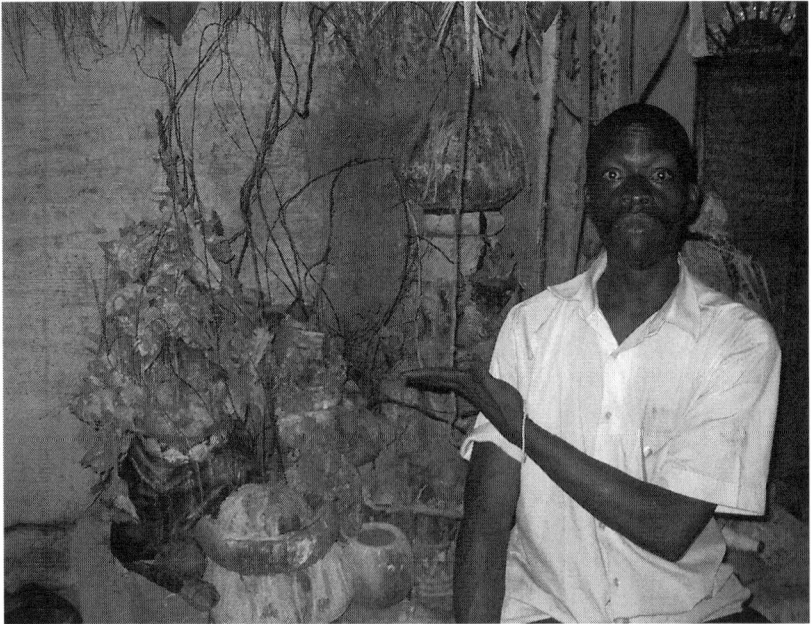

FIGURE 5. A healer shows off his shrine, while expressing pride in African occult powers. (Photograph by the author)

magically travel back to Abomey to make sacrifices to his *vodũ* (spirits). Here we see the sense of pride and nostalgia for the monarch's traditional powers, made all the more poignant by the story of opposition to the French colonial rulers, over whom he gained a supernatural and moral victory in spite of his military defeat. One of the earliest kings in the Fon royal dynasty was Houeg-badja (1645–85), who is also associated with occult powers (Blier 1995, 317). On two separate occasions, informants cited the historical proverb "Huegbaja ká su do; mɛ ɖe nɔ hǔ kpɔ̌ ǎ" (Houegbadja's calabash is closed; nobody can open it). This expression presents the calabash as a metaphor for the king's hidden power, and because the power of *àzě* is contained within a calabash, this implies that King Houegbadja was an *àzètɔ́*.

Suspicions and stories abound regarding contemporary politicians who consult diviners or use witchcraft in order to ensure success (Landry 2015); thus the occult is never far removed from discussions of politics (see also Ellis and ter Haar 1998).[24] Perhaps the most prevalent story about the confluence of political and occult powers relates to a more recent historical event involving President Nicéphore Soglo, the first democratically elected leader following Mathieu Kérékou's seventeen-year dictatorship. Prior to his 1991 inaugura-tion, Soglo became critically ill and spent time at Val-de-Grâce Hospital in Paris. I have heard several people discuss the circumstances of his illness and recovery, but I will relate one such telling from my friend Maxime, whose account goes as follows:

> Before Kérékou left office, he stated the proverb "the branch will not break while in the chameleon's hands." This is more than a proverb and is actually an incantation intended to sabotage anyone attempting to be Kérékou's suc-cessor. Because Soglo was a proponent of medical science and rejected tradi-tional African powers, he placed his trust in medicine, but to no avail. He languished in the Paris hospital for months, in danger of missing his inaugu-ration before ultimately conceding that he needed supernatural assistance. The supernatural intervention was the only thing that saved him and proved that he needed the help of traditional African powers. (See also Banégas 2003; Constantin and Coulon 1997, 154–55; Ngokwey 1994)

Informants also complained of Europeans dismissing African religious knowledge. Christianity has become popular among Benin's professional and elite classes, and staunch Christians regularly condemn adherents of the Vodun religion as devil worshippers (Claffey 2007). Although Vodun practi-tioners are relatively tolerant of Christianity, there is a movement to restore the indigenous religion's value. An Abomey healer asserted that Christians have mistakenly equated the divinity Lĕgbà with the devil. He argued, "We must get closer to our indigenous values/resources." Rodrigue the artist said that all imported beliefs and customs are lies, that it is all a business. Surprisingly, even a Beninese Christian pastor said that colonists and missionaries should not have imposed their foreign beliefs on Africans. He told me of a colonial official in Abomey who accused some local men of stealing one of his possessions. The official ordered the men bound, and he tried to force a confession out of them, but to no avail. Local people told him they would consult Fá to find out if the accused were really guilty. When they performed the consultation, Fá indicated that the Frenchman was himself responsible for the disappearance of the object. The man laughed and declared that Fá really was powerful, for he had indeed taken the object in order to test the oracle. This pastor's respect for aspects of indigenous religion and culture is not unusual in academic and religious circles. In 1970 Catholic priest and scholar Barthélémy Adoukonou founded a theological-anthropological movement to reconcile Catholicism with indigenous Fon culture. Dubbed the Sillon Noir (Black Furrow) in French and Mewi Hwendo (Huĕdo) (Black People's Furrow/Customs) in Fon, the movement promotes respect for "traditional" culture by incorporating Fon customs into Catholic liturgy (Adoukonou 1993; Babatounde and Adoukonou 1991; Noret 2010, 54, 139–40).

Indigenous religious and occult powers (including Fá, vodŭ, and bŏ, but especially àzĕ) are the focus of people's pride and hope, and a number of comments reflected this sentiment. People want to restore pride and revive the disappearing knowledge that they said was their heritage, created by their grandparents. Àzĕ is "an African power" that some note is now recognized by yovó who come to Benin to be initiated. After the French soccer team won the 1998 World Cup tournament, stories circulated that representatives from that team had visited specialists in Benin to acquire supernatural advantages; people stated with confidence that it was, in fact, African powers that won the cup. This pride in the superior strength of African àzĕ was evident in expressions such as "The African doesn't need a knife to kill" and "L'Afrique est dense" (Africa is dense/rich). While I was preparing to leave an interview with a court official, he stated that after talking to me he realized that àzĕ is worthwhile, saying, "It's something that we created." There is a sense of regret that indigenous powers are disappearing in the face of modernity, but there is also a desire to revitalize them as part of indigenous culture, one of the few items of value in a poor country without natural resources (see Jean Comaroff and John Comaroff 1993). A forceful expression of pride in African occult powers surfaced during a 2016 seminar at the University of Cape Town. The exchange, captured in a YouTube video, featured a young South African woman arguing that Western science disrespects African knowledge, such as the ability to "send lightning to strike someone" (UCT Scientist 2016). Her comments included a plea to decolonize Eurocentric science by recognizing African ways of knowing. I witnessed a similar desire to recognize the value of indigenous knowledge during a seminar at the University of Benin, where I attended two presentations that received heated comments from audience members who questioned the speakers' focus on European writers and values. These attendees saw this as a weakness and an affront against African values and intellectual contributions. An Abomey healer put a similar sentiment in terms reminiscent of a growing academic language by saying that people need to get back to their roots by embracing *valeurs endogènes* (indigenous values), a term already in circulation among African scholars seeking greater respect and recognition for the productive potential of African technologies and ways of knowing (Hountondji 1997a, 2002). Indeed, as discussed above, many of my informants stated wistfully that Africans could use the occult for productive ends, and it is this optimism that Mikael Karlström (2004) urges us to embrace rather than solely paying attention to the negativity, fatalism, and destruction in Africans' use of witchcraft.

Science, Morality, and Ambiguity

The conceptual rapprochement between science, on the one hand, and witchcraft, on the other, is an indicator of the merging of categories and the desire to revitalize African indigenous knowledge. Beninese philosopher Paulin Hountondji (1997a, 2002) has been an outspoken proponent of reconciling traditional and scientific knowledge (see also Hoppers 2002). Although he does not refer explicitly to occult knowledge, he does juxtapose "tradition" to "science" and laments the fact that there has been no effort to fuse them: "Should we not explore the possibility of harmonizing them in a more viable composite, bringing them into a local union, and thus finding out if they can in theory and practice yield coherent concepts and technical procedures that might at the very least prove minimally meaningful?" (1997b, 14).

Beninese psychiatrist Gualbert Ahyi (1997) also discusses the difficulty of combining "African" and "Western" models. This creates a tension between competing systems of knowledge, and it reaffirms clichés about African thought shared by both Westerners and Africans alike. Ultimately, unless Hountondji is right about the potential for fusion, this tension leads to the notion of two separate and incompatible worlds, with science on one side and spirituality on the other (Hund 2003). And the spiritual world is consistently linked to Africa; another Beninese psychiatrist has written, "Africa is a land of many mysteries. . . . Of these mysteries sorcery has a particularly powerful grip on the continent's population" (Adjido 1997, 266).

In an attempt to demystify occult beliefs, I have tried to show that while Beninese people may occasionally echo these essentialist images, the grass-roots is giving rise to a different formulation, which holds that science and witchcraft are extraordinarily similar, although different, manifestations of the same universal force. Despite the tendency to regard science and indige-nous knowledge systems (IKS) as incompatible, Lesley Green (2007) reports that South Africa has implemented a new policy to integrate the two systems in the country's educational programming. Green acknowledges that the pre-sumed incommensurability may discourage African scholars from conduct-ing research into IKS, but she rejects the idea of a dichotomy between science and indigenous knowledge. Green contends that the idea of an isolated "in-digenous" knowledge reifies and marginalizes the indigenous as static, tradi-tional, natural, and bound to a particular geographic place. Therefore, she objects to the implications of the term "indigenous knowledge systems," arguing that it is inherently contradictory; on the one hand, it attempts to valorize formerly colonized peoples, but on the other, it marginalizes them from the modern scientific world. Instead, she advocates for integration to prevent people from thinking in the predictably dualistic terms of science versus IKS, rationality versus enchantment, and modern versus primitive.

Beninese are proud of their reputation as masters of the occult. Their com-parisons between "traditional" and "modern" ways of knowing spark feelings of nostalgia and pride for the indigenous powers of their forebears (see Noret 2008). But many want to recapture those disappearing abilities and systematize them in the same way that Westerners harness technology. James Smith (2008) has offered an excellent analysis of the ways that witchcraft beliefs in Kenya are part of a broader rethinking of development, tradition, and modernity. His informants, frustrated by political corruption and their inability to get ahead, are searching for new resources, and, in what Smith calls "tempopolitics," they are questioning and critiquing old and new strategies to achieve knowl-edge and progress. Smith's work demonstrates the interesting and compli-cated ways in which witchcraft plays with ideas of temporality and permeates discourses of development, governance, alterity, education, and good and evil.

In this chapter I have explored articulations between witchcraft and Beni-nese ideas of science and the morality of self and other. In the Western con-ception, science, technology, and development are typically associated with progress and social benefit, but in Benin there is an explicit recognition of the moral ambivalence of technological innovation, which can serve productive purposes but can also destroy. Similarly, *àzě* (or *bǒ*) is considered a type of science representing both positive and negative potentialities. For Beninese, good and evil coexist and transform into one another; they are inescapable aspects both within and between individuals. Loving family members can harbor envy or jealousy and turn on each other. Friends become foes and then sometimes friends again. Healers are admired as heroes until they are corrupted and transformed into bloodthirsty villains. It turns out that the ambiguity between healers and witches is a broad trend common to both Africa and the European witch-finding movements of the Middle Ages, but that trend seems to find especially strong expression in Africa (Geschiere 2013; Larner 1984; Thomas 1971).

Beninese understand that good and evil are dangerously close but that they maintain a precarious balance. A Cotonou healer who travels internationally explained to me that opposite forces are always at work in the universe, and he equated them with the complementary and interdependent yin and yang. In spite of its extremes, the occult is about finding balance between opposing forces, viewpoints, and characteristics. Given *àzě*'s association with the struggle between opposites—day and night, masculinity and femininity, good and evil, kin and nonkin, white and black, healers and witches, righteousness and guilt, love and hate, rich and poor, health and sickness, gain and loss, admiration and repulsion, human and animal—it is clearly a theme on which countless meanings condense. *Àzě* is a total social fact, to be sure, but one that cannot be totally grasped, for its meanings are infinitely deep.

As I have shown, Beninese discourses about science, the occult, and nature's forces carry important messages about the natural and supernatural worlds. But the discourse is also about the social world of Africans in a postcolonial setting where people have a complicated relationship with white foreigners whom they sometimes admire and at other times resent. Good and evil occult powers are described as white and black magic, but these color categories also apply to the association of white people with good witchcraft and black people with malevolent witchcraft. Yes, the occult in Benin is very much about selfishness, greed, and spite. Despite claims that *àzètɔ́* are compelled to sacrifice beloved family members against their will, people affirm that targets of witchcraft and sorcery are chosen based on family grudges invariably related to financial inequality. In a poor country like Benin, where one child's success may come at the expense of another, the zero-sum game is an unfortunate consequence of stagnant poverty. But instead of focusing solely on internecine rivalries exacerbated by growing inequalities inherent in the transition to a market-based, development-oriented society, I see Beninese exploring scientific, magical, religious, and occult practices in response to global inequalities. In an effort to radically transform their poor country into a wealthier one, some Beninese people are beginning to see the occult as a force of good, as a typically African capacity for change and reversal. While the negative imagery surrounding Beninese *àzě* is still apparent—and often spills over in the troubling and unflattering ways that people speak about the African mentality—the effort to retool *àzě* is empowering and displays a remarkable optimism about the potential for change. On the secular side, this optimism is part of the political language calling for *changement* (change or transition). In recent years, politicians and bureaucrats have been promoting a strategy of *changement* to fight corruption, to change business as usual, to develop a new civil society that emphasizes productivity, efficiency, cleanliness, honesty, and transparency. Though it may amount to political posturing on the part of Benin's leaders, the countless seminars and public service announcements on television, radio, and street signs have generated sincere interest among the citizenry who desire a (peaceful) social revolution. But for those who have irretrievably lost faith in the government, it may be their faith in spiritual options that offers hope of reversal and social transformation. *Àzě* is the most obvious candidate for the force to begin this process. It beckons one to explore the imagination, to consider the unimaginable and even the impossible. And this recalls Judy Rosenthal's (1998) description of the power and ecstasy of Togolese Vodu possession—the spirit's ability to take over the adept's body, to become the adept, to replace the adept. Although I may be stretching the interpretive limits here, this may be a fundamental source of the relationship or conflation between *àzètɔ́* and *vodũ*, both of which change, possess, and do unbelievable things.

In exploring the discourse of the occult, I have suggested interpretations and metaphors, with hints of psychological, feminist, structuralist, interpretivist, and postcolonial perspectives. But bear in mind that aside from the explicit statements about dualism and moral equilibrium, most people would not acknowledge all of my observations about the occult, so these remain potential readings, consistent with what people say, though not necessarily a part of everyday discourse. And there are other possible readings both by participants of the culture themselves and by different observers. Furthermore, despite some generalizations, it should be clear that Benin's culture is rife with heterogeneity and ambiguity when it comes to occult views. Some say occult practices are increasing in their prevalence, while others say no.

Some acknowledge that the occult has changed dramatically, while others argue that it is static. Many say *àzĕ* is stronger than *bŏ*, but a few claim the opposite. Some believe there are both positive and negative occult forces, yet many maintain that all are evil. Some say that *àzĕ* and *bŏ* are related, while others say they are distinct. Some suggest that the occult is linked to the Vodun religion, but others disagree. Some say whites do not have *àzĕ*, though most say they do. What is more, no matter what people believe at any given time, they are likely to alter their views over the course of their lives. These discrepancies are expected, even unavoidable, when dealing with guarded esoteric knowledge, but they are also a product of *àzĕ*'s inherent potential for transformation, for embracing opposites. As Rosenthal (1998) notes for the Ewe of Togo, the rampant uncertainty and heterogeneity, the continuous process of transforming, of doing and undoing, of becoming and un-becoming, of opposites and opposition, all show the dynamic postmodern sensibility that is so well developed in this part of the world. Every story has its counterpart; every perspective has an opposing one. And "truth" can be created, shaped, and reshaped. Perhaps *àzĕ*'s potential for transformation and reversal is what opens the door for benevolent occult uses. Though *àzĕ* has mostly been the epitome of evil, it may be its dynamic nature that allows for its potential to be a force for good in the world. *Àzĕ*'s strength is its very capacity for undoing itself, turning itself on its head. As the international Cotonou healer mentioned above told me in richly symbolic terms, knowing how to use *àzĕ* and accepting its power means embracing reversal, learning to walk on your head.

chapter three

Whose Reality?

Any discussion of spiritual forces, including witchcraft, sorcery, magic, and God, raises difficult epistemological and ontological questions, and the case of Benin's mystical environment is no exception. In the years that I have been conducting research in the Republic of Benin, I have never met a Beninese who does not believe in witchcraft—or, I should say, for whom witchcraft is not real, since theological concepts like belief and faith have little meaning for them. There are plenty of reasons for an anthropologist to be skeptical about the existence of supernatural entities, but it is common anthropological practice to accept different cultures' beliefs and customs, to suspend disbelief. Indeed, cultural relativism is a hallmark of anthropological inquiry, prompting us to avoid judging or discrediting other people's traditions. But this does not mean that anthropologists automatically accept other people's supernatural worlds as real; indeed, scholars typically sidestep epistemological issues by referring to other people's "beliefs," "traditions," or "conceptions" about spiritual forces or entities. We implicitly compare our beliefs to those of others but tend to assume that we understand what it means to believe. Rodney Needham (1972) points out that anthropologists typically do not define belief; instead, they treat belief as a universal concept despite the fact that belief is a hidden phenomenon of the mind (see James [1890] 1913). How do we really know what people believe, and are their beliefs comprehensible to us?

Although belief is sometimes acknowledged as a barrier for anthropologists negotiating their relationships within religious communities (Blanes 2006), in their writing, researchers rarely express their own views or reservations about whether other people's deities actually exist. Official and established religions are especially immune to this type of hand-wringing on the part of scholars, but when it comes to "witchcraft" and related occult forces, writers often feel compelled to comment on the reality of these phenomena

(Houtondji 2008). Beginning with E. E. Evans-Pritchard ([1937] 1976), anthropologists have often professed disbelief in witchcraft, and it is worth exploring how anthropologists' beliefs interact with those of their interlocutors and how these interactions shape ethnographers' sensibilities and the ethnographic project. This chapter looks at the question of occult reality in anthropological literature for my Beninese friends and for me personally. I attempt to move beyond facile descriptions of other people's "beliefs" or terms like "the occult imaginary" by seeking to learn not only what Beninese believe but also *how* they believe it. Another way of describing this approach might be to say that for me, this has been more than an intellectual journey; therefore, I attempt to share some of the feelings and uncertainties I experienced living in a world inhabited by witches.

Some readers may find the reflections in the latter part of this chapter unusually personal and certainly provisional. But it is increasingly common for anthropologists to divulge how their fieldwork encounters transformed them and even unsettled them, so I hope readers will indulge me in this effort. I also draw courage from the pathbreaking work of scholars like Paul Stoller (Stoller and Olkes 1987), who unabashedly declares his acceptance of witchcraft reality, and Harry West (2007), who candidly reveals details of his experiences and struggles with witchcraft belief and reality.[1] I realize that in painting myself into the picture of a world with witches I run the risk of appearing to claim that I "understand" witchcraft or that I have come to think like a native. That would be a flattering assessment of my endeavors, yet I must admit that I will probably never completely understand my friends' views of witchcraft or how it feels to live constantly in fear of it. As described in previous chapters, witchcraft is a fluid and contested phenomenon that defies definition, and everyone's experience is unique. Nevertheless, if ethnography is of any value, it is because we have attempted to become friends with people, made an earnest effort to take their views seriously, and wrestled with the comparisons to our own culture. This chapter is the imperfect result of these wrestlings, musings, and other efforts to grasp my friends' and informants' perspectives. Although it is undoubtedly safer to sidestep the question of reality (Ashforth 2008) or to simply refer to informants' "beliefs" and be done with it, I maintain that there is value in sharing with readers the messiness and uncertainty of ethnographic research. In the end, I cannot claim to know what reality is; there will remain unanswered questions and unfinished interpretations to remind us how complex and multifaceted humans and their culture are. This is not to say that other peoples or their cultures are entirely unfathomable; if that were true, then ethnography would be little more than a flirtation with curiosity, and anthropologists would be little more than cultural tourists trafficking in exoticism. While I acknowledge the limits of our understanding, I believe strongly that ethnography provides us with meaningful experiences that bring us closer to our interlocutors. This chapter begins by reviewing the ways that anthropologists have approached the problem of belief and reality, followed by more personal and narrative experiences with witchcraft.

The Status of Witchcraft Reality

Witchcraft studies hold a prominent position in the history of anthropology, for witchcraft represents one of the most exotic foreign beliefs in a discipline originally founded on the quest to uncover cultural and human oddities and present them to a curious world. Nineteenth-century anthropology often used magic and religious typology as benchmarks of the progress of civilization (Frazer 1890; Spencer 1897). With African people's spiritual reality containing magic and witchcraft, the continent was placed on the lowest rungs of the evolutionary ladder. For racist theorists, the "dark continent" epitomized their conception of primitive, irrational humanity.

Evans-Pritchard's *Witchcraft, Oracles and Magic among the Azande* ([1937] 1976) was among the first studies to usher in a new age of anthropological treatment of witchcraft. A progressive work for its day, Evans-Pritchard's account held that Azande witchcraft was not an irrational belief; instead, it was a logical explanation for events that were beyond scientific comprehension (see Kapferer [2002] for a review). In the classic example, all Azande understand that a granary can fall as a result of termite damage, but there is no scientific explanation for why it falls on a particular person at a particular time. Witchcraft fills this epistemological void. Despite the relativist possibilities implied in his writing, Evans-Pritchard classified Zande spirituality as irrevocably foreign, writing, "The Zande notion of witchcraft is incompatible with our ways of thought" ([1937] 1976, 31). And he failed to disguise where his ontological sympathies lay, saying, "Witchcraft is an imaginary offense because it is impossible" (1935, 417–18). Thus, although it was rational, witchcraft was relegated to an exotic and mistaken belief in imaginary forces. As Byron Good notes for Evans-Pritchard and other Western scholars: "Quite reasonable, even if mistaken: that is how the beliefs of others seem to be" (1994, 18).

Later functionalist anthropologists argued that witchcraft was a symptom of social and mental stress (Marwick 1964; Middleton and Winter 1963b; Nadel 1952), or else it served the purposes of maintaining social order (Beattie

1963) and acting as an economic leveling mechanism (J. Rush 1974). This fit with a Durkheimian notion of society as a group of people with common goals and values benefiting the community. Because the functionalist approach reduces witchcraft to a sociological rather than a physical phenomenon, it contains an implicit rejection of witchcraft's reality. Yet, like Evans-Pritchard, some functionalists felt compelled to comment explicitly on the reality of witchcraft. John Middleton argued that witches do not exist, but "what do exist ... are the beliefs, fears, suspicions, and accusations of witchcraft and sorcery" (1963, 266). Belief remained the dominant model for dealing with witchcraft ontology.

Though anthropology lost interest in witchcraft for a couple of decades, with the publication of Jean Comaroff and John Comaroff's *Modernity and Its Malcontents* (1993), a new wave of anthropologists began dealing with witchcraft but treating it less as a tool of social control than as a product of modern social turmoil. These writers claimed that expanding neoliberal policy, inequality, modernization, and rapid social change have engendered uncertainty, confusion, and envy, resulting in the proliferation of witchcraft fears and accusations (Moore and Sanders 2001; J. Smith 2008; Stewart and Strathern 2004). Thus, while earlier modernists predicted a decline in witchcraft owing to the spread of technology and Western education, the consequence of rapid social change has instead seen an increase in inequality, jealousy, and envy and therefore of African preoccupations with witchcraft (Pels 2003). Contemporary scholars rightly point out that African witchcraft is not a vestige of a timeless and "traditional" past associated with uneducated rural villagers; instead, witchcraft is a dynamic and fully modern phenomenon that articulates with current urban politics and society (Geschiere 1997). Recent studies draw on earlier functionalist frameworks, but with a new reading, since they portray witchcraft as a product of social tension and envy rather than as a force for conformity and social harmony (Falen 2007; Kapferer 2002; Moore and Sanders 2001).[2] If witchcraft is a manifestation of uncertainty, inequality, and socioeconomic changes, its existence could be interpreted as a social-psychological phenomenon (belief or fantasy) rather than a physical phenomenon (a reality). As James Siegel argues, "Western philosophical tradition depends on banishing magic and on basing knowledge on what reason can comprehend" (2006, 9). This, he says, prevents outsiders from understanding witchcraft as anything more than superstition and myth. Although some writers are sensitive to the seriousness with which witchcraft is taken by Africans, they are often hampered by the persistent question of belief—on the part of both Africans and themselves (see Fratkin 2004, 63). In his book on witchcraft in South Africa, Adam Ashforth confides that he does not exactly believe in witchcraft. He quotes a white South African physician who says, "The difference between you and me is that you talk about witchcraft as if it could be real. I know that it *is* real. And it's helluva dangerous" (Ashforth 2005, 317).[3]

Kwame Anthony Appiah (1992) discusses the central role that African "traditional religion" and witchcraft have played in philosophical debates about modernity, rationality, and reality. Following Keith Thomas (1971), Appiah argues that "religion" in industrialized nations has changed dramatically since the Enlightenment, such that science replaced many of the practical, materialistic aspects formerly contained within the religious sphere. This restricted religion to symbolic rather than literal significances, but, he argues, "it is peculiarly unsatisfactory to treat a system of propositions as symbolic when those whose propositions they are appear to treat them literally" (Appiah 1992, 115–16; see also Good 1994). Togolese psychiatrist Léocadie Ekoué addresses the effect of different disciplinary methods.

> Westerners always have their own notions of sorcery and the way it has functioned in Europe and the U.S., and they use that frame to investigate African sorcery, but that simply does not work. The questions themselves are full of traps so that the answers are pulled into a discourse that has its own agenda and cannot result in an African interpretation. Sorcery . . . as interpreted by Westerners is always about trials, the law, judgment, and capitalism. It is as though when we speak of sorcery in terms of sociology . . . we use a huge fishing net for catching sharks, when we should be using a fine spider web made of silk. (Ekoué and Rosenthal 2015, 130)

West (2007, 45) has pointed out that one of the pitfalls of the dominant social science tradition derives from Émile Durkheim's and Karl Marx's depiction of religion as symbolic and illusionary. As West notes, these models see African witchcraft as a metaphor for envy, wealth differential, and disenchantment with capitalism; in other words, witchcraft is a symbol for other social-psychological phenomena.[4] West criticizes these views and acknowledges that phenomenological approaches are more accommodating of native beliefs. His realization was inspired by a Mozambican's reaction to a talk he gave about the symbolism of sorcery lions. After the talk, the Mozambican audience was stunned and silent until one of them finally told him, "I think you misunderstand . . . these sorcery lions you talk about. . . . They aren't symbols—they're real" (2007, 5).[5] Peter Geschiere reports a similar experience at a conference on witchcraft in Cameroon where he was criticized by a priest for using the idea of different discursively created realities to explain witchcraft. Geschiere writes: "My line about witchcraft as a discursive practice was for him completely beside the point" (2013, 204). As these examples illustrate, recognizing the gap between us and our informants does not automatically make it easier to accept the reality of witches. And as Geschiere makes clear, the contradiction between native and foreign views can lead to reproducing a vision of African false consciousness (2008a) or of reifying an essentialist view of African difference (2013, 170). The use of metaphorical or discursive constructions to interpret witchcraft is the product of anthropologists' honest attempts to deal with different lived worlds, but it risks reaffirming the notion of incommensurable cultures.

Some recent scholars of African witchcraft take a more explicit position on the question of belief, claiming not only that witchcraft is a fantasy but that responses to witchcraft beliefs are unlawful and dangerous—in other words, if witchcraft acts are imaginary, then witchcraft accusation is a violation of human rights. Gerrie ter Haar's edited volume *Imagining Evil* (2007) unequivocally operates from the position that people are welcome to *believe* whatever they like, but human rights dictate that they cannot *act* however they like toward suspected witches. This position derives from reports documenting how accused witches are increasingly being driven from their homes, beaten, and even killed by angry mobs (Niehaus 2001). For ter Haar, the fault lies not only with the mobs but with anthropologists who may unwittingly reinforce local witchcraft beliefs by accepting the reality of witchcraft.[6] While I agree that witch hunts represent a crisis, I do not accept ter Haar's conclusion about anthropologists' culpability, for, as I noted, most anthropologists portray witchcraft as an imaginary social construct rather than a reality. Moreover, as Geschiere (2013, 106) points out, anthropologists and missionaries historically tended to collapse ambivalent local occult terms into the single negative word "witchcraft," thereby silencing the diversity of meanings. And most anthropological writing is read in Europe and North America, so it seems unlikely that ethnographic work would have an impact on folk beliefs in Africa. Furthermore, if successive waves of missionaries, schoolteachers, and colonial legal systems have been unable to eradicate witchcraft ideas in Africa, then I doubt that the work of anthropologists would influence the status of belief on the continent.

The issue of witchcraft epistemology has a long history in anthropology, and scholars have noted the problem of "reality" in ethnographic interpretation (Ashforth 2005; Douglas 1970; West 2007). In *Structural Anthropology,*

Claude Lévi-Strauss (1963) attempted to make sense of an account by Matilda Coxe Stevenson (1904) about a Zuni boy who confessed to witchcraft after previously denying it. For Stevenson and Lévi-Strauss, it seemed clear that the boy's confession was a lie motivated by the thought that it was his last hope for escaping the death penalty.[7] The youth embellished his story with a mesmerizing tale and a demonstration of witchcraft that impressed his judges and reaffirmed their certainty that witchcraft was real. Lévi-Strauss concluded that much magical thinking gains strength from psychological motives and the "social consensus" about magic's reality. According to this line of reasoning, confessors and shamans are performers offering reassurance of a (false) reality. Lévi-Strauss concluded that a shaman who achieves results is triggering a psychosomatic reaction in his patient and that this reinforces a belief system that relieves anxiety by explaining the otherwise inexplicable (cf. Evans-Pritchard [1937] 1976; Malinowski 1948). This is not unlike Evans-Pritchard's message that, however wrong Azande belief in witchcraft, it was still rational.

In a provocative article drawing on Evans-Pritchard's work, Karen Fields (2001) dissects the concept of rationality to compare belief in witchcraft to the belief in racist ideas (which she calls "racecraft"). She points out that even as he denied the truth of witchcraft, Evans-Pritchard defended Azande rationality in an effort to undermine Western racism, and this has become common practice in the social sciences. This is paradoxical, she says, because social scientists present racism as false and therefore irrational. She argues that if Azande witchcraft is false but rational, then so too must be racism, unless we accept that Africans and Europeans are fundamentally different. This invokes the debate about the psychic unity of humankind, which might otherwise appear self-evident. Fields concludes that witchcraft and racecraft are in fact similar phenomena because they are both false but rational. Their rationality is predicated on a model of reality constructed collectively through social consensus.[8] Although the evidence for witchcraft, as for racecraft, is always debatable and selectively evaluated, Fields emphasizes that it is always available. She adds that even scientists who refute the truth of racist ideology cannot deny that race is a social reality in our world. This view is echoed by George Clement Bond and Diane Ciekawy, who argue that reality is irrelevant to the study of witchcraft; since people believe in it, the scholar's challenge is to find "analytic loci which have meaning for the academic observer and the actor" (2001, 7). In other words, witchcraft is like any social domain that can be subjected to scientific examination through appropriate metaphors, analogies, classifications, and terminologies that create meaning. Fields suggests that the analogy between racecraft and witchcraft indexes the psychic unity of humankind, the acknowledgment of which can help us better understand the social reality of witchcraft, regardless of our view of truth or reality.

In *Naming the Witch* James Siegel also views magic as imaginary, but he has a different take on the psychic unity of humankind. He argues that we should avoid trying to minimize the differences between cultures and that anthropology embraces difference because it "structures the study" (2006, 17). He adds that the objective of explaining and understanding witchcraft is unrealistic and misplaced: witchcraft is incomprehensible, in the first place, and anthropologists do not end up believing, practicing, or protecting themselves from it, in the second. For Siegel, witchcraft "remains inaccessible" (21), an example of unknowable and impenetrable culture: "The 'truth' of sorcery presumably lies in the transformation between inchoate feelings and the delimitation of these in such a way that they are tellable" and brought to the surface only through language (25). Thus, "truth" is a discursive creation based in the process by which people attribute meaning to social phenomena.

On the other hand, Geschiere (2000) acknowledges that the persistence of witchcraft in so many domains of African life compels academics, perhaps now more than ever, to tackle the question of reality rather than treating it as irrelevant or unknowable. I have attempted to answer Geschiere's call by taking witchcraft seriously. Conceiving of witchcraft as Africans do is one strategy for grasping their reality, though, as noted, this is probably only partially achievable because of the extraordinariness of it. However, Peter Pels (1998) has cautioned against depicting African witchcraft in the exotic fashion so common in the West, arguing that for Africans, it is a quite ordinary phenomenon. He urges us to abandon our Western perceptual tendencies and risk feeling what magic is like to Africans. Unfortunately, because Western academics often see occult beliefs as a symbol for something or as a collective fantasy, it is difficult to put ourselves in Africans' shoes, particularly if we assume that such a process involves a fundamental transformation of ourselves into "others." Instead, one strategy of rendering witchcraft more comprehensible might be to imagine Africans in *our* shoes, making sense of *our* belief systems. In other words, what ordinary Western customs and beliefs might Africans recognize as similar to witchcraft? Pels (2003) notes that Ruth Benedict and Bronisław Malinowski compared magic to such Western practices as political oratory and advertising. Likewise, Geschiere (2003) suggests that Western political spin doctors perform a role similar to African witch doctors in their control of information and their exercise of power. In fact, he has argued that the Western world is full of "modern" types of enchantment that are similar to those in Africa (Geschiere 2000). As I have noted, using the meanings expressed in popular literature and films about vampires, superheroes, and mystical abilities is indeed one way of gaining an entrée into witchcraft sensibilities, but I am wary of equating fictional characters with real people.

The problem with trying to put ourselves in African shoes is that we are never quite sure we succeed, particularly if we keep the supernatural realm at arm's length. One solution for encountering the reality of witchcraft firsthand would be to get initiated and actually acquire supernatural power, as described by Stoller (Stoller and Olkes 1987). Despite such examples of magical apprenticeship, the academic literature remains reluctant to engage with the reality of witchcraft.[9] Although I am unsurprised by the small number of Western academics willing to declare the reality of witchcraft, I would expect to find more African scholars expressing their convictions about witchcraft (Mbiti [1969] is an exception). Ter Haar's (2007) edited volume includes several African contributors living in Africa, and the book's introduction states that these authors were selected for their ability to offer a more authentic African perspective on witchcraft. Interestingly, none of them demonstrates the belief in witchcraft that I am familiar with in Benin. One of them even takes a decidedly pejorative and paternalistic tone, writing, "Witchcraft beliefs foster a naïve attitude among the members of the Bakwaya society" (Nyaga 2007, 264). An edited volume by South African law professor John Hund (2003b) is one recent work that treats witchcraft as real and includes contributions from African authors in the traditional healing profession (Chavunduka 2003; Mutwa 2003). There is also a host of theological and self-published literature in Africa that accepts the reality of witchcraft, but these works are generally not written by mainstream academics (e.g., Agossouza n.d.; Aza n.d.; Dagnon n.d.; Hebga 1979; Kuassi n.d.; Kunhiyop 2003; Mbuy 1989, 1992; Mukundi 1983; Zawa 2006). In fact, the writings I see in Benin are often produced by mystics and healers who stand to gain clientele through the propagation of witchcraft beliefs, so they are not necessarily impartial observers.

So why do so few African academics declare a belief in witchcraft? For some, in light of the numerous witch hunts, to acknowledge witchcraft's reality may be politically incorrect or dangerous. There may also be a generational factor at play, since many senior scholars were educated in the Western tradition during a time when witchcraft was labeled a superstition and discouraged. But young, educated Beninese with whom I talk show little ambivalence about acknowledging witchcraft. My adoptive Beninese brother and former research assistant, Chams, says he knows university professors in Benin who believe in and even use *àzě* and *bǒ*. But he feels they are reluctant to reveal their beliefs publicly for fear of being regarded as irrational (see Green 2007).[10] This would mean that African academics adhere to a "don't ask, don't tell" policy when it comes to witchcraft belief. Indeed, since the academy is dominated by Western rationalism, which is discursively pitted against a prerational traditionalism (Kapferer 2002), the admission of witchcraft's reality might be seen as professional suicide. This suggests a dual model of reality—one scientific, rational, modern, and Western and the other magical, irrational, traditional, and African. Indeed, Terence Evens (1996) holds that Africans truly inhabit another world that remains unfathomable without a complete transformation of ourselves (see also Needham 1972). This would mean that the notion of two separate worlds is an enduring barrier to understanding African witchcraft.

In addition to the problem of divided worlds, witchcraft is subject to an important status handicap. Because witchcraft beliefs and accusations are seen as destructive, they have come to be viewed as a social problem to be corrected (ter Haar 2007). Moreover, magic appears as a belief system anterior to science and even to religion, so witchcraft has a hard time getting a foothold in academic legitimacy. Religious scholars and anthropologists rarely, if ever, undermine the reality of people's gods or deities in the way they question witchcraft. Just as modern-day Western "cults" have missed the mark of being regarded as established religions, witchcraft continues to be seen as something inferior, illegitimate, and cultlike. But as I have argued, there are signs that witchcraft is becoming more official, more public, and more established in Beninese society, perhaps laying the foundation for a new status.

Beninese Experiences with the Occult

As noted, I have never met a Beninese who does not treat witchcraft as real. One man I met in Abomey told me there are some who disbelieve, but he admitted they are rare. He went on to tell me about his father, a principled defender of scientific rationalism who inculcated in his children the view that witchcraft was nothing more than foolish fantasy. However, my informant went on to say that, despite his father's teachings, as he grew up and began to experience the world on his own, he came to realize that witchcraft was real. This man's life represents two poles in an imaginary contest between absolute belief and total rejection. In reality, most Beninese I know fall somewhere in between the two extremes, displaying occasional skepticism amid a backdrop of long-term acceptance of the reality of witchcraft. People are convinced that witchcraft is real, but they do not necessarily accept that every suspected witch is guilty. It may appear contradictory for people to question individual

instances of witchcraft while otherwise possessing the overwhelming conviction that witchcraft exists, but as Thomas Kuhn (1962) reminds us, belief systems can withstand considerable doubt and counterevidence before being
abandoned. But this is a tension to which Beninese readily admit. My friends
and informants struggle with how to determine in which cases witchcraft has
really occurred and in which cases it is merely the paranoid search to blame
somebody for misfortune. In 2008 I visited the Beninese director and assistant director of the Benin headquarters of an international nongovernmental organization (NGO). When I told them about my research on witchcraft,
they became excited, saying they were extremely interested in my findings.
One of the issues the NGO deals with is the status of women, and the officials
explained that their problem is trying to distinguish between actual witchcraft and false accusations against women. They hoped that I could assist
them in protecting innocent women by shedding light on ways to identify
guilty witches. Unfortunately, I had to say that I had not uncovered this secret,
which nearly everyone is seeking in Benin. In many ways, the skeptical perspective so often associated with Westerners is alive and well in Africa but
concentrated in less personal cases, which can be treated more abstractly. For
cases involving the death of an immediate family member and in the face
of severe grief or the observation of startling coincidences or confession, it is
harder to take a removed critical stance. I will now turn to some of these
pieces of evidence that convince people of witchcraft's reality.

Evidence

Like the officials in the NGO mentioned above, most Beninese lead a continuing search for proof or evidence that witchcraft exists, that a particular
event was caused by witchcraft, or that a suspected individual really is a witch.
People are generally aware that Westerners deny witchcraft's reality, and they
claim that the legal system also fails to acknowledge it, so there is occasional
insistence on the part of people who want to affirm that witchcraft exists. For
Beninese, one of the most convincing pieces of evidence for witchcraft is an
untreatable illness. Time and again, I have learned of people who fall ill and
visit medical doctors only to be told that no illness can be detected. When
medicine fails, this is considered a sure sign of supernatural causes. In fact,
as noted in chapter 2, doctors freely admit that there are cases they cannot
treat, and many of them suggest that patients try their luck with traditional
healers. A medical doctor believing in the power of spiritual healing might
seem odd to Westerners who create a neat dichotomy between a scientific,
medical reality, on the one hand, and a supernatural belief, on the other. But

for doctors who grew up in Benin, there is no conflict in their respect for both systems of healing, since, like ordinary people, they recognize that there are invisible forces that transcend medical knowledge. One of the differences between the way Westerners and Beninese perceive these issues rests on the importance of personal experiences, relationships, and testimony in accounting for witchcraft's existence. Whereas Westerners might be inclined to trust only observable, scientifically verifiable evidence (which Beninese also desire), my Beninese friends tend to place equally important weight on information garnered through their own experiences or learned from others. One need only talk to Beninese for a short time before hearing stories of witchcraft attacks, suspected witches, or measures taken to avoid witchcraft. The following vignettes offer a sample of the many pieces of evidence reported by friends and informants.

In 2008 I met Jérôme, a man in his thirties who was underemployed, working as a day laborer at the port in Cotonou. At the time, he occasionally did odd jobs for my adoptive mother, Mouni, when she came to Cotonou to stay with her daughter. Jérôme had already had a difficult life, and Mouni told me he was a sad case, trying to raise his family in little more than a lean-to shelter on the outskirts of town. Jérôme told me about his spiritual history, which demonstrated a life of hardship beginning early on. When he was a child he suffered from asthma, but he learned that his case had supernatural origins. Having been ensorcelled, he was brought to a healer in the coastal town of Grand Popo. Jérôme said the healer hit him solidly on the chest, and the ailment was gone instantly. This type of miraculous cure is a recurring theme in cases of what Beninese call "provoked" illness. In the case of a physiological condition, people say it would have to run its course or be treated with biomedicine, but supernatural illness can be cured as mysteriously as it arrived (see chapter 5). When he was a student at twenty-four years old, Jérôme had a problem with headaches. For a month and a half, every time he started studying, he experienced intense headaches, preventing him from continuing his work. In addition, he developed a sinus infection for which pharmaceutical medicine brought little relief. After consultation with a diviner, he learned that this was also a supernatural attack designed to prevent him from succeeding in his studies. He found a Chinese book on healing in a library, and in it he learned of a recipe calling for him to submerge a bay leaf in a bamboo cup and drink the contents twice a day for three to four days. He was pleased that this had a positive effect, but since his problem was more than physiological, he knew this treatment was only a temporary solution. Most people agree that mystical forces will prevail eventually unless countered with stronger magic. He returned to his childhood healer in Grand Popo, who lifted the spell and cured him.

Laurent, a retired elderly friend in Abomey, told me the following case he was involved in through his role as a government-appointed dispute media- tor, someone who tries to resolve cases outside of the official court system. In one of his cases, a woman came to him complaining that her son was being mystically attacked by her aunt. The boy was noticeably sick, and the family was so incensed that they wanted to kill the aunt. They explained that a diviner had already identified her as the guilty party. Laurent said he took the aunt aside and told her that the safest thing for her was to release the child. He told me that although she initially denied responsibility for the boy's illness, she admitted privately that she was angry that the boy's mother did not show her the proper respect owed to an elder (a clear motive). When pressed, she finally consented to prepare an infusion to help the boy. The next day, the family came and told my friend that the child was cured.

Jean is a longtime friend from a village south of Abomey. Since my arrival in the summer of 2008, I saw him once or twice in the village, where I learned that he had lost his daughter to witchcraft a few years earlier. I was eager to interview him, but I had difficulty getting him to commit to a time and loca- tion. His natal home and family are in the village, but he also has a house and a second wife in Abomey, and he worked as a civil servant in Bohicon. This meant that he was constantly on his motorcycle traveling the fourteen- odd kilometers between each of these locations. Although he was friendly and cheerful when I saw him, I was also concerned that the topic was too emotional and raw and that he may have preferred to avoid me. He finally agreed to meet in his Bohicon office before going to a nearby restaurant for lunch. Despite my concerns, he spoke candidly and at length about the loss of his eleven-year-old daughter. Here is an edited passage from our interview, conducted in French.

J: Here's how it happened. I have a cousin; she was staying with us. I have to say that she had already gotten into witchcraft, but I didn't know. . . . And from time to time, she didn't completely get along with my wife. But while we were all there, she was already making a plan for one of my kids, but I didn't know, and their mother didn't know either. Do you see? And one evening, she was already getting ready to take the child. One evening, returning from the fields, when I arrived, the child was in good health. The child was in good shape; she's even the one who said, "Welcome home, Papa," and I saw her. I wanted to wash and get ready to go out, to go for a

walk, and then come back. And when she [the cousin] noticed that I had
left, she attacked the child in an extraordinary fashion. The child who was
in great shape leaving the house, when she returned, she fell right there at
the gate.

DF: She died on the spot?

J: When she fell, without having anything wrong with her, from the moment
we took her, until the hospital in Goho [Abomey], she didn't say another
word until her death [in the hospital]. And after some research, after consultations and research, we realized that it was that lady there who's a
witch.

DF: You consulted Fá?

J: We consulted Fá, we consulted *vodū*. There are *vodū* people consult. We also
consulted that religion Gbigbɔwèwé [Celestial Church of Christ], who told
us that there was a witch involved. And they all said nearly the same thing.

DF: And what did you do to the woman?

J: We made a *bŏ*. We went to see a *vodūnɔ̀*, a healer, to know if she was really
a witch. We went to see a *vodūnɔ̀*, who told us, if she is really a witch, we'll
know. He prescribed a number of things. We bought all these things. We
spent nearly 100,000 FCFA [$200]. That thing [the *bŏ*], he came to do it
in the middle of the night. We dug a hole at least sixty centimeters deep in
the woman's courtyard, we buried the thing there. Such that . . . in fact, the
next morning, when the lady woke up, she started speaking like a crazy
person. Everything she said, she couldn't even know. And that's what the
vodūnɔ̀ told us, that she would start talking, and everything she said, even
she wouldn't understand. And in fact the next morning, when she started
opening her door, right away she started yelling loudly: "Oh, I see a lot of
things! Leave me alone! Why are you doing this to me? No, no, no! You
have to let me go! Why?" And we were saying, "What did I do? I didn't do
anything to you."

DF: Did she know the thing was buried there?

J: No, she didn't know! Because she was sleeping when we went. . . . I buried
that thing there myself. . . . She refused to stay in the house. She fled the
house!

DF: So you confronted her finally?

J: Finally, we called her. We said that what happened, it was her! She left and
went to stay with her dad.

Solange, a woman in her late thirties, related an account of her aunt being
a witch. When Solange was about twelve, she had a little sister who was getting

ready to dance. But their aunt grabbed the sister, then let her go. By that night, the girl had a high fever. The next day, the family took her to the hospital. On the third day, the fever was so strong that she was urinating blood. She died soon after that. Solange's father was approached by a specialist, who performed a ritual used to identify witches. The ritual consisted of Solange's father putting a medicine in his eyes, after which he and the specialist were transported to a large house, where people were cutting meat and fish [a common metaphor for witches' consumption of human souls]. He saw the aunt and learned from her that she had killed the child to pay a debt. Another medicine was applied to his eyes, and he was returned to his bed. The specialist recommended a ritual preparation involving a substance in a bottle, which would attract the guilty witch. Soon after the bottle was prepared, the aunt appeared. Solange's father confronted her and hit her in the face, knocking out four teeth. After three months of yelling and talking about the attack on the child, Solange's aunt died.

Pulchérie, a twenty-five-year-old administrative assistant in Cotonou, told me about her boss being harassed by witchcraft. The wealthy boss was the victim of a series of fires at his house. The first fire was in his garage, but it was extinguished with little damage. The next day, the man was at work discussing the mysterious fire with his employees when the phone rang. It was his wife saying there was another fire but in a different room, and she told him to call the firefighters. Again, the fire was put out without significant damage. The following day, Pulchérie was at work while everyone was still talking about the sad events of the previous two days. The phone rang and she answered, only to learn that her boss's wife was again reporting a fire, but this time it was even more serious and had spread throughout the house. When Pulchérie and her employer arrived on the scene, they found the house in ruins, with many of their possessions destroyed. Nobody could understand how this could happen, since none of the residents smoked cigarettes, the kitchen was not in use, and the children were all at school. People unanimously declared that this was not natural, for a series of unfortunate and unlikely events so close together were the obvious work of witchcraft. The man was urged to consult a diviner to get to the bottom of his problems, but instead he summoned a Catholic priest to pray for him. The priest called a family assembly for the prayer, during which he had a vision that the man's twelve-year-old maid was behind the fires. Pulchérie explained that those suspicions were confirmed when the girl began shaking and crying during the ritual. The priest told the man his maid was responsible, and he wanted to hold an exorcism, but the girl's family refused and took her away.

A retired elderly schoolteacher in Abomey told me about a six-year-old girl he knew to be an àzètɔ́. One of the powers often attributed to àzètɔ́ is a type of X-ray vision that allows a witch to see inside people. In this case, the girl looked inside a woman's abdomen and correctly told her she was pregnant before the woman even knew.

My friend Simon, an educated rural man in his forties, has a wife with a history of illness, usually of supernatural origin. He told me that when his wife got very sick once, a mysterious old man came to see him, saying that his wife's sickness was unnatural (i.e., provoked by supernatural means). The man claimed to have mystical powers, and he brought this information in order to help Simon's wife. After that, Simon visited a healer to discuss the mysterious man's claims. The healer performed a spiritual investigation and concluded that the old man was himself responsible for the ailment. The healer performed a ritual, and Simon learned a few days later that the mysterious visitor had died suddenly.

The stories I have related here are not extraordinary either in frequency or in gravity. For many people, illness and misfortune provide clear evidence that witchcraft is real. Though dramatic incidents are rare, other people have witnessed incredible superhuman feats that make bǒ and àzě unmistakably real. But occult problems and solutions are everywhere, to the point that one need not have experienced a supernatural attack or witnessed a magical demonstration personally in order to have details about such events. While educated Westerners may attach importance to personal observations and statements by authorities, Beninese accept the testimony of trusted friends and family more than official news sources (Ellis 2002). To outsiders, this appears as gullibility, a lack of critical perspective, but in Benin this is part of a broader cultural pattern, sometimes called *radio trottoir* (sidewalk radio) among Africanists (Ellis 1989; Nkashama 1987). While the types of personal contacts that disseminate information are unusually strong and far-reaching in Africa, such that the informal sidewalk networks can rival or surpass the scope of official media, use of the term *radio trottoir* carries the unfortunate implication that it is merely a rumor mill for exaggerated or fabricated stories passed between unsuspecting dupes (Geschiere 1998; Nyamnjoh 2001).[11] There are undoubtedly many such invented and embellished accounts, but the official media are likely to report their own share of misinformation, so people are often left to sort out reality on their own (Ellis 2002). Of course, fictional witchcraft videos produced in Nigeria for popular consumption could be interpreted by undiscerning viewers as documentaries, and this information then gets propagated as evidence of occult activity. But it would be unfair to suggest that

Africans are somehow naïve victims of commercial films and rumors. As noted, Beninese do not accept all evidence at face value, but they may use popular videos as symbols or demonstrations of the manner in which witches operate, even though they know full well that the films are staged performances. But when these films correspond to events Beninese have already encountered among their own friends and families, then the information can indeed reinforce understandings of how occult forces work.

Confession

Perhaps the single most compelling piece of evidence for witchcraft's reality is confession. The reasons for confession remain something of a mystery to informants. Readers will recall from chapter 1 that some people suggest that witches confess on their deathbed because they are compelled by an involuntary urge to do so. But to explain other confessions, many people often shrug their shoulders and say that when the evidence mounts against witches, they simply admit to what they can no longer deny. A court official told me that àzĕ used to be more secretive but that confessions are now more common because child witches cannot keep secrets, and they expose the people who transmitted àzĕ to them. Few scholarly accounts attempt to understand confession or its consequences. As Mary Douglas (1970) notes, confession is likely to perplex Westerners, since they see witchcraft as an imaginary offense. But some academic interpretations of witchcraft confession suggest that it is a product of social or psychological pathology (Hallen and Sodipo 1997). For example, most accused and confessed àzètɔ́ are poor, older women, and one might suppose that such women are often marginalized, powerless individuals in their communities. Therefore, confessing to powerful acts (albeit malicious and imaginary ones) would be one way of acquiring power and respect (Piot 2010, 115). I admit to being tempted by this explanation, but the problem with this rationale is that exposed àzètɔ́ do not have an opportunity to enjoy their status, since confession renders them powerless (see also Bastian 2001). Furthermore, they are unlikely to be treated well by their families, who may disown them or simply begin distancing themselves socially from a confessed witch. In some cases, àzètɔ́ are even brought to court and sentenced to prison for their acts. More extreme retribution might include vigilantism leading to a witch being killed by her own family. So these results do not sound like incentive for someone to confess, though confessions could be a way of avoiding impending vigilantism. A second interpretation is that confessions could come from psychologically troubled individuals willing to admit anything, whether they did it or not (Omoyajowo 1965). Unfortunately, I do not have data to address all the potential motivations for confession. But more to the point, these are concerns that would appear unimportant to most Beninese, for whom confessions are authentic evidence of witchcraft.

Aside from deathbed declarations, there are three other types of confession. First, witches may confess after divination has identified them as *àzètɔ*. As in the examples provided above, anyone who has a sick child or mysterious bad luck is likely to consult a *bokɔnɔ̀* (diviner), a traditional healer, a church pastor, or other specialist with the ability to detect *àzètɔ* attacks. Individual diviners and spiritual leaders may have different abilities, so people often go to multiple specialists of different religious persuasions to achieve consensus that an *àzètɔ* is truly guilty (as in Jean's case above). Once an *àzètɔ* is detected, those concerned might begin acting differently toward the suspect, making insinuations or outright accusations, leading to the confession. The second type of confession involves someone caught in a suspicious act, possessing suspicious items, or exhibiting unusual behaviors and abilities. For example, people sometimes report witches turning into a bird or owl. In other cases, suspected witches are caught carrying magical paraphernalia, especially the *àzě-ká* (*àzě* calabash). Of course, there are also accused individuals who deny culpability, and this may lead to strained relations and mistrust within families. In some cases, certain family members may be convinced of the accused's guilt, while others defend her. The third variety of confession is when *àzètɔ* wish to convert to a new religion, often Christianity. In such cases, they may join the new religion in order to exorcise witchcraft and remove the desire to harm others. According to a friend in the Celestial Church of Christ in Cotonou, former witches converting to his religion confess regularly in church. My Beninese brother, Chams, and other friends have told me that they suspect that some people falsely confess to being witches for the purposes of attracting converts to churches. According to this model, a pastor hires people to visit communities where they are unknown, and then they confess to horrible acts before being saved by the pastor and his church. I have no evidence to confirm or disprove this possibility.

In 2009 Gaston told me a story about a witch encounter a few years prior in a town north of Abomey. Gaston was visiting an elderly head of a family when a boy came racing in and told the old man that he was being summoned to go to the fields alone. The man was alarmed and confused by this request, so he asked Gaston to accompany him, since Gaston was educated and might be useful if this was a legal matter. When they arrived in the fields, they found a man standing above a grave-like pit holding a gun to his own mother. He accused her of killing two of his children and attacking a third child who was

critically ill. He explained to the others that he had consulted Fá and determined that she was responsible. Gaston told me that the woman confessed,
claiming that she attacked the children because her son never gave her any
money. Her rationale was that at least the children's funerals would mean that
she would receive some money as part of the ritual protocol. Her son asked
her to name her accomplices, and they were also brought to the field, where
the three were asked to save the child. One of the accused women left to
retrieve some leaves, and when she returned, she made a medicine out of the
leaves and gave it to the child, who recovered quickly. They did not pursue
any further punishment for the accused.

   In the introduction, I described the case of a woman and two children who
confessed on the radio to being witches and to having killed multiple people.
When one journalist rapped the woman's knuckles with a stick, I mentioned
to the reporter next to me that this looked harmful and unnecessary, and some
others I spoke with later agreed that such punishment is cruel. But those
on the scene insisted that the woman desired to be punished. I wondered if
she felt this option was preferable to a more severe beating she might incur
elsewhere. I will never know whether these individuals were put up to their
confessions or whether they truly believed they were àzètɔ. To me, broadcast-
ing the confession on the radio was the most intriguing aspect of the whole
affair, since I could understand a witch being caught and even confessing, but
I could not understand why they would want to announce it on the radio.
It occurred to me that this could be an example of the scenario Chams proposed of churches trying to drum up converts, but I wanted to know more
about the circumstances leading to the event. My friend Odette told me that
such media confessions are not uncommon, and I know that they contribute
significantly to the body of evidence people use to assess the reality of witchcraft. When I asked Odette why people would offer public confessions, she
said that maybe they do it in order to show people that witchcraft really exists.
This is a troubling paradox: though everybody accepts witchcraft's reality,
Odette suggested that people need to be convinced that it really exists. Like
so many aspects of the occult, there are numerous uncertainties surrounding
confessions. While I am still unsure exactly why people confess, it is clear that
confession is an important piece of the puzzle in understanding how witchcraft can be so overwhelmingly real.

Àzĕ and the Law

One of the more controversial aspects of the reality dilemma for African
witchcraft is what ramifications the acknowledgment of occult power might

have on the legal system. A body of literature has documented how some countries take explicit account of witchcraft in their legal codes, making it a punishable crime. The legal treatment of witchcraft has been especially developed in Cameroon, where witchcraft is criminalized and traditional healers and mystics act as expert witnesses against accused witches (Fisiy 1998; Geschiere and Fisiy 1994). In Benin there is also a recent history of state interaction with witchcraft, since after a military coup in 1972, the regime led by President Mathieu Kérékou carried out an intensive antiwitchcraft campaign during the 1970s. According to Jeffrey Kahn (2011), in an attempt to develop a modernist Marxist-Leninist state, Kérékou vowed to eliminate the primitive, antisocial, individualistic tendencies incarnated by witches. The government rounded up and imprisoned hundreds of suspected witches throughout the country. The accused were sometimes beaten into confessing and paraded in public as a way for the state to make an example of the antirevolutionary elements. In waging the campaign against witches and other representatives of traditional religion, the Beninese state recruited witch-finders in their efforts, but because possessing witchcraft is often required in order to identify and oppose witches, the witch-finders were themselves suspected of possessing witchcraft (Kahn 2011). Of course, another irony in this campaign and all state prosecution of witchcraft is that, in their efforts to eradicate witchcraft, the state empowered priests of the very traditional religion they were opposing and actually legitimized the fear of witches, thereby reinforcing a belief system from which they were intending to distance themselves.

Although memories of Kérékou's antiwitchcraft era remain, most respondents did not believe the state has an official policy on witchcraft. When I asked Beninese what they think about the idea of prosecuting witches, most maintained that this would be ridiculous. They claimed that witchcraft accusations do not meet legal standards of proof. The law, they maintained, cannot recognize invisible occult acts and therefore has no business arresting or prosecuting witches. But some people, including a number of healers, expressed a desire to make Benin's legal system more like Cameroon's. One healer told me that legislation is under review by Benin's government to begin prosecuting witchcraft. The irony in these widespread claims of the law's disregard for witchcraft is that the courts in Abomey have been prosecuting witchcraft all along, but most people seem to know nothing about it.

During my visit in 2009, Gaston had a matter to resolve at the courthouse, and he invited me to join him, saying that he had a friend who was a judge, and we might take advantage of our visit to ask him a few questions about witchcraft. I took him up on his suggestion, despite the fact that I had no expectations of learning anything new. I already had the unanimous opinion of every interviewee that the legal system had nothing to do with the occult. When I arrived in the courthouse I was stunned to learn just the opposite. I spoke with two male court officials, both of whom stated matter-of-factly that witchcraft is absolutely a crime under the law, and they showed me the legal code by which the courts prosecute people accused of witchcraft and *charlatanisme* (Azalou n.d.; see also Topanou 2009). According to the officials, accused witches vary in age and gender, but the vast majority of them are poor, old women. They reported that they see on average ten witchcraft cases per month, and that number has been increasing in recent years. Though the officials said they investigate accusations in a scientific manner, it was unclear exactly what proof would be acceptable. They told me that the court considers the reputation of the accused, as well as any objects that might be discovered—principally the *àzě-ka*. But ultimately they admitted that the primary information upon which convictions rest is confession. One official stated that it was basically impossible to prove guilt without a confession. The judge said that the law prescribes sentences from fifteen to thirty years of labor detention but that sentences are usually around ten years. When I asked the officials how the court deals with vigilante justice, they said that such cases do occur and that they have prosecuted people who attacked accused witches. But one wonders what percentage of vigilantism cases are actually brought before the law. A healer in Ouidah told me that he knew an old witch discovered by her family. According to him, she was locked in her house to die of thirst and starvation. Since the whole family was complicit, there was nobody to bear witness to any wrongdoing. Even if the police suspected foul play, they would have no evidence to pursue. So while the courts may intervene to protect accused witches, it remains unclear how many other cases go undetected.

When I asked the judge whether he believed in witchcraft, he looked at me as if this were a silly question and said, "I'm African." The clerk voiced a similar view, stating, "It's something we created."[12] Such comments from legal professionals demonstrate just how pervasive and ingrained occult realities are in Beninese society, potentially setting the stage for more widespread state intervention in witchcraft.

Monsters, Whos, and Witches

One day in July 2009, a couple of weeks after returning from fieldwork in Benin, I had just finished reading Harry West's provocative book *Ethnographic Sorcery* (2007), dealing with the question of reality and belief, when my four-year-old daughter spontaneously said to me, "Papa, monsters are real, right?"

Despite my efforts to explain that monsters are fictional beings in books and fables, she insisted that they were real. I could not help noticing the irony in the fact that I assertively maintained the nonexistence of something so real to her while my professional persona is more equivocal about whether monsters (i.e., witches) exist for others. That same evening, another example of ontological discord came to my attention when my two daughters were watching the 1970 Dr. Seuss cartoon *Horton Hears a Who*. In the story an elephant named Horton discovers a tiny planet with inhabitants so small as to be imperceptible to everyone but Horton, whose heightened auditory abilities allow him to hear the defenseless, microscopic Whos living in Whoville. Horton is first ridiculed and later persecuted for insisting on the Whos' existence. Eventually the Whos were able to create enough noise so that Horton's neighbors also heard them, thus vindicating Horton's heretofore outrageous claims.

In the case of my daughter's monsters and Horton's Whos, we are faced with two similar situations. Both involve someone believing something that others find impossible, but there is one crucial difference: in Horton's case, he succeeds in convincing the naysayers. One lesson we can derive from these examples is that skeptics are likely to disbelieve anything they cannot observe, whether it is a Who, a monster, or witchcraft. But what would have happened if Horton's companions had never heard the hapless Whos? Horton would have been imprisoned and his version of reality permanently silenced. A Western rationalist who believed in Whoville would find this outcome a disturbing concealment of the truth, but postmodernists, while equally sympathetic to Horton, might be more willing to accept that there are multiple potential realities. In a postmodern world, "reality" is merely the product of a contest for the power to control the discourse defining the terms of that reality. Silencing the elephant could mean that Horton's Whos cease to exist. Although Horton wins in his world, in my world adults define reality, so children eventually lose their claim to monsters and are forced to adhere to a different reality.

For anthropologists who want to respect and legitimate other people's beliefs, the postmodern solution of multiple discursively created realities offers some relief from the troubling "ontological chasm" (Ashforth 2005, 317) separating worlds with witches from those without. We can describe African beliefs as logical within a different discursive cultural system, and this goes a long way for the purposes of cultural interpretation. Philosophers Alfred Schutz (1962) and William James ([1890] 1913) are among those who suggested that reality is subjective and constructed, allowing some to claim the existence of multiple realities (see Tambiah 1990, 101–5). Yet as Geschiere (2000) concludes, a discursive construction of lived worlds is no longer enough;

researchers increasingly have to confront the problem of reality. I, too, cannot help feeling unsatisfied with a purely discursive explanation of reality, for it seems to sidestep Africans' desire that witchcraft be taken as an actual, physical reality. Recall that Harry West's Mozambican friend told him that supernatural beings are real, not symbols or metaphors. Furthermore, concluding that there are multiple realities might generate a division in cultural ontology that would render the ethnographic endeavor pointless. Why would we dedicate our careers to studying other cultures if they were completely impenetrable and fundamentally incomprehensible? As for me, I confess that, despite vast differences in language and culture, I believe we can understand other people and find common ground. And my Beninese informants seem to agree that the search for understanding is worthwhile, because they repeatedly urged me to recognize witchcraft as real, to seek out scientifically verifiable evidence, and to see things from their perspective. I cannot prove that I have succeeded, but I think that I have made progress. I have learned that it is one thing for an anthropologist to dismiss children's belief in monsters, Santa Claus, and the tooth fairy, but Africans' claims that their children were killed by witchcraft is another thing altogether. For my Beninese friends, witchcraft exists not merely in words or discourse but in cold, hard actions and results. If I take a more rationalist view of reality in my daughter's case, then I may adopt the temporary indulgence of a parent humoring a child, but only until she attains the cognitive sophistication to see through the myth. But for Africans who suffer from a legacy of military colonialism and the constant threat of intellectual colonialism (Mudimbe 1988), it becomes obvious that equating a child's fantasy with witchcraft beliefs reconstitutes a paternalistic and patronizing variety of anthropology.[13] It is spectacularly offensive to suggest that Africans are like children who grew up without the guiding, rational voice of their parents. Seeing witchcraft as a social "problem" unavoidably places the West in a parental role. And while cultural relativists may have noble intentions, they are not automatically more accepting of witchcraft's reality than is the fleeting indulgence of a child's faith in Santa Claus. What I want to avoid most is equating witches with children's imaginary friends or cartoon characters. Witches and accused witches are real people living as family and friends in every community.

Though Beninese people rarely asked me if I believe in witches, I suspect they sensed my ambivalence, since they know most Western visitors are skeptical. As I mentioned, one obvious way of gaining an inside view of the occult would be to become initiated into the àzètɔ́ society. In fact, a number of my informants suggested I become an initiate, and a couple of healers offered to initiate me, but as discussed in the introduction, I declined these invitations. The irony, of course, is that if I were more dismissive of witchcraft reality, I might have been more willing to undergo initiation. Other informants suggested that if I wanted proof of occult forces, all I needed to do was test some magical formulae and witness magical acts with my own eyes. Occasionally, specialists spoke of such demonstrations, though only in one case did the offer come to fruition in the following way. A female healer informant showed me a powder that she poured onto a kola nut, which she then submerged in a jar of water. When she pulled it out of the water, she asked me to touch the powder, and I noticed that it was completely dry. Though the powder does not necessarily represent witchcraft, this demonstration is consistent with the notion that natural substances have mystical properties. Informants urged me to document such demonstrations to make witchcraft and sorcery a scientific field of inquiry involving the study of plants, minerals, and the spiritual properties of the universe. In their view, to study supernatural domains in a systematic fashion would not only offer the hope of beneficial recipes but would also bring witchcraft fully into the realm of the real, the concrete, and the scientific.

Despite my reservations about believing in witchcraft and becoming a practitioner in the occult world, long-term exposure to other people's ideas does have an effect, and I have been deeply transformed by the accumulation of experiences and testimony garnered since I first visited Benin in 1996. Through my relationships, I have not only begun to learn what social conditions are associated with Beninese beliefs in spiritual forces but also become sympathetic to how they feel about them. Even a skeptic like me was occasionally able to set aside my reliance on scientific evidence and become seduced by the possibility of a different reality.[14] The willingness to experience and immerse oneself in the lived world of others is one feature of the phenomenological approach in anthropology. Beginning with my first trip to Benin, my curiosity led me to participate in Vodun ceremonies, and occasionally I visited diviners, but as a social scientist I mostly kept my friends' spirituality at arm's length. However, in 2008 I experienced something altogether new during a ceremony in Tchetti, a Nago town a few hours north of Abomey. My adoptive sister's husband, Antoine, was receiving an advanced initiation to become a priest of the deity Trɔ̀. Trɔ̀ is a relative newcomer in most of Benin, having arrived from Ewe-speaking areas of Ghana and Togo into Ouidah (Bay 2008; Montgomery and Vannier 2017; Rosenthal 1998; Tall 1995b). Antoine was preparing to become a vodŭnɔ̀ (called xunɔ̀ for Trɔ̀), so the ceremony involved the installation of a new deity at his home. After a few hours on the road from Abomey (a trip lengthened by our car's mechanical troubles), a caravan including me, my brother, Chams, some Trɔ̃ adepts, and a few Trɔ̃ priests from Ouidah finally arrived in Tchetti around 5:00 p.m. Tired, hungry, and hot, we had no time for relief, for the ceremony started immediately. The first phase was a ritual at the front gate of the home, where a series of sacrifices were made and some sacred objects were buried. Next, the congregation moved inside the family compound to the new shrine Antoine had recently completed to house his deity, right next to a huge new home he was constructing. I do not have the space to describe every aspect of the ritual, but it involved the burial of large stones, huge quantities of kola nuts, and many sacrificial cats and chickens in the floor of the shrine. The shrine contains an opening in the roof where light and rain can enter to nourish the kola tree that takes root in a Trɔ̃ shrine. During this lengthy process, there was joyful singing, and many of us danced in the hot antechamber across from the more sober religious events taking place in the interior room of the shrine.

In total, the ceremony lasted about three hours, and by that time I was thoroughly drained and starving, since I had not eaten since 10:00 that morning. Soon afterward, a feast was presented to attendees with several courses, including rice, chicken, fish, and black yam paste, with a selection of beer and soda to drink. When we were all sated and relaxed, we looked for somewhere to sleep. Those of us lacking a claim to a privileged place in one of the houses began migrating to the large, unfinished house by the shrine. My adoptive sister led me through the raw concrete structure to look for a comfortable spot. I suggested that I might sleep on the top story of the house, where I could enjoy the cool night breeze in the open, roofless house. Unfortunately, the floor was so littered with construction debris and cement chunks that this was impossible. I decided to take the grass mat she loaned me and join the other men on the ground floor. Eight or ten of us dropped our mats on the floor of what one day would be a spacious living room. Lying there with only a couple of millimeters between me and the cement floor, I was remarkably comfortable, despite the extreme fullness from the feast. Oddly, I felt a strong camaraderie lying there beside these men and Trɔ̃ adepts whom I did not know but with whom I had just shared a very moving religious event. One of the last things I noticed before falling helplessly to sleep was that there were no mosquitoes whining in my ears or biting my ankles. What happened next was one of the most interesting and spiritual sensations I have ever felt. At some unknown time during the night, I woke suddenly to see a young, bare-chested man standing over me. People in the room were chanting as the man pushed a perfumed finger against my forehead. I tried to raise my head, but the pressure he applied was too great. I was frozen. As they prayed, they said in unison *ampa*, the Ewe word for "amen," which is repeated constantly throughout every Trɔ̃ ceremony. As I tried harder to lift my head, I eventually succeeded, but I immediately noticed that the man was gone and my companions were all sound asleep.

In the morning, I told this story to a gathering of people, including a *bokɔ́nɔ̀*. The *bokɔ́nɔ̀* told me without hesitation that this was no accident, that Trɔ̃ had greeted me with a blessing. Those present expressed pleasure and even a touch of awe that this *yovó* (white person) had just had a spiritual encounter. Though I cannot speak for all my Beninese friends, it seems to me that this is the type of event that they see as evidence of supernatural powers. Of course, it is easy enough to conclude that my experience was merely a dream, but I admit that I felt comfort at the thought that a spiritual force had taken an interest in me, and I experienced a powerful sense of community with the people around me. Furthermore, I had seen a supernatural entity in the same way that many Beninese do—through a nocturnal encounter. Though I am not altogether comfortable labeling my experience a dream, it would not be inconsistent with how Beninese people communicate with spiritual forces, and for them, dreams are not necessarily juxtaposed against reality. In fact, in Benin and elsewhere, dreams are a powerful and recurring medium of interaction with the divine and the occult (see Meyer 1999, 194). Dreams are one of the ways that witchcraft victims are sometimes able to see their attackers. And it is often via dreams that new witches are inducted into the society. Many healers also use dreams to find attacking witches and intervene on the victim's behalf. Whether or not I classify my experience as a dream or as real is irrelevant to me personally and to my task. Instead, I see my encounter with Trɔ̃ as a powerful spiritual moment allowing me to understand for the first time in my life what religious faith feels like. And I would add that I see no distinction between having faith in a recognized deity and having faith in the existence of witchcraft. Perhaps I have an advantage in coming from a nonreligious background, since these different types of supernatural thought feel similar to me. This is also why I am troubled by the tendency of some academics to treat "religion" as legitimate but "witchcraft" as fantasy.

My experiences in Benin have also brought me closer to understanding occult fears. Ever since I began investigating witchcraft in Benin, my friends and informants have told me to be careful, to watch out for negative reactions of people who feel threatened by intrusive questions. They warned me that my research put me in danger of attack. Some urged me never to drink or eat anything offered in the house of elderly people suspected of possessing occult knowledge for fear that I would ingest witchcraft substance and become a witch myself. When I first began visiting Benin, my immunity was fairly secure by virtue of the fact that I was a *yovó* without any witches in my family (recall that until recently, witches primarily operated among kin). But in recent fieldwork, I could only downplay the risk, reassuring my friends that I asked very few probing questions, never solicited secret formulae, and tried to show respect for everybody. I added that I would be careful but that I was confident everything would be all right.

I continued to reassure my distressed friends with these same words, but due to another event, I now understand their concerns and how people can be afraid of mystical attacks. Though I had heard years of testimony from friends about the existence of mystical forces, magical powers, and invisible spirits, an illness sparked more than an intellectual curiosity in these forces. In the middle of my 2009 fieldwork in Abomey, I suddenly got sick with a headache, sinus inflammation, fatigue, and body aches. I felt the illness coming on one evening, and the next morning, I was too sick to leave the house. Although these symptoms are fairly consistent with a bad cold and could have been the product of my constant outings under the sun on the backs of motorcycles while inhaling large quantities of road dust, the illness came on quickly and felt different from the colds I was accustomed to. I spent the day resting and worrying about how long the illness would last, whether it would worsen, and whether it would jeopardize the rest of my fieldwork. (A few weeks later, I remembered the swine flu pandemic and realized that this was another concern I probably should have entertained.) But while I lay there suffering, thinking, and worrying, my thoughts suddenly turned to all my friends' cautions about spending too much time with old people "in the villages." It was true, I liberally drank *soɖabì* palm liquor with my hosts, and sometimes I ate the food they offered me. But, I thought, the people I visit are all so friendly and interested in sharing their experiences. Why would they have anything against me? Still, my illness felt strange, and it was possible that a healer or *vodṹnɔ̀* felt slighted by something I did or said. Some healers are competitive with one another, and I may have gotten caught in the middle of a rivalry. Some may have wanted to use me as a contact to develop greater prestige or as an outlet for foreign aid. Others may simply have felt threatened in the way my friends suggested. Daydreaming, but with some real anxiety, I started wondering what I would do if this was a supernatural attack. I began to ask myself who my enemies were, who disliked me, and whom I had inadvertently wronged. Suddenly the world became dangerous, unknown, and filled with people of questionable trustworthiness. But as it turned out, the following day my illness passed just as quickly and mysteriously as it arrived. Although I am inclined now to conclude that this was merely a brief cold induced by dust and smoke in the air, in contrast to Siegel's (2006) claim that foreigners are unable to enter the witchcraft mindset, I realize instead that it is not so far-fetched for a Western, scientifically minded academic to entertain the reality of witchcraft and supernatural powers. Furthermore, one wonders what would have happened if my illness had persisted and doctors were unable to help me. This, in fact, is more in keeping with the evidence used by Beninese people to conclude that they are being attacked mystically. One could even argue that my friends are probably more skeptical than I, since they are likely to wait much longer with a more mysterious and persistent illness before suspecting witchcraft.

Another anxiety-laden experience occurred in 2009. My brother, Chams, took me to see Maurice, a healer he knew outside the town of Ouidah. In the presence of Chams, Maurice's son, and another young man, I began the interview by asking the elderly man some basic questions about the nature of *àzě* and *bǒ*. When I mentioned that Westerners often doubt the reality of occult forces, Maurice suddenly adopted a different tone, both matter-of-fact and ominous at the same time. He told me, "If you want, we'll do a test." One of the other men started snickering as Maurice continued, "I'll show you what witchcraft is. Then when you see it, you'll be better able to talk and write about it." The others erupted in laughter, but the old man remained stone-faced. Although I was doubtful that this man, whom I had just met a few minutes before, was willing to offer a demonstration (and I made a point to avoid requesting such demonstrations), I attempted to play along, stating that I would be happy to see whatever he wanted to show me. Maurice looked at the others, saying, "He doesn't understand." Trying to defend myself, I insisted that I had understood. They asked me what I understood, and I explained that he offered to show me something that would convince me that witchcraft is real. A discussion arose, with occasional nervous laughter, the old man now declaring that I understood, while the others argued that I had not. He continued, "You agree? You agree? So we can do the test, right?" Sensing the pregnant meaning in his questions, coupled with the laughter and the way the old man seemed to be baiting me, I paused and then grasped what he was getting at. I backpedaled, stating that while I understood, it was my right to reflect before making a decision. Laughter continued. In case I had not figured it out, Maurice then made the terms of the test more explicit by recounting a story about some foreigners who came to see him.

I was doing a consultation three or four months ago for some whites like you. I said, "If you want my power—" The woman has two children. I think the man has three children. "If you want me to hand over my power, you'll have to give me the name of one of your children. We'll be here, and the child will die, and I'll give you—" Ah! And they pulled back. [*More laughter arose from Chams and the others.*] They weren't ready for that! But they want my power. That's witchcraft!

In the following minutes, Maurice pressed me, only half-joking, urging that if I were to return to my country to tell people about witchcraft, then I had to know it personally, which meant that I would have to sacrifice a loved one. I insisted that it was my intent neither to sacrifice anyone nor to obtain his power. I tried unsuccessfully to offer some levity and deflect his questions by indicating that my colleague Chams would perhaps be better suited to such a test. Maurice was undeterred, arguing that my brother grew up and lived with àzĕ on a daily basis and therefore needed no convincing. It was foreigners who would have to be taught this lesson. I was finally rescued when he received a call on his cell phone.

Maurice's proposition was another situation in which the warnings of friends corresponded to a potential threat, reminding me that there was a reason they cautioned me about getting too close to àzètɔ̀. Clearly, the old man was enjoying himself, trying to rattle his guest's nerves, and he was probably even more pleased that he was able to shake the scientific calm of a foreigner, but I found it hard to avoid a touch of anxiety. Most of the time, I am unafraid of being personally affected by witchcraft, but on this occasion somebody had actually made a threat against my family. And like the white visitors who reportedly preceded me, no amount of disbelief was sufficient for me to dare this man to kill someone I love. Does that mean I believe? Again, I find such a question unproductive when it comes to witchcraft. Everything depends on context, including the mood of the discussion, the old man's tone, and my own state of mind. But beyond that, the stakes of his wager were so high that there are probably few people willing to take the risk. And here is a crucial element that I suspect operates in the minds of Beninese people. Many have witnessed nothing equivalent to "proof," but the stakes for ignoring àzĕ are so high that most people would suggest that it is best to keep an open mind about àzĕ. Without getting bogged down in questions of what it means for me to "believe," this is advice to which I also subscribe. One might argue that faith makes the supernatural real, and some of my informants admitted that if you do not believe in magic, then it cannot harm you. Informants have offered a

Fon expression to illustrate this principle: "Mɛ wɛ nɔ̃ ɖi bŏ, bŏ nɔ̃ ɖi" (Bŏ only work on those who believe) (Adjido 1997, 276). But I would caution the reader that this expression does not deny the reality of bŏ; instead, it serves as a model for how you can protect yourself from magical forces. Even if people admit that faith is a factor in the efficacy of bŏ, other expressions paint a different picture for àzě: "Xó ɖe nu àzě ma flĩ wè o" (Pray that witchcraft does not remember you) and "É nɔ̃ gló àzě ǎ" (One cannot stop witchcraft). Although other anthropologists have declared their position on witchcraft, I break with that tradition by not pronouncing a conclusive statement on my "belief." I do this in part because beliefs can change, and there is no reason to think that I have a final answer. But I also maintain that, despite the Fon proverb, the idea of "belief" is not entirely relevant to Beninese lived worlds. For my informants, natural and supernatural forces simply exist, and there would be no more reason to question the existence of witchcraft than to question the existence of God, the wind, or the trees. For people with a practical view of the world, faith is a foreign concept (Brown 2001).

Rationality and Incommensurability

Before heading off to Benin in 2009, I held a number of Internet discussions with Chams. I explained that I was continuing my investigation of àzě and bŏ and that I hoped he could propose some additional people to visit. In one exchange, he told me that several of his friends whom I had met the previous year said they were sure that I was an àzètɔ́. I was taken aback, because this was the first time I had heard or even imagined such a claim about me. I asked Chams if he had assured his friends that I was not an àzètɔ́. He responded by saying that he was not altogether sure himself. Based on our long-term friendship and joking tendencies, I thought he was kidding. Perhaps he was indeed exaggerating, but the "joke" continued for the remainder of our discussion, and then he confessed to being interested in acquiring àzě himself. When I arrived in Benin and confronted him with our earlier exchange, he dismissed it, claiming that he had never really thought I was a witch and that he was uninterested in acquiring witchcraft. Perhaps he really had been joking, or else he changed his mind or decided it was too dangerous a topic to discuss in person. In any event, this brought me face-to-face with the troubling consequences of witchcraft reality and accusation.

Later, after my 2009 fieldwork, I reminisced with Chams about our earlier exchanges and his friends' suspicions, and he confided that his friends were not the only ones who suspected that I had àzě abilities. According to Chams, before the death of his mother (Mouni, my adoptive mother in Benin), she said she thought that I possessed the good form of àzĕ. She never mentioned this to me, but Chams told me that she developed this theory to explain why I was able to circulate among healers and other spiritually powerful individuals without being harmed. As noted, she believed that associating with mystically powerful people exposed me to these forces, making it inevitable that I would acquire them (see Kahn 2011). And since I am regarded as a wealthy foreigner, people no doubt assume that I can afford to purchase the expensive benevolent witchcraft. After hearing the news of his mother's suspicion, I asked Chams again if he thought I had àzĕ, and he said no, but this time he supported his position with the verdict reached after he consulted Trɔ̃ about me several times. Apparently, his suspicions were serious enough for him to seek a more trusted arbiter, and each time he asked if I was a witch, Trɔ̃ said no. Moreover, Chams added, the fact that I have entered the Trɔ̃ temple must mean that I do not have àzĕ; if I were an àzètɔ́, Trɔ̃ would never have permitted it.

Like West (2007), I recognize that studying witchcraft and acquiring a certain level of knowledge make one a target of suspicion, since knowledge of witchcraft is tantamount to being a witch. But unlike West's account from Mozambique, Beninese do not conceive of witchcraft as a discursive creation; in Benin, being a witch is thought to be a matter of concrete acts, even if those acts are involuntary. Therefore, people think that either someone is a witch or she is not, and the key is finding the proper evidence. Nevertheless, being on the receiving end of even a lighthearted suspicion makes one even more conscious of the danger of false accusations. I am obviously sympathetic to human rights activists who want to protect people from persecution and mob killings, and most Beninese agree that these kinds of excesses are unwarranted. Yet legislating against witch hunts is unpromising, because witchcraft is so real among citizens, police, and government officials that people will continue to condemn and ignore any law that fails to treat witchcraft as real. Using the legal system or a mediation process to confront accused àzètɔ́ may relieve some of the vigilante justice, but it will also legitimize witchcraft reality and potentially exacerbate fears and accusations.

I have no solutions or policy recommendations other than to suggest that in the case of occult forces, anthropology is well positioned to make use of the information we collect to reduce cultural barriers. Whatever approach human rights advocates propose, they cannot blindly dismiss witchcraft's reality or otherwise suggest that Africans are misguided, irrational, and superstitious. Instead, taking witchcraft seriously and even acknowledging it as a religious or scientific belief might bolster its legitimacy and allow people to apply more positive meanings, thereby decreasing occult violence and establishing a new religion, alternative healing, and fresh models of development. The world has already witnessed how previously derided practices like Haitian Vodou, ethnobotany, and acupuncture have gained a more positive standing in the West. New Age religions like Neopaganism are finding greater public acceptance in Western societies, often appealing to white, middle-class individuals (see Freedman 2009; Jorgensen and Russell 1999).[15] Geschiere (2013) points out that the Brazilian religion of Candomblé was until recently regarded as witchcraft or black magic, but today, after a concerted effort to institutionalize Candomblé, it enjoys the status of legitimate religion.[16] Perhaps it is only a matter of time before a new generation of African scholars fosters a similar legitimacy for witchcraft. In some ways, as noted in chapter 2, this has already begun through grassroots efforts to institutionalize and legitimize witchcraft, and in some cases, people have called for the creation of schools for witchcraft training.

Doing research on witchcraft is fascinating but a little scary at times. Sometimes I find myself unsettled by the sensation that I am trying to inhabit two worlds as I travel back and forth, both physically and intellectually, between Benin and the United States (see Stoller 2008). However, conceiving of cultures as incommensurable worlds with incompatible modes of thought can unfortunately deepen the divide between *us* and *them*. This would lead anthropologists to fix their gaze on one world at a time and then turn quickly to the other, hoping to retain a view of the first. We would spin in circles, as if straining to see the reflection of the backs of our heads. I admit that I have wrestled with my rational upbringing to make sense of the astonishing claims that I have heard from friends and informants in Benin. Byron Good astutely points out just how central the question of reality is to anthropology, a discipline charged with translating ontology between cultures: "Do we argue that members of traditional cultures live in wholly different worlds, and their statements are true in their worlds, not ours, or even that they cannot be translated intelligibly into our language?" (1994, 10). Stanley Jeyaraja Tambiah shares these concerns and argues that the "translation of cultures . . . raises not only the question of the mentality of us and other peoples, but also ultimately the issue of '*rationality*' itself, and the limits of Western 'scientism' as a paradigm" (1990, 3). The matter of language and words is crucial here, because even if anthropologists feel successful in understanding another cultural perspective, how can we write about that other world in a language outside of the cultural context? Needham (1972) concluded that we can never truly understand another culture's perspective or modes of thought and that language proves unreliable in our attempts to translate cultures. Benjamin Lee Whorf (1956) was the best-known advocate for the notion of linguistic relativity, suggesting that the language we speak shapes our thoughts and reality. Indeed, he argued that science has reached its linguistic limits because the language of science cannot be translated or understood in non-European languages (Whorf 1952). Although I acknowledge the challenges of translation, and I would not rule out the possibility of some extreme examples of untranslatable languages (see Everett 2005), I remain optimistic that anthropology can make productive efforts to convey meaning and understanding across linguistic and cultural barriers. People from different countries are not identical, to be sure, but I am convinced that we have enough in common to make anthropological inquiry and ethnographic writing worthy endeavors, and scholars have offered possible solutions to the challenge.

Although Alasdair Macintyre (1970) and Needham (1972) were pessimistic about the potential for establishing understanding between cultures, some anthropologists and philosophers have argued that it is a worthwhile and achievable goal. To avoid the problem of rationality's presumed incompatibility with magical ontologies, Bruce Kapferer (2002, 23) proposes accepting the existence of a "virtual" realm where there is a different truth or reality (see also Hund 2003). Similarly, Tambiah (1990) draws on Lucien Lévy-Bruhl (1926) in positing two modalities of thought: participation and causality. Causality is associated with systematic, scientific, and logical thought, whereas participation is manifest in aesthetics, religious faith, emotions, and relationships between people. But rather than conceiving of one mode of thought as characteristic of a particular people or culture, he argues that all peoples and cultures exhibit both causal and participatory thinking, a view that reaffirms the psychic unity of humankind and gives hope to the ethnographic enterprise. Tambiah (1990, 111) states that social scientists can develop a "double subjectivity" in order to understand the other and translate these views into another language. Peter Winch opposes the positivist view of an objective reality that merely awaits discovery, advocating instead a transformative strategy that creates new ways of knowing and thinking within the researcher: "Seriously to study another way of life is necessarily to seek to extend our own—not simply to bring the other way within the already existing boundaries of our own" (1970, 99).

Drawing these various threads together leads me to the prospect of alternate realities. Following Kapferer's (2002) suggestion of a virtual or "phantasmagoric" reality, I have begun to entertain the idea that there may be an alternative truth or rationality of witchcraft. As noted, various scholars have offered versions of this postulate, including Lévy-Bruhl, James, Tambiah, Winch, and Kapferer. Not all of their models are identical, but their acknowledgment of different modes of thought or realities appears to be the most promising path out of the epistemological forest. As noted earlier in this chapter, postmodern thinking has already proposed the existence of multiple, discursively created realities, but this is still insufficient. I recognize that we acquire our reality through language and socialization, so I cannot deny the power of discourse in the creation of reality, but I want to work against the idea that realities are merely discursive constructions that make anything we say come true. Instead, I prefer a more interactionist view that focuses on people's relationships and beliefs while acknowledging that discourse is the vehicle for communicating these beliefs. In other words, reality may be shaped through discourse, but that reality resides in a body of beliefs shared by a group of people. Lévi-Strauss (1963) emphasized social consensus, and Lévy-Bruhl (1926) referred to participation as the foundation of this type of reality, and what these ideas have in common is a shared connection between people, which is the type of relationship that should be cultivated during ethnographic work. To address the idea that we inhabit incommensurable worlds, Tambiah (1990) argues that the reality created through participation, like that exhibited by aesthetics and religion, may be different from a scientific, rationalist reality, but because Westerners have not abandoned the participatory sense of reality, we are capable of understanding the other. This means that anyone has the potential to exercise Tambiah's double subjectivity. And in fact, I have actually had the sensation of thinking and perceiving in different modalities. I sometimes have the impression of a bifurcated self that straddles a scientific reality and the supernatural reality of my Beninese friends. Thus, I answer the doubts of Evens (1996) by saying that intense fieldwork can be productively transformative. Transformation, however, does not necessarily consist of the loss of one type of rationality or one part of the self; instead, it can be an extension of one's mode of thinking (Winch 1970), a process generated through long-term and intensive contact with people. The challenge, then, would be to find ways of connecting to another people, to participate in their lives and share in the consensus generated through intimate association with them.

Stoller (1998) advocates a phenomenological approach as a way to create connection, blend realities, and find common ground across difference. In general, phenomenology involves putting experience, sensation, and perception at the heart of one's analysis and using this "experience-near" perspective to generate meaning. This philosophical movement merges with a related trend in postmodern anthropology that emphasizes reflexive writing that blurs the line between anthropologist and subject. For Stoller, the phenomenological method means attempting to understand other cultures through lived, embodied experience and writing about his emotions and sensations in the field. Taking his example, I immersed myself in my Beninese friends' world, taking seriously the notion that witchcraft *is* science and that science *is* witchcraft, bringing both realms into sight simultaneously and without whiplash.

Rather than describe other people's "worldviews" (i.e., how they represent the real world), phenomenologists focus on lifeworlds, which vary by one's experience. Steven Friedson critiques symbolic or representational analyses, saying, "Searching deeper and deeper into cultural symbols, peeling off layers of interconnected meaning, is a metaphor for going the wrong direction" (1996, xiv). Following Maurice Merleau-Ponty, Friedson argues that ethnographers must start with bodily sensation, stressing the "lived experience" involved in fieldwork. Focusing on embodied experiences and the "being-in-the-world" of their interlocutors is a hallmark of phenomenological methods (Katz and Csordas 2003), often leading anthropologists to accept different realities in the field setting by suspending or "bracketing" their own beliefs (Desjarlais and Throop 2011).

The phenomenological concern for the lived worlds of others necessarily involves an interrogation of reality and existence, or "ontology," turning away from the anthropological concern for culture or "belief" (Viveiros de Castro 2013). Indeed, in some ways, my approach might appear to reflect what has been called the "ontological turn" in anthropology. The ontological turn refers to a renewed interest in alterity, in making sense of others' reality, accompanied by the acknowledgment of multiple realities or worlds (see Henare, Holbraad, and Wastell 2007; Heywood 2012; Paleček and Risjord 2012). In other words, this theory holds that the anthropological question should not be epistemological (how others think of the world) but ontological (what world they live in). Supporters of the ontological approach view epistemology as the study of the many ways that cultures depict a single reality, whereas the ontological approach is more radical in acknowledging different realities. Of course, anthropology was founded on the study of difference, and the concern for reality has always been central to the discipline, so this is not necessarily a novel perspective, and it may even be an expected outcome of anthropologists' enduring concern for emic understandings. But in other ways, contemporary ontological concerns are a noteworthy expression of the dissatisfaction some anthropologists feel with cultural theory to date. And as with the phenomenologists, ontologists' dissatisfaction lies with the positivist stance of functionalists or materialists, as well as with the representational enterprise of interpretivists and the constructivist path of postmodernists. I am not interested in whether my work fits within a current fad or fashion in anthropology, but insofar as the recent interest in ontology encourages us to take our informants seriously, I appreciate this trend because it demonstrates the attempt to reckon with native perspectives, whereas previous theoretical approaches have a tendency either to explain away local understandings of the world as fictions, representations, and symbols or to ignore local understandings altogether. Martin Holbraad (2010) states that most anthropological theories treat different realities encountered in the ethnographic setting as "wrong." He claims that even relativists and postmodernists, whose apparent aim is to express respect for cultural alterity, reduce difference to alternative representations of a single true world. The ontological turn is intended to avoid portraying that "disagreement" between the native's and the anthropologist's realities as a sign that the other is "wrong" and to admit that it is instead a sign of the anthropologist's inability to develop conceptual categories that permit him or her to accept the existence of another reality. For example, with regard to Evans-Pritchard's (1936) description of the Nuer people's claim that twins are birds, there has been much anthropological debate about how to reconcile this claim with our own definition of twins (see Evens 2012; Littlejohn 1970). Holbraad (2010) writes:

> Rather than asking why the Nuer should think that twins are birds, we should be asking how we need to think of twins, birds (and all their relevant corollaries, such as humanity, siblinghood, animality, flight or what have you) in order to arrive at a position from which the claim that twins are birds no longer registers as an absurdity. . . . This, then, is what an "ontology" is: the result of anthropologists' systematic attempts to transform their conceptual repertoires in such a way as to be able to describe their ethnographic material in terms that are not absurd. (2010, 184–85)

Holbraad's sentence could be rewritten with "science" and "witchcraft" in the place of "twins" and "birds," and this would capture the spirit of my efforts in this book: taking emic ethnographic data at face value and attempting to transform my concepts of "science" and "witchcraft" (along with "religion" and "magic") so as to see Beninese people's claim of the conceptual equivalence between the two in a way that is no longer absurd (see also Viveiros de Castro 2013). Critics of the ontological turn argue that it creates a dangerous relationship of incommensurability between different worlds, which, if true, would render the ethnographic endeavor useless (Vigh and Sausdal 2014).

Although I recognize the risk that positing multiple realities may distance *us* from *them* and could result in an othering tendency, I find the ontological stance bold and refreshing. Separate worlds certainly pose a problem for anthropology, but I argue that long-term, immersive fieldwork can allow anthropologists to bridge these worlds.

Although the ontologists disagree with the interpretivists, whom they criticize for their representational qua fictional conclusions about culture (Van Heekeren 2015), Clifford Geertz's interpretivism was not naive and in fact laid the groundwork for much of the postmodern criticism in anthropology, which ultimately led to the ontological questions that have recently been raised. Geertz (1973b) held on to the notion that anthropology was a science, but he admitted that it was an imprecise, nonpredictive, and ultimately contestable practice, consisting of anthropologists' constructions of other people's constructions of their lives. Thus, perhaps without realizing or intending it, he opened the door for the critique of science and the ontologists' claim that there is not one truth or reality but rather many potential worlds or realities. While postmodernists are often criticized for treating culture as constructed and therefore unreal, I do not think that all postmodernists would characterize constructedness as an absence of reality (see Latour 1999); therefore, I see the ontologists' and phenomenologists' search for multiple realities as consistent with the postmodern rejection of positivist singularity. By recognizing some of the common threads between interpretivism, postmodernism, phenomenology, and the ontological approach, I feel no discomfort employing a range of theoretical tools. Indeed, though I have drawn on ontological and phenomenological perspectives, much of my analysis rests on the interpretivist idea that witchcraft expresses important themes in the lives of Beninese. For example, I argue that witchcraft is an expression of the duality of good and evil in the world, as well as a critique of Western development and a symbol of African pride. However, what makes this argument consistent with my overall mission is that these interpretations derive largely from my informants' own testimony, and although they might not state it in exactly these terms, I believe these ideas conform to my informants' views of witchcraft; therefore, these ideas are not merely fictions constructed by the anthropologist.

In joining together the phenomenological and ontological claims for alternative realities, along with Tambiah's view that we all possess both participatory and rational modes of thought, we are faced with the possibility of the coexistence of two realities or even the merging of two realities. The case of Benin is instructive because my friends do not perceive religious and scientific realities as separate, and this might be how other Africans see these two supposedly separate worlds. Yes, witchcraft is invisible to most people, but so is much of science, from particle physics to deep space astronomy to molecular biology. These scientific "realities" are our Whos, and scientists are our Horton. Put another way, our scientists are like Beninese healers and diviners, who serve as experts knowledgeable of processes invisible to most of us. As Roy Wagner (1981, 144) suggests, anthropologists should endeavor to apply relativity to their own cultures, recognizing that one version should not be privileged over others (see also Viveiros de Castro 2013; West 2007, 82). Bruno Latour (1988, 1993) also advocates turning the anthropological gaze on Western scientific culture to unsettle our assumptions about universal truth and about the distinction between the natural and social. To disrupt our biases, I concur that we must be willing to question the foundations of our own ideas. What if someone were to study the reasons for Westerners' belief in medical diagnoses? How can we explain that we continue to visit doctors and buy medication, even when it fails? In such cases, why do we believe in microscopic pathogens rather than in supernatural forces? These are the same types of questions leveled at African witchcraft and sorcery, but they might be disquieting when directed at our own beliefs. Indeed, Tambiah (1990, 30) reports that science "resorts to defensive strategies" to explain away results that are inconsistent with scientific expectations. Catherine Elgin offers the following more pointed critique of scientific truth.

> Science routinely transgresses the boundary between truth and falsehood. It smooths curves and ignores outliers. It develops and deploys simplified models that diverge, sometimes considerably, from the phenomena they purport to represent. Even the best scientific theories are not true. Not only are they plagued with anomalies and outstanding problems, but where they are successful, they rely on laws, models, idealizations and approximations that diverge from the truth. Truth-centered epistemology . . . easily accommodates anomalies and outstanding problems, since they are readily construed as defects. The problem comes with the laws, models, idealizations, and approximations which are acknowledged not to be true, but which are nonetheless critical to, indeed constitutive of, the understanding that science delivers. Far from being defects, they figure ineliminably in the success of science. If truth is mandatory, much of our best science turns out to be epistemologically unacceptable and perhaps intellectually dishonest. (2004, 113–14)

Although I do not take such a critical view of science, Elgin's point is instructive, for it prompts us to question our assumptions and, possibly, to recognize that science is itself a belief system (Tambiah 1990). I am just as capable as the next person of critically analyzing witchcraft, but I offer little of such thoughts in this book, since they are not conducive to building understanding across difference. Of course, I occasionally had discussions with my friend Gaston and others about whether witches were truly capable of such acts as shape-shifting and teleporting. Gaston, a social studies teacher with a master's degree and an intense curiosity about different ways of life, has a healthy skepticism of things people say about witches. Yet for most people (Gaston included), this skepticism serves mainly as an intellectual exercise that cannot shake their conviction that witchcraft does indeed exist. While they may question individual cases of suspected witchcraft, they rarely question the existence of witchcraft itself.

I take seriously Olivier de Sardan's (1988) caution about the potential that a personal ethnographic account will overly dramatize and exoticize quotidian features of African religious life, though I agree with Stoller (1989) that the occult in Africa can indeed be dramatic. With respect to the debate of whether the occult is either banal or extraordinary, I contend that it is both. In the same way that technological achievements are both fantastic and commonplace at once, witchcraft is a phenomenon that people marvel at, even though they encounter it everywhere. People's fears and speculations about fantastic supernatural abilities and threats are indeed dramatic, but they are also a part of their everyday lives. Like soldiers who face the potential for disaster with anxiety and trepidation while still going to work and even making jokes, Beninese people face their own dangers. But since they have no choice, they make their way as best they can and accept that they live in a world with witchcraft.

chapter four

Religion and the Occult

OPPOSITION AND CONNECTION

Given the recent media attention to and the academic evidence for the growing prevalence of witchcraft in Africa, one of the questions I asked my informants was whether witchcraft has increased in recent years. This is a difficult question because it requires speculation about something that is often hidden. While people had differing opinions, my friend Gaston drew an interesting distinction between witchcraft activity and the talk about witchcraft. In one conversation, he argued that witchcraft itself is no more common than before but that people today talk about it more openly. He said that when he was younger, almost nobody talked about *àzĕ*, mainly out of fear. Even in the relatively short span between my 2000 and 2006 field seasons, it seemed to me that the talk about *àzĕ* had increased dramatically. Gaston credited Christianity and the new Trŏ̃ cults with the recent changes, saying that both religions publicize *àzĕ* and its threats as a way of attracting adherents. His interpretation is not without merit, for there is certainly a great deal of buzz around *àzĕ* in these new movements, and scholars of African religion have come to similar conclusions (Marshall-Fratani 1998; Meyer 1999; Newell 2007). But the discourse of *àzĕ* permeates many sectors of society beyond religion, much of it reflecting an urgent fear of this pervasive and pernicious force in the world.

While Beninese people accept that *àzĕ* is everywhere, this does not mean that they willingly submit to its dangers. There are numerous folk practices to combat and repel witchcraft attacks. People also call on their gods for protection and salvation, and nearly all of today's popular religious movements, including Catholicism, Pentecostalism, the Celestial Church of Christ, Eckankar, and Trŏ̃, make spiritual combat central to their message. Competing for a share of the religious market requires leaders to promote their religion's opposition to witchcraft as a key feature in their proselytism efforts.[1] This suggests a firm dichotomy between people's notions of "religion" and "witchcraft." But because àzĕ is the strongest force there is, many people said that any religion that succeeds in neutralizing witchcraft must itself be utilizing the same force. Healers, Vodun priests, and Christian pastors are all suspected of possessing both good and evil forms of àzĕ. This leads to increased moral ambiguity about religious leaders, their gods, and religion in general, reinforcing notions that witchcraft is everywhere and that supernatural forces are all part of the same universal energy. The relationship between witchcraft and religion is controversial in Benin, particularly given the West's history of portraying the Vodun religion as a form of black magic. From the time of the first European contacts with this part of West Africa, Westerners and missionaries in particular have conflated the worship of indigenous deities with evil supernatural deeds (Henry 2008b). But in an ironic twist, it now seems that the slippage between witchcraft and religion has been extended to include Christianity, fueling Christian theological battles over hypocrisy and syncretism in the different churches.

This chapter addresses the wide range of religious activity surrounding witchcraft, including how both Christianity and "indigenous" religions depict and combat the occult.[2] As for Vodun's relationship to witchcraft, I examine whether such claims are merely ignorant racist rhetoric or whether Vodun actually has something to do with the occult. Though staunch Christians diabolize Vodun, equate it to witchcraft, or reduce it to superstition, many of my informants who practice Vodun admit to certain links between the indigenous religion, àzĕ, and bŏ. Of course, most people portray Vodun as distinct from the hidden mystical practices, and I urge readers to bear in mind that magical and religious spheres remain separate in many ways. Nevertheless, I report people's testimony of how the public Vodun religion articulates with the more secretive occult activities, and I draw on reports of similar connections between religion and the occult in Haitian Vodou and Brazilian Candomblé. While scholars have identified these links, such findings remain controversial because they could fuel long-standing Western stereotypes about African-derived religions. Furthermore, given the contemporary demonization of these religions by evangelical movements, this is a spiritually and politically charged issue (see Hackett 2003). I must emphasize that while I accurately report my informants' claims, there are others with good reasons to dispute them, reasons based on both observation and ideology. I share their concerns but feel compelled to present this important cultural phenomenon that contributes to the ongoing trend of universalizing religious, occult, and scientific systems of knowledge.

Opposing Witches

Before addressing the religious practices people use to contend with witch-craft, I first outline some of the many secular and folk solutions for super-natural threats. Not everyone practices a religion or has access to religious specialists. Furthermore, because diviners, healers, and Vodun priests demand payment for their services or require costly sacrifices, many people cannot afford to call on professional assistance. But lacking access to religious rituals does not mean people are helpless. Ordinary individuals say there are meth-ods for detecting àzètɔ́, protecting themselves from potential attacks, and combatting attacks that have already been launched. Of course, some people are said to be naturally resistant to àzĕ without recourse to any magical pro-tection, but most people believe that one is best served by maintaining vigi-lance, first by recognizing witches and then by taking action against them and protecting oneself from future attacks.

One of the most commonly reported ways of detecting or identifying an àzètɔ́ is simply by accidentally witnessing her in the process of transforma-tion or teleportation.[3] Àzètɔ́ transform into animals (often a bird or an owl), and sometimes they accidentally get caught out too late at night and regain their human form at daybreak, naked and outdoors, where they are seen by people beginning to leave their houses in the morning. An Abomey hair-dresser told me she learned of a woman found perched atop a wall overlook-ing a family compound. The woman who noticed her screamed at the dis-covery and claimed that the intruder had just transformed from a night bird. Others held that an attacking witch becomes visible in one's dreams and that by paying attention to dreams, one can recognize one's vulnerability.[4]

After having identified an àzètɔ́, there are a number of things one can do. For example, people claimed you can stop an àzètɔ́ during her nocturnal dream journey while her spirit is away from her body. One way of accom-plishing this is to apply salt to her sleeping body's eyes and nose, making these orifices too "hot" for the witch's soul to reenter her body. To prevent an àzètɔ́ from embarking on her nighttime travels altogether, one man suggested tak-ing the cloth that she uses in her outings. But for most people, the simplest way of ridding oneself of àzètɔ́ and preventing future attacks is to banish them, beat them, or kill them. Numerous informants admitted that even if àzĕ is the most powerful supernatural force in the world, àzètɔ́ are quite ordinary when it comes to physical threats and violence. My friend Simon said that àzètɔ́ are afraid of mean-spirited, quick-tempered, violent people. Because àzètɔ́'s magic works slowly, they cannot respond to an immediate physical threat;

therefore, àzètɔ́ can be physically harmed, provided that they cannot predict the attack in advance and prepare countermeasures. Àzètɔ́ are often discussed in the same breath with thieves, and because thieves are capable of violence, they are àzètɔ́'s strongest adversaries. As noted in chapter 1, thieves and àzètɔ́ share a number of characteristics because both groups belong to secret societies that are unpredictable, operate at night, and disrupt the social order. In their illegal activities, thieves regularly confront supernatural forces because most people have antitheft bǒ protecting their homes. Mouni's home was burglarized once while we were all away, and before the thieves left, they pulled down the bǒ she hung over the doorway and in defiant mockery left it on the ground outside the house. Although thieves' disregard for bǒ may not translate into immunity from àzě, it shows their willingness to defy supernatural powers.

Comments about using physical force against àzètɔ́ were repeated by numerous people. It should be obvious that such claims pave the way for the type of vigilante justice that most troubles human rights activists. In fact, an Abomey friend of mine told me he knows a man who threw his own mother down a well after becoming convinced that she was an àzètɔ́. And as mentioned in the preceding chapter, a healer in Ouidah informed me of a similar case where an accused witch was locked inside her home and starved to death by her own family. These are the most extreme examples of vigilante justice, and I judge them to be uncommon, though there are many other less severe sanctions against the accused. For example, I once witnessed an old woman in Bohicon being chased through the streets by children banging pots and pans. I was riding in my adoptive sister's car when she turned to me excitedly and said, "Douglas, look, there's a witch!" In addition to physical attacks, at the very least, some accused àzètɔ́ face the threat of social marginalization or exile from the family home.

Some people rely on semireligious or magical practices to protect themselves from witches. Christians might cross themselves or say a prayer prior to consuming anything that might be suspected of containing witchcraft poison. One woman explained that after such an act, if you bring a contaminated drink toward your mouth, the glass will break suddenly before you can ingest anything. There are also "treated" (magical) leaves and formulas (bǒ) that allow one to identify witches, and when these substances are applied to one's eyes, they permit one to see all the àzètɔ́ in the community as they go about their nefarious business. One old healer in a village north of Abomey gave me the following recipe to allow one to see àzètɔ́ during one's dreams: combine two vulture feathers, a piece of a cadaver's skull, a weaver bird, a pigeon, and

a rooster. After making this formula, all *àzètɔ́* in the neighborhood will come
to you and inform you of where they are going. He added that this essentially
makes one the boss of the local *àzètɔ́*.[5] An Abomey journalist provided a different recipe with the same purpose: take a *wútútú* bird hatchling and leaves
from a *jelelemã̀* plant, a *kpamã̀* plant, and a *xaixaimã̀* plant.[6] Mix these ingredients together, put them on your head, and lie down nude with a white cloth
across your body. This formula allows you to travel where the *àzètɔ́* are, and
you become their chief. These recipes imply that even ordinary people have
access to occult secrets and that anybody can take measures to protect themselves from supernatural attacks.

Despite people's attempts to prevent *àzètɔ́* attacks or to assault accused
àzètɔ́, numerous informants admitted to being skeptical about the possibility of removing *àzě* from a witch. Although some thought an outed witch is
automatically stripped of her ability to harm people, many still suspected that
a witch is always a witch. Even a number of healers and other ritual specialists
told me that they can stop an *àzètɔ́* from carrying out an attack but cannot
remove *àzě*. As one healer south of Abomey said, removing *àzě* might be possible, but it would mean the death of the *àzètɔ́*. He told me that anyone who
claims to be a former *àzètɔ́* is lying, as is anyone who claims to have removed
àzě. In sum, while there are many tactics said to protect people or combat *àzě*,
witchcraft remains a domain of great uncertainty and contradiction.

Christianity and the Occult

Christianity has a complex relationship with the occult. There are numerous
churches and denominations throughout Benin, and as they do in other African nations, many of them attract followers due to their claims to protect
people from witchcraft (Henry 2008b; Newell 2007; Surgy 2001; Tall 1995b).[7]
The Catholic Church is the oldest and largest denomination in Benin, representing 27 percent of the population (INSAE 2003). Though there were
several failed mission attempts along the coast beginning in the seventeenth
century (Labouret and Rivet 1929), the first permanent mission was established in Ouidah in 1861, followed by Cotonou in 1901 and Abomey in 1902
(Alladaye 2003).[8] The Catholics also established the first schools, training a
class of educated Catholic civil servants and paving the way for the religion's
prominent place in society. Today, Catholic churches are among the most con-
spicuous architectural structures in the country, especially in Cotonou, which
boasts a large cathedral and numerous other churches, some of which have
given their names to the neighborhoods where they are located. The second
largest denomination, with 5 percent of the population, is the Celestial Church

of Christ (INSAE 2003, 21), an indigenous African church founded in Porto-Novo in 1947 with a considerable following in Nigeria and other countries throughout West Africa and the world (see Adogame 1998; Ayegboyin and Ishola 1997; Henry 2001; Mary 2002, 2005; Obafemi 1986; Tade 1980; Tall 1995b). In addition, there are Protestant denominations and a growing number of evangelical and Pentecostal churches (see Alokpo 1996; Surgy 1996). Christianity has been steadily gaining ground in Benin, particularly in urban areas and among elites. According to the 2002 census, 23 percent of Beninese practice indigenous religions, 24 percent are Muslim, and 43 percent claim to be Christian, though where I work in the South, Islam is much less common, making Christianity and Vodun the main religions (INSAE 2003).[9] Even compared to a few years ago, Christian identity has become noticeably more important and visible. Today, weddings, baptisms, and christenings are lavish ceremonies accompanied by costly receptions where hundreds of invitees eat and drink their fill. Benin's national television station broadcasts Christian programs that show preaching and play religious music, including American gospel singers. Christian musical groups have become popular, and now one hears their music blaring from radios on the streets and in taxis.

Nearly all Christian denominations appeal to people's sense of spiritual insecurity, which manifests in concerns over ordinary misfortunes. Informants reported that the reasons for conversion include the desire for wealth, peace, health, and children. Insecurity is experienced by both men and women, but almost universally, people said that women are more susceptible to these fears, making women more numerous in church congregations (Falen 2008). For example, a woman may seek out a minister if she is unable to conceive or if she has health problems, and a successful outcome may prompt her to attend the church regularly. Although these mundane desires are common the world over, in Benin people routinely attribute chronic health problems, bad luck in business, and any other misfortune to the work of àzètɔ́. Behind all the ordinary anxieties there is nearly always a supernatural cause motivating the search for new religions or new spiritual influences. Christianity in Africa also involves an interest in achieving a more "civilized" or modern lifestyle (Marshall-Fratani 1998; Sargent 1989). There is a tension between Vodun and Christianity that extends to a broader battle between modern and traditional identity. Christians associate their religion with education, urban life, and bureaucratic employment, all of which project an identity of enlightenment and sophistication, which they oppose to the dark, traditional, agricultural, backward, and diabolical ways of Vodun. For their part, many Vodun worshippers I spoke to demonstrated remarkable tolerance for Christianity, though a

FIGURE 6. The Catholic church Saint Jean-Baptiste, Cotonou. (Photograph by the author)

number of my informants responded to the demonization of Vodun by portraying Christianity as a foreign, intrusive, "white people's religion."

Some Christians suggested that their religion automatically protects them from the evil that resides in rural Vodun practices. A driver for an NGO told me that he learned from his father that it is better to worship God than to pay attention to the occult. He said that if you do not believe in witchcraft, then it cannot harm you. A young male student said that Christians think about àzĕ and bŏ less and therefore are less troubled by these negative forces. However, most people acknowledged that moving out of the village and belonging to a church are only the first steps. Christians must also cultivate a sincere faith in Christ if they want protection; some churches use special protective prayers, but people said these are ineffective without true faith.[10] Two hotel administrators in Cotonou admitted that faith conquers all, but they also felt that people must have unfaltering faith and be without sin in order for it to work. They concluded by saying that nobody is perfect; therefore, nobody is safe.

Other people believe that churches provide active protection through efforts at identifying and exorcising àzètɔ. Their effectiveness varies depending on the church or the person performing the ceremony, but many held that churches and their leaders are successful in fighting àzètɔ. One informant told me that, apart from thieves, churches are the only thing àzètɔ are afraid of. However, many people said that some of the worst àzètɔ, those who have eaten the most victims, actually take refuge in churches after being publicly identified, and since àzĕ cannot be removed, this makes church a dangerous space occupied by witches (see Newell 2007). It is often said that witches join church congregations to prey on the unsuspecting members, and people claim this accounts for why àzètɔ are so much more numerous in churches than anywhere else. A Protestant pastor expressed doubt about his own church's effectiveness in removing àzĕ, explaining that converted àzètɔ must be monitored closely to ensure that they remain free of àzĕ; backsliders are especially dangerous, because they can draw on both àzĕ and the power of the church.

Despite skepticism, many people declared that àzètɔ confess in church and successfully abandon àzĕ in favor of Christian faith. There are witnessing programs on the radio, during which former àzètɔ confess and proclaim their new Christian faith. Many Catholics expressed pride in their church's record at combatting àzètɔ and removing their àzĕ power, saying that Jesus Christ's word is more powerful than witchcraft. In 2006 I spoke with a Catholic priest who had studied in a seminary in the United States, and he told me that although Americans do not take witchcraft seriously, the Beninese Catholic Church acknowledges this reality and performs exorcisms. He said he was skeptical at first but has since witnessed people vomiting needles and snakes, so he feels the church is justified in taking witchcraft seriously.

When I asked interviewees which denominations are most successful in combatting witchcraft, I received a range of responses. Some claimed that Catholicism is best, while others touted what they called the "new" evangelical or Pentecostal churches. But the Celestial Church of Christ has the strongest reputation for spiritual protection. Indeed, one of the church's hallmarks is spiritual combat and healing (Henry 2008a, 197). People suffering from unexplained illnesses who have found no relief from healers, diviners, hospitals, or *vodŭnɔ̀* often turn to the Celestial Church, where they may be kept for days or weeks at a time to receive treatment through intensive prayer and rituals to expel evil forces (203).[11] During this time, the person may be forced to abandon his or her job and must rely on friends and family to supply food. Mouni told me about her nephew who became sick and was taken to the Celestial Church, where they tied him up and whipped him to chase off the evil.[12] The Celestial Church's efforts at spiritual security also consist of ritual offerings to persuade the Holy Spirit to help the victim. Offerings include candles and sweet items like fruit, honey, and sugar (see figure 7). In spite of its leaders' insistence that the Celestial Church has nothing to do with "traditional" religion and that it is an authentic church strictly following scripture, the use of offerings forges an association with the indigenous religious heritage and invites condemnation from other denominations that claim that the Celestial Church embodies syncretism (Henry 2008b).[13] Their disputes are based on the Celestial Church's acceptance of polygyny, the use of offerings, and mutual accusations of hypocrisy and inauthenticity (Falen 2008). Rodrigue the artist likened the Celestial Church to the Afro-Caribbean religion of Santería, labeling it a syncretistic religion because its leaders rely on visions and trance that resemble Fá divination and spirit possession. Nevertheless, many Celestial Christians insist on their church's effectiveness in combatting *àzĕ*, and I have heard that *àzètɔ́* regularly confess in order to be purged of *àzĕ*.

But as noted, even if occult attacks can be prevented, some people said that witchcraft can never truly be removed from someone. This is one reason why there is skepticism about Christianity's spiritual victories. Furthermore, claims that churches have become a haven for witches hiding in the congregation ironically suggest that churches are more dangerous as a result of their exorcism efforts. Others said that because *àzĕ* is the strongest supernatural power, then only *àzĕ* can combat *àzĕ*. They argued that if church leaders are capable of opposing witchcraft, then they must themselves possess *àzĕ*. People contended that Celestial Church leaders actually use *àzĕ* in their spiritual battles

FIGURE 7. Offerings of fruit, honey, and sugar in a Celestial Church of Christ, Cotonou. (Photograph by the author)

and that many of them used to be traditional healers and still rely on traditional healing techniques or even on their former colleagues. Although they may acknowledge that the church uses benevolent àzě, they imply that there is a single and supreme supernatural force at the root of both witchcraft and Christianity.[14] Hervé told me that Celestial Christians secretly use good àzě; they bury the ká gohŭ (the smaller, bumpy àzě calabash) at the site of a new church, and this is the power that attracts converts. He added that he knows pastors from the Celestial Church who admitted to this and to performing other magical acts. When I asked a Protestant pastor if his church's power is like àzě, he simply said, "Of course!"[15] In sum, many see a thin line between Christianity and àzě.

Statements about àzě being the source of Christian power give rise to rampant accusations of hypocrisy in the competitive quarrels between denominations over who practices the more "authentic" Christianity. For example, one newly founded Christian movement derives much of its appeal from these suspicions and accusations of inauthenticity and hypocrisy. The Very Holy Church of Jesus Christ of Banamè was founded by a former Catholic woman named Parfaite. According to her followers, in 2009, at the age of eighteen, Parfaite was plagued by witchcraft and sought help from a Catholic exorcist. After her successful deliverance from these supernatural attacks, Parfaite herself began performing miraculous cures and gaining a reputation both within and beyond the Catholic Church. When she declared that she was the receptacle for and manifestation of God himself, the Catholic Church became alarmed and distanced itself from her.[16] She subsequently denounced Catholic priests as witches and even accused the pope of being the most notorious witch in the world. In a few short years, she has attracted an enormous following (perhaps hundreds of thousands) and has risen to national prominence as a controversial figure boasting a spiritual war against Catholicism, Vodun, and all other religions. Not surprisingly, Parfaite's detractors have also pointed to her miraculous accomplishments as evidence that she herself possesses *àzě*.[17]

Battles over authenticity are not limited to churches' connections to witchcraft but include their stance on Vodun religion. Catholics often contended that the Celestial Church's reliance on offerings makes it a disguised continuation of Vodun, while Celestial Christians maintained that the Catholic Church is contaminated by its attempt to assimilate indigenous culture through its Mewi Hwendo policy (see chapter 2). Many informants stated that Catholicism is so popular precisely because of its priests' tolerance for indigenous culture (Alokpo 1996). My Beninese brother, Chams, knows Catholic priests who even employ Fá divination and keep Fá accoutrements hidden in their homes. Although Catholic priests forbid *bǒ* and other occult activity among their congregations, people said priests secretly use these magical strategies themselves. Much as people claimed about the Celestial Church of Christ, evangelical leaders are accused of burying a *bǒ* before building a new church as a way to attract additional members and generate money. Others claimed that priests' (and all Christian ministers') power is actually rooted in Fá, and Timothy Landry (2015) reports witnessing a Christian pastor being initiated into Fá divination. If religious leaders are themselves unable to abandon Vodun, then their congregations interpret this as an unspoken justification for church members to maintain their ties to Vodun. Therefore, even if Christian leaders preach the rejection of Vodun, people might not feel motivated to separate the two traditions in their everyday life.[18] There is reportedly a prominent healer in Cotonou who claims equivalence between a black Jesus and the *vodǔ* named Sɛgbo-Lisá. Didier offered a telling example of Vodun's ambivalent relationship with Christianity. He said he knew a woman studying for her catechism who asked the Vodun spirit Lɛ̌gbà to ensure her success. Such phenomena have inspired a widespread expression that people practice

Christianity by day and Vodun by night, suggesting a coexistence between the two religions.[19] Maurice, the menacing Ouidah healer discussed in chapter 3, told me that the "imported" Christian religions force people to perform a pretense, but, he stated, "Le vodun est incontournable" (Vodun is incontrovertible). He also referred to an idiom about churches being full in the morning, while people still visit the *vodŭnɔ̀* at night, adding that priests and pastors are among his clients, so Jesus must not be very powerful. He himself was once Catholic, but when he married his second wife and became polygynous, he voluntarily stopped receiving Communion. He condemned others as hypocrites for hiding their polygyny and continuing to receive Communion.

While Christians generally denounce Vodun and deny any connection with it, Rodrigue the Cotonou artist argued that the Vodun deities are tolerant of Christianity, or else they would never have allowed churches to be established. He noted the presence of a Catholic cathedral directly in front of the python temple in Ouidah. As for Christianity, he accused churches of seeking money and using false testimony about miracles to dupe unsuspecting converts. When asked about supernatural forces, he stated that Westerners use their powers to cure illness, adding:

> Nous, notre seul dommage, c'est qu'on n'a jamais su que c'est une force qu'on pouvait mettre au profit de la population. On n'a jamais su que c'était une force qu'on pouvait mettre au profit du développement. Oui? On a toujours traité ces gens là de maléfiques. On a toujours traité ces gens là de mauvais, parce que la religion, le christianisme, elle a fait son lit, et son lit préféré. Tu vois? Oui, parce qu'il faut détruire ça, il faut donner une mauvaise opinion de ça. Or, moi, j'ai plutôt une mauvaise opinion du christianisme que de tout, et de l'islam que de tout. Parce qu'on ne peut pas dire qu'au nom d'Allah on va tuer des gens. C'est mauvais. . . . Au nom de quoi? Du même Dieu. Dieu n'a jamais dit ça. Dieu n'a jamais dit ça. Dieu n'a jamais dit, "Tapez-vous les uns les autres. Tuez quelqu'un en mon nom." Dieu n'a jamais dit ça. Dieu a dit "pardonnez." Et que les hommes n'ont jamais pardonné. Donc pour moi, ce n'est plus des religions. Et quand tu parles de religion aujourd'hui au Bénin, moi je te dis qu'il y a toujours une seule religion au Bénin. C'est l'animisme, eh? C'est le vodun, eh? . . . Je peux te donner pleins d'exemples. Quand ça ne va pas dans la journée, là, les gars que tu vois en train de prier à l'église là, le soir ils sont tous chez les bokɔ́nɔ̀ pour savoir ce qui se passe, parce qu'ils ont tellement peur. Ils ont tellement la trouille qu'ils sont obligés de se protéger. Demande-moi pourquoi un député de l'Assemblée Nationale, quand il quitte ses fonctions, et il a son quatre-quatre, a l'état, et pourquoi [unintelligible] ne

prend pas le quatre-quatre et il demande à ce qu'on lui achète un autre quatre-quatre? Eh, c'est quoi la raison? Eh? Pourquoi il fait changer tous les meubles du bureau? Là ou son prédécesseur a travaillé, parce qu'ils ne sont pas du même clan? Pour quelle raison? Pourquoi dans toutes les maisons, dans *toutes* les maisons, dans toutes les maisons sauf les nouvelles maisons construites, dans toutes les maisons familiales, pourquoi il y a un vodũ? Il y a toujours un vodũ, si tu fouilles là, il y a un vodũ. Ceux qui nous disent qu'ils sont évangélistes aujourd'hui, comme Yayi Boni, il est quoi? Pour moi il est païen. Il est rien du tout. Il imagine qu'il est évangéliste, mais [unintelligible] vas chez lui, là bas, fouille chez lui et tu trouveras des vodũ. Et puis quand ça ne va pas, il sera le premier à . . . Ils sont tous des chefs d'état là, ils ont tous de vrais marabouts, des gens qui les protègent. Parce qu'ils ont peur. Ils savent réellement ce que c'est. Eh oui!

[As for us, what's a shame is that we never knew that it's a power that could benefit the population. We never knew that it's a force we could use in the interest of development. Right? We always treated these people [who use the occult] as evil. We always treated them as bad, because the religion, Christianity, established itself and took the upper hand. You see? Yes, because you [they] have to destroy it [traditional religious belief], you [they] have to create a negative impression of it. As for me, I have a more negative opinion of Christianity than anything, a more negative opinion of Islam than anything. Because you can't say that you're killing someone in Allah's name. It's wrong. . . . In the name of what? Of the same God. God never said that. God never said that. God never said, "Beat each other up! Kill someone in my name!" God never said that. God said "Forgive." But people never forgave. So for me, these aren't religions. And when you speak about religion in Benin today, I'll tell you that there has always been a single religion. It's animism, right? It's Vodun, right? . . . I could give you plenty of examples. If things aren't going well during the day, those people you see praying in church, in the evening they're all visiting the *bokɔnɔ̀* to learn what's really happening, because they're so scared. They're so terribly afraid that they have to protect themselves. Ask me why a deputy in the National Assembly, when he leaves his [previous] job, and he gets a 4×4 from the government, and why [unintelligible] doesn't take the 4×4 but asks that they buy him a new one? Huh? What's the reason? Huh? Why does he have all the furniture replaced in his office, where his predecessor worked, because they're not from the same clan? For what reason? How come in every home, in *every* home, in every home except the newly constructed houses, in every family home, why is there a *vodũ* [i.e., deity]? There's always

a *vodǔ*, if you look around, there's always a *vodǔ*. The people who tell us
they're evangelicals today, like [President] Yayi Boni, what is he? For me, he's
pagan. He's nothing. He imagines that he's evangelical, but [unintelligible] go
to his house. And there, look around, and you'll find the *vodǔ*. And then when
things aren't going well, he'll be the first to ... All the heads of state, they all
have real marabouts, people who protect them. Because they're scared. They
know what's really going on. That's right!]

This interviewee is an intellectual who is more comfortable than most in discussing such issues and offering candid opinions. But his interview is significant because it captures a number of themes that recur in conversations with
other informants, especially with Vodun adherents. For example, he expresses
indignation over missionaries who demonized indigenous religion, and he
regrets that people have failed to develop more positive uses for supernatural
power. He highlights the fear and spiritual insecurity prevalent in all walks of
life, right up to the president of Benin. And he rejects Christianity (and Islam)
as a foreign facade hiding people's authentic faith in Vodun. While not everyone would agree with his assessment, he poignantly portrays the sometimes
uneasy coexistence between Vodun and Christianity that leads to rampant
accusations of Christian hypocrisy. My friend Gaston, who identifies with the
Vodun religion, once told me he finds his own Christian siblings' denuncia-
tion of Vodun to be offensive, and he wonders why they favor an imported
religion over their own heritage. These are the primary issues in the religious
battles involving Christianity, and despite some Christians' insistence on their
separation from Vodun and witchcraft, many informants remain convinced
that Christianity retains important traces of African culture and spirituality.

Debates over Christian denominations' authenticity, connections to Vodun,
and ambiguous relationship with witchcraft index a complicated and even
symbiotic relationship between Christianity and other supernatural forces.
In her seminal work on Ghanaian Christianiy, *Translating the Devil* (1999),
Birgit Meyer reveals how Christianity maintained entanglements with indigenous witchcraft beliefs. Meyer explains that missionaries to Ghana, similar to
those to Benin, translated "devil" using a local word that bore connections to
indigenous gods and witchcraft, which meant that despite missionaries' preference to avoid engaging with witchcraft, their own cultural and linguistic
translations virtually guaranteed that witchcraft would occupy a central role
in Christian life. The links between Christianity and witchcraft discourses are
well documented in West Africa, where other scholars suggest that Pentecostalism is especially influential in fomenting fears of witchcraft. For example,

Sasha Newell (2007) observes that Pentecostal churches in Ivory Coast are attempting to distance themselves from witchcraft while simultaneously perpetuating and even constituting witchcraft discourse through their claims to protect their members. Likewise, Ruth Marshall-Fratani writes that Nigerian Pentecostalism "directly addresses the problem of the forces of evil and incites public testimony about the workings of evil forces" like witchcraft (1998, 304). Therefore, these scholars suggest that as Pentecostalism has become more popular in recent years, its public emphasis on fighting evil and providing protection from witches has the ironic effect of amplifying witchcraft fears and discourses and embedding witchcraft into the very fabric of Christianity. In Benin similar circumstances likely explain why people rarely consider the likelihood of eradicating witchcraft; instead, they test different denominations' and Vodun's ability to protect against it. According to Meyer (1999), in Ghana conversions between Christian and indigenous religions made the devil a shared symbol articulating with both indigenous and foreign religions and paving the way for further ambiguity between "traditional" and "modern" modes of thought. This ideological fusion of witchcraft and Christianity is bolstered by the common suspicion that Christian churches and their pastors are themselves endowed with witchcraft. In Benin these suspicions have ensured that Christianity and indigenous religion operate with similar supernatural goals and within a witchcraft paradigm that emphasizes the ambiguity and ambivalence of supernatural forces. Meyer's analysis suggests that it may not be a coincidence that witchcraft fears seem to have grown in tandem with the popularity of Christianity in Africa. In Benin preoccupations with witchcraft seem to have accelerated during a period when Pentecostalism, with its emphasis on evil, has been gaining momentum. Therefore, a religious explanation for the surge in African witchcraft may be a viable addition to the modernity school's focus on neoliberalism, inequality, and social turmoil.

Trɔ̃ the Protector

Besides Christianity, another prominent religious import engaged in spiritual combat is the deity Trɔ̃. Trɔ̃ and related divinities had arrived in Ouidah by the 1940s via Ghana and Togo (Bay 2008; Tall 1995b; Montgomery and Vannier 2017; Rosenthal 1998), but it took longer to spread farther north. One informant in his forties said that Trɔ̃ did not exist in Abomey when he was a child but that it began arriving in the 1980s and 1990s. Trɔ̃ exists in two forms in southern Benin, the first version called *kpetɔ deka* and the second called *kpetɔ ve*.[20] Some informants suggested that there may also be a *kpetɔ atɔ̃* (third version), highlighting the deity's ability to multiply and transform in response to

different religious or political pressures (Rosenthal 1998). Though Trɔ̃ is usually referred to in the singular, initiates and laypeople alike acknowledge the
existence of other named deities associated with Trɔ̃, such as Kunde, Banguele,
Gambada (Garbala/Gabada), Djogbe, Sakla, Kofi, Sogbedji, and Agbizounon.
With the exception of Kunde, Gambada, and Banguele, who are sometimes
considered specific types or partners of Trɔ̃, it is unclear whether or not most
of these deities belong to a Trɔ̃ pantheon or simply perform similar functions. It may be Trɔ̃'s dynamic quality that allowed it to adjust to the changes
in àzě, propelling it to the forefront of supernatural battles. The term Ajavodũ
(meaning a vodũ from the Aja region, southwest of Abomey) is another umbrella category frequently used to refer to Trɔ̃ and the entire collection of
antiwitchcraft spirits that came to Benin via the southwestern Beninese prov-
ince inhabited by Aja people.[21] Some people refer to Ajavodũ as a purer, more
authentic power, and one informant contrasted "true" Ajavodũ with what he
considered the simple imitations spreading through Benin from Ouidah.
Indeed, some healers talked about the Aja region as the most authentic source
of supernatural power.

Trɔ̃ is also sometimes called a gorovodũ (kola nut divinity) and has achieved
wide popularity throughout southern Benin due to its powers of opposing
witchcraft (Tall 2005). Before arriving in Benin, the gorovodũ tradition arose
in Togo and Ghana near the end of the nineteenth century as an antiwitchcraft movement that developed into a collection of deities that specialized
in healing. The deities' origins are in the Muslim North of Ghana and Togo,
and they incorporate Islamic names and symbols (Montgomery and Vannier
2017). Though Beninese Trɔ̃ is not identical to Togolose gorovodũ, my Beninese informants also acknowledge Trɔ̃'s Muslim heritage.[22] Hervé told me
that although he was not initiated into Trɔ̃, in the course of his research for a
program he learned that Trɔ̃ came from a Fulani or Hausa man in Ghana,
a Muslim who ate kola nuts. According to his story, the Ghanaian man was
in the bush and discovered how to hit a stone to exorcize witchcraft from
himself. Afterward the man sought out a home where witchcraft was strong,
bringing the stone and kola nuts with him. He eradicated the witchcraft, and
the family adopted his new religion, which then spread from Ghana to Togo
and eventually to Benin.[23] The majority of informants said that Trɔ̃ is among
the most powerful forces in protecting people and eradicating àzě.[24] Chams
told me that Trɔ̃ is so attuned to witchcraft that any àzètɔ́ who approaches
the deity's shrine will be prevented from entering. At the Trɔ̃ installation
ceremony I attended in 2008 (see chapter 3), the visiting xunɔ̃ (Trɔ̃ priest)
from Ouidah recited a series of prayers commemorating the new shrine, and

one of the most forceful prayers he pronounced again and again was "Àzètɔ́ lɛ tēkpɔ̃ ɔ, Trɔ̃ na wli!" (If witches try anything, Trɔ̃ will catch them!). Indeed, David, whose two-year-old daughter died from an àzĕ attack, told me that he called on Trɔ̃ to find those responsible. During the ritual, Trɔ̃ possessed a devotee and identified the two family members who had killed the child.

Trɔ̃'s reputation creates financial incentive for religious specialists to acquire shrines and become xunɔ̃ in order to take advantage of the lucrative demand for spiritual healing. But buying Trɔ̃ from another priest in Aja or Ouidah is a serious investment, and most people told me that the cost can surpass several hundred thousand FCFA. A xunɔ̃ I know in a village near Abomey told me that he paid another xunɔ̃ in Aja 2 million FCFA ($4,000) for his Trɔ̃. According to Gaston, this xunɔ̃, who was already a healer, admitted that he only added Trɔ̃ to his repertoire for the business it promised. Ordinary people become initiates of Trɔ̃ for its protection and for the good luck that it provides. Trɔ̃ is very much in fashion with intellectuals and the upwardly mobile urban population. Many of my friends and informants have been initiated into Trɔ̃, and for a fee of 20,000 FCFA ($40) Chams was initiated into one of the early stages to achieve the rank of kpējigā.[25] He said that his motive for becoming an initiate was to improve his relationships and professional opportunities as a master of ceremonies. Rival emcees and his coworkers at his customer service job seemed to dislike him, and he feared for his career. Soon after his initiation, his situation improved. He got a good job as an emcee at a ceremony, and his coworkers suddenly befriended him and began confiding secrets to him. Aside from the financial expense, initiation comes with a host of taboos. Chams's taboos included avoiding the consumption of pork, catfish, and certain greens; not answering someone who calls for him while he is bathing; not having sex with bare feet on the ground; and not killing snakes. A Cotonou Trɔ̃ initiate gave me another list of taboos: never pursue another man's wife, avoid arguing with àzètɔ́, avoid eating pork, and never visit the Trɔ̃ shrine after having sex. Though some people surely take all the taboos seriously, Chams confided that it is difficult to respect them all.

One of the features distinguishing Trɔ̃ from Ewe gorovodũ and the traditional Vodun deities is that Trɔ̃ does not dance in groups at large public possession ceremonies. However, I have witnessed some Trɔ̃ possessions and heard about others. For instance, a friend once invited me to a Trɔ̃ shrine outside of Abomey, where I met a xunɔ̃ carrying the priest's requisite saber—a short decorative sword with a wide blade. As a noninitiate, I was required to remove my shirt to enter the shrine. I offered the xunɔ̃ 700 FCFA ($1.40) to buy a small bottle of gin for the deity. When the bottle arrived, he put it to his

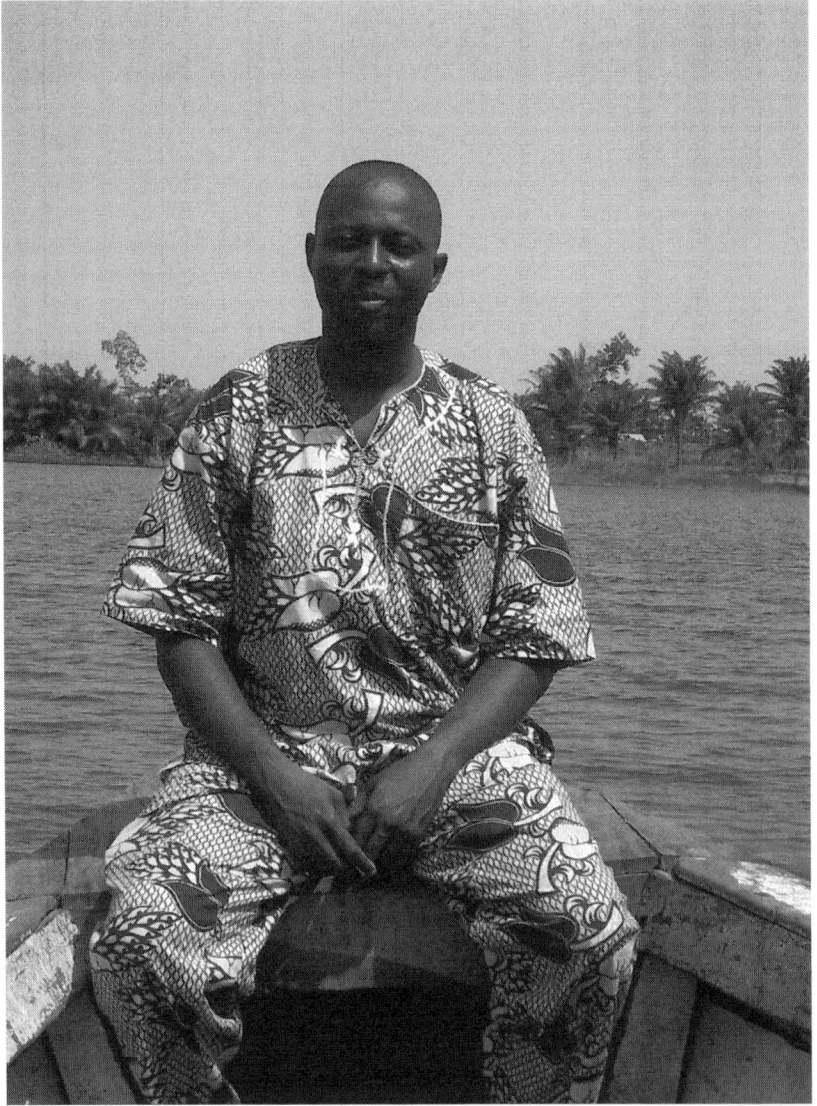

FIGURE 8. My adoptive brother, Chams, in the canoe crossing the lagoon to Tohounou. (Photograph by the author)

mouth and then sprayed gin atop the conical cement mound representing the deity Banguele. I was asked to buy cigarettes, which we lit and blew on Banguele's mound, then we left them atop the cone until they burned out.[26] A female adept possessed by Banguele arrived carrying a trident; she was dressed in red and white, and her face was completely covered in white powder. I gave 100 FCFA ($0.20) to Banguele and 100 FCFA to the *xunɔ̀* for the divination he was to perform. Next I was told to cut a bit of my hair and place it atop the conical mound representing Banguele's shrine. Banguele spoke calmly in another language but barely opened her mouth. The *xunɔ̀* said she was speaking Mina (Gɛ̃) mixed with some Yoruba. Another woman came to interpret for Banguele and told me that the spirit's message was that I had a friend back home pursuing my wife. They offered to perform a ceremony to address the problem, but I politely thanked them and declined. On the way out, the *xunɔ̀* showed me Trɔ̀'s chamber, where a kola tree grew from the earthen floor. He threw in a few kola nuts and some water. Trɔ̀ shrines usually have an earthen-floored chamber where kola nuts are thrown as offerings. The shrine's roof is left open above this chamber so that light and water can nourish the nuts, which grow into kola trees.

On several occasions when I visited various Trɔ̀ shrines, the *xunɔ̀* offered to consult Fá for me. Each time, I would remove my shirt, though initiates remain clothed. When I entered the shrine I was instructed to greet Trɔ̀ by kneeling and touching the floor, my forehead, and my chest three times in succession. Then I offered the *xunɔ̀* some money. Instead of the *àgŭ màgà*—the divination chain with which a *bokɔ́nɔ̀* consults Fá—a *xunɔ̀* uses split kola nuts (*goro*). The *xunɔ̀* took the nuts and touched them to my forehead, then banged a stone on the cement at the base of the shrine before casting the nuts on the ground. He then read the sign and told me its meaning. With the exception of Banguele's message noted above, all of the readings were positive, saying that my health and activities held good promise.

On another occasion, I consulted Trɔ̀ when my adoptive brother, Chams, invited me to visit the large shrine in Tohounou, near Ouidah. This is a site that some people call Benin's Trɔ̀ headquarters, and its leader, the *xunɔ̀gá*, is head of the *kpetɔ deka* version of Trɔ̀. From the main road to Ouidah there is a narrow dirt road that leads north to the edge of the lagoon. Entrepreneurs run a few large canoes, ferrying passengers across. On the other side, it is a short walk through the village up to the *xunɔ̀gá*'s shrine. The shrine is housed in a large brick-and-cement building with bas-relief sculptures on the terrace walls, a receiving room for the *xunɔ̀gá*, and an attached hallway leading into the shrine, which consists of the kola tree chamber, a waiting room, and a consultation room, whose walls are lined with a cement bench. Chams had become friends with the *xunɔ̀gā* and had even proposed to record religious songs and produce a CD that the *xunɔ̀gā* could use to commercialize his activities in Haiti and elsewhere (though this never happened). Chams and I removed our shoes as a required sign of respect and entered the receiving room. The *xunɔ̀gā* was friendly and welcoming. I was surprised that he suggested I accompany Chams into the shrine room, even though I had not been initiated. I took off my shirt and followed Chams along the hallway and past a number of smaller chambers where people were doing other consultations and praying. I heard one woman praying rapidly, asking for assistance. Chams was beckoned to the other side of the kola chamber, while I sat on the bench in the adjoining waiting room. An elderly *xunɔ̀* was helping Chams consult with Trɔ̀, and a few minutes later the *xunɔ̀gā*'s son came and told me to join them to observe the proceedings. I kneeled down and touched my hands to the ground, to my head, and to my chest three times in a row. When it was my turn, the *xunɔ̀* bid me wash my hands, and he placed four kola nuts in my left hand. I was instructed to hold the nuts and move my hand around my head and over my body and then hand them back. He threw the kolas, and all four landed face up, an unambiguously positive sign; he then said, "A ɖo ɖagbe" (You're good/all right). He told me that Trɔ̀ liked me and predicted good things for my future. After the consultation, the *xunɔ̀* dipped his fingers in a wet, sandy, gray, charcoal substance, which appeared to be mixed with ash, and dotted my head, cheeks, chest, arms, and back with it. Then he sprinkled perfume on his hands and rubbed them over my body. He handed me two kola halves and told me to eat them, and he then asked if I had any questions for Trɔ̀. Based on my previous nocturnal encounter with Trɔ̀ (chapter 3), I was toying with the idea of becoming an initiate. So I asked the *xunɔ̀* if Trɔ̀ wanted me to be initiated. He was a little surprised, saying that of course Trɔ̀ approved, that this in fact was the result of my consultation and the four open kolas. He added that his own vision had also told him that I should be initiated, and within eight days. I never did become an initiate, for a variety of reasons. For one, I was concerned about the expense, but in general I am wary about initiations and have refused all of them because I worry that some people might find it disrespectful for a foreigner to pretend to belong to their sacred community. I am also concerned about contributing to the practice of seeing foreigners as spiritual tourists to be enticed into joining groups that they do not truly understand or believe in.

Despite my concerns about intruding on sacred territory, Trɔ̀ appears to be one of the most open and welcoming deities. A year after meeting the *xunɔ̀gā*,

Chams and I returned to Tohounou for a brief visit, and the *xunɔ̃gā*'s son, not realizing that I was still uninitiated, nearly invited me into the shrine without getting permission and without asking me to remove my shirt. He told Chams that I seemed to belong and that he was sure I was already an initiate. Like those of other deities, Trɔ̃'s society is secret, so theoretically, membership is controlled. But people tell me that faith, religious affiliation, and skin color are unimportant, so virtually anyone is eligible to be initiated. Chams echoed this sentiment, telling me that Trɔ̃ accepts people who belong to any religion. Another *xunɔ̃* from a village near Bohicon also urged me to become an initiate, saying that anybody can benefit from Trɔ̃'s protection, including Christians, Muslims, and members of any other religions. Indeed, Trɔ̃ is uncompetitive with other religions or the local deities, and Edna Bay (2008) learned of a Trɔ̃ spirit that insists that initiates fulfill ritual obligations associated with Christianity, Islam, and Vodun. Chams told me that during one of his consultations, Trɔ̃ recommended that he go to his paternal home and feed the family spirits. And during a Trɔ̃ healing ceremony outside of Abomey that I attended with Gaston, I learned that Trɔ̃ was acting as an intermediary, asking the deity Dā to accept an offering and help a sick child. This inclusive attitude is unsurprising when one considers Trɔ̃'s explicitly heterogeneous origins, which fused northern Muslim spirits and southern Ewe gods in its trek across West Africa.[27] Moreover, the ethos of inclusion mirrors the universalizing tendencies that I have already discussed with respect to witchcraft and science but that are also noticeable in the realm of organized religions, where people often state that all religions recognize the same God.

Another example of this universalizing trend is that Trɔ̃ is often said to be undergirded by *àzě*. In the same way that Christian priests and pastors are suspected of using *àzě* to fight *àzě*, people said that *xunɔ̃* are only able to cure their witchcraft-stricken patients through the use of *àzě*. Again, the rationale is that there is nothing stronger than *àzě*. A number of informants made these statements, including several healers, a rural businessman, and a female member of the Eckankar spiritual movement. Of course, some said that Trɔ̃ uses good *àzě* to fight the evil variety, but as I showed in chapter 2, there is significant ambivalence about the existence of distinct good and bad *àzě* because people frequently said that *àzě* is neutral, so individuals' morality is what accounts for the good or evil results. Though many healers admitted to using *àzě*, one *xunɔ̃* denied this association, saying that there is no *àzě* in Trɔ̃. For a number of informants, Trɔ̃'s relationship to *àzě* was also contingent on the version of Trɔ̃. Surprisingly, all of my informants who stated a preference for one of the versions of Trɔ̃ held that the first version (*kpetɔ deka*) was the pure and benevolent kind that combats *àzě*, while the second version (*kpetɔ ve*) was malevolent *àzě* itself.[28] Hervé told me that Trɔ̃ *kpetɔ deka* does not use the *ká gohŭ* (*àzě* calabash) and does not have any inherent relationship to *àzě* but that some benevolent *àzètɔ́* have begun acquiring Trɔ̃, creating the impression that Trɔ̃ and *àzě* are identical. Despite the contradictions, it is clear that even as it combats *àzě*, Trɔ̃, like Christianity, maintains ambiguous connections to witchcraft.

Vodun and the Occult

Trɔ̃'s African origins, divination, possession, and requirements for offerings demonstrate obvious similarities to the established Vodun deities of southern Benin. At the same time, Trɔ̃ is imported and possesses different characteristics, leading academics to refer to Trɔ̃ and related deities as neo-Vodun. Unlike the preexisting Vodun gods of southern Benin, Trɔ̃ consumes vast quantities of kola nuts and prefers sacrificial kittens. But compared to other deities, Trɔ̃'s antiwitchcraft appeal and ambiguous relationship with *àzě* appeared to be the most distinctive and novel features. Before beginning this research, I understood the cosmological system of Vodun to include numerous deities with no connection to the occult. Witchcraft and sorcery, I thought, were undeniably separate from the polytheistic religion of Vodun. However, during my inquiries, I learned of a number of important connections between these two spiritual domains. For example, a few years ago, when I had just begun asking informants about *àzě* and *bŏ*, several of them mentioned the word *àzěvodŭ* (witchcraft *vodŭ*), a term that immediately surprised me because it implied that these two seemingly distinct domains were related. I first interpreted it to mean a *vodŭ* spirit responsible for creating or using witchcraft, but I later learned that *àzěvodŭ* was much more ambiguous in that people described it as a deity responsible for both using and combatting *àzě*. In this regard, *àzěvodŭ* resembles some of the ambivalent characteristics people attribute to Trɔ̃ and the Celestial Church of Christ. In this section, I will outline what *àzěvodŭ* and other features of Vodun demonstrate about the relationship between Vodun and witchcraft.

The ambiguity bears a striking resemblance to that found in Vodun's New World cousin, Haitian Vodou, whose cosmological system also suggests a blurring of the lines between official religion and illicit magic. I follow New World religious scholars in facing the ethical challenge of acknowledging these links while expressing caution about reinforcing popular stereotypes that characterize African and diasporic religions as witchcraft and black magic. Given the long-standing sensationalism surrounding Vodun and related religions, and given the current academic and popular interest in African witchcraft, this topic carries important theoretical and ethical implications about the distinction between magic and religion (Styers 2004). Although scholars of Haiti have produced a body of work challenging North American media stereotypes about Haitian Vodou, there are few comprehensive ethnographies of African Vodun.[29] There are many works on the occult in Africa, but in most places, indigenous religion is disappearing in the wake of Christianity and Islam, so there is little exploration of the occult's interaction with indigenous religion. By contrast, in Benin, Christianity and Vodun exist side by side, and both of them have important interactions with occult beliefs. As in Haitian Vodou, many informants claimed that the source of both religious and occult powers is the same and that religious leaders are frequently suspected of being the same individuals who perform occult acts.

When it comes to Haitian Vodou, there is an established scholarly tradition of combatting negative media portrayals and popular misconceptions about the religion. Early European encounters with Vodou produced heavily biased and sensationalized accounts, like that of Spenser St. John, who claimed in the nineteenth century that Vodou was a tradition born of fear, magic, and murder (see also Moreau de Saint-Méry 1798). St. John wrote: "It appears incredible that sorcery, poisonings . . . , and cannibalism, should continue to pervade the island" (1884, 228). The U.S. Marine occupation in the early twentieth century brought Haitian Vodou into the American consciousness, leading to Hollywood's obsession with images of zombies, snake rituals, witchcraft, and of course Voodoo dolls. Thanks to video games and feature films like *The Serpent and the Rainbow* (Universal Studios, 1988), contemporary conceptions of Haitian Vodou continue to focus on zombies, witchcraft, and black magic, and popular conceptions of Beninese Vodun employ similar imagery.

In response to these images, most ethnographic accounts of Haitian Vodou make a point of highlighting practitioners' service to the spirits and their search for success and protection. Scholars point out that popular American notions are unfounded, misleading, and often racist (see Brown 2001; Desmangles 1992; Farmer 1992; Price-Mars [1928] 1983). Alfred Métraux acknowledged the ethnographer's uphill battle, stating that Vodou "usually conjures up visions of mysterious deaths, secret rites—or dark saturnalia celebrated by blood-maddened, sex-maddened, god-maddened negroes" ([1959] 1972, 15, cited in Farmer 1992, 3). Although some of the most outlandish claims about cannibalism might be dismissed altogether, scholars admit that the Haitian cosmological system does include magical acts. Early in the twentieth century, Melville Herskovits ([1937] 1971) argued that serving the spirits and performing

magical acts are both parts of Haitian spiritual life, though they are theoretically separate. Paul Farmer (1992) also admits to the existence of magical
beliefs in Haiti, but he strongly denies their connection to the religion's practice of spirit possession and service to the deities. Ideally, the Vodou priests,
known as *hungan* and *mambo*, receive their calling from the spirits, and in
turn they can call on the spirits for help; but the black magician, or *bocor*, is
said to "purchase" illegitimate power rather than be given benevolent power
(Brown 2001; Herskovits [1937] 1971; Pierre 1977). Despite these distinctions,
Herskovits ([1937] 1971) noted that some priests are known to serve with both
hands, a metaphor for performing both official religious and unofficial magical acts. Although the *hungan* may be conceptually distinct from the *bocor*,
scholars admit that in many cases, they are one and the same person (Hurston
[1938] 1990). In Brazilian Candomblé, there is a similar ambiguity between
legitimate religious rituals and occult activities. Pentecostal pastors make a
point of demonizing Candomblé and equating it with *macumba* (black magic),
but even scholars admit that some priests engage in magical acts (Birman
2011; Hayes 2011; Parés 2013). For indigenous Amazonia, Neil Whitehead and
Robin Wright (2004) argue that scholars have failed to address the negative
aspects of shamanistic activities. The authors claim that the urge to romanti-
cize indigenous religion has prompted researchers to whitewash the fact that
shamans sometimes engage in ritualistic murder and cannibalism. Although
Vodun priests and healers in Benin are usually not associated with this level
of violence, it is undeniable that their performance of magical acts comes
with an ambiguous moral valence.

Acknowledging this ambiguity puts ethnographers in a bind regarding the
politics of representation. As noted, one way to counter the stereotypes is to
dissociate "religion" from the unofficial "magic" that exists alongside it, thereby
legitimizing the public rites honoring the spirits while delegitimizing the selfish magical acts. Although Western popular culture continues to use exotic
images of Vodou and Voodoo, this strategy has achieved notable success in the
domains of academia, the arts, and alternative spirituality. Karen McCarthy
Brown's friend and Vodou "mother," Mama Lola, became known internationally following the publication of the first edition of Brown's book in 1991.
And perhaps partly due to that publication, Haitian Vodou has achieved
more public exposure and legitimacy, generating interest within the academy
and museums (Cosentino 1995) and among spiritual seekers. While Vodou
practitioners and observers used to be divided along racial lines, today many
whites have become curious about Vodou, and some of them undergo initiation, even traveling to Haiti or Benin (Forte 2010; Landry 2013). Despite the

public relations successes in focusing on the official religion, the magical facet of the Vodou cosmology remains an important part of Haitian beliefs and practices but is often paid less attention in the literature, perhaps because of the fears about reinforcing negative stereotypes.

Interestingly, on the African continent, the opposite seems to prevail, but with similar results. Rather than ignoring the occult, we see that in the midst of widespread proliferation of occult fears and accusations, witch trials, and vigilante killings, scholars and the media have shown overwhelming interest in the unofficial occult acts of witchcraft and sorcery, but there is little examination of the connections between the occult and indigenous religion. Scholars may be motivated by the same concerns as their colleagues in the diaspora, hoping to combat popular notions of African religions and malevolent magic. However, given the religious pluralism in Africa, there are important questions about how the official and unofficial religions interact. Indeed, I have noted that studies acknowledge that occult fears and rituals persist right alongside the growth of Christianity on the continent, suggesting that magical beliefs can be associated with any religion, not merely "traditional" African religions (see also Farmer [1992] on Haiti). But it is more common for Africanist anthropology to highlight the surge in Christianity being fueled by the occult than it is to investigate the occult's connections to indigenous religion.

As in the diaspora, West African Vodun has a long history of being portrayed as irrational, exotic, barbarous, and demonic. Precolonial European travelers to Dahomey produced tales of a godless, primitive religion. In 1793 Archibald Dalzel labeled the Vodun tradition "a jumble of superstitious nonsense" and described the magical charms and amulets as "crude mis-shapen images, tinged with blood, besmeared with palm oil, stuck with feathers, bedaubed with eggs, and other absurd applications of which a particular account would be both tedious and unprofitable" (1793, vi). In 1847 John Duncan claimed that people "worship . . . images, but here they are more disgusting than in any other part of Africa I have yet visited" ([1847] 1968, 1:124). And in 1851 Frederick Forbes wrote that "the priests and priestesses . . . assemble within a ring, in a public square; a band of discordant music attends; and after arranging the emblems of their religion, and the articles carried in religious processions, such as banners, spears, tripods, and vessels holding bones, skulls, congealed blood, and other barbarous trophies, they dance, sing, and drink until sufficiently excited" (1851, 1:172). Although Western laypeople today are more likely to be unaware of traditional African religion than to subscribe to such specific imagery, the media's coverage of African religious thought often focuses on child witches, mob killings, and other supposedly irrational aspects of African culture (Houreld 2009; Karimi 2009; Oppenheimer 2010). For their part, Christian missionaries to Dahomey explicitly linked indigenous religion to devil worship and black magic, an association that endures today (Claffey 2007; Meyer 1999). Indeed, following missionary rhetoric, many of my informants casually translated one of the most important deities, Lĕgbà, as Satan (see Ekoué and Rosenthal 2015). Given the problematic association of traditional religion with evil magic and superstition, there is good reason to use caution when mentioning Vodun and the occult in the same breath. Despite these cautions, and despite the ideological separation between Beninese Vodun and the occult, informants suggested a much more ambiguous relationship between the two spiritual domains.

In order to make clear the distinctions and similarities between the religious and magical domains, I must first offer a brief description of the Vodun religion.[30] In the Fon language of southern Benin, vodṹ means "spirit" or "deity," and there are countless vodṹ.[31] I use the capitalized proper name Vodun (with conventional academic spelling) when talking about the religion and the lowercased vodṹ (phonetic spelling) when referring to the deities. Some of the more prominent deities include the god of the earth and smallpox (Sakpatá), the god of thunder (Xɛbiosò), the god of iron (Gŭ), the trickster/messenger god (Lĕgbà), the mermaid goddess (Mami Wata), the snake/rainbow god (Dã), the god of the sun (Lisà), and the god of rivers and stillborn children (Tɔxósú), as well as the cult of twins (Hoxo), the royal cult (Nɛ̃súxué), and the ancestor cult (Kútító). All the vodṹ are under the authority of a supreme god named Măwŭ.[32] As Haitians serve the loa, Fon people serve their vodṹ through offerings of food and alcohol and animal sacrifices representing either gratitude or a request for assistance with problems in their lives. Although anyone may make appeals and offerings to the deities, practitioners called vodṹsì (wife of the vodṹ) undergo a secret initiation to learn the dances, language, and secret characteristics of their deity. Vodṹsì can be possessed during ceremonies where the vodṹ inhabits their bodies and they dance to the deity's rhythms before an audience. Vodṹsì are led by a vodṹnɔ̃ (owner/guardian of the deity), a priest who organizes ceremonies and manages the troupe. Ordinary individuals learn about their fate and the spirits' will through consultation with a diviner (bokɔnɔ̃), who reads the signs of Fá, the Fon divination system, and prescribes offerings directed toward the vodṹ. For Vodun adherents, the deities are like natural objects that exist without question; the notion of belief or religious faith in the gods is unfamiliar.

A notable difference between Vodun and the occult is that Vodun is a public religion involving rituals and offerings calling on the power of named spirits, whereas the occult involves private acts emanating from an individual. Apart from the staunch Christians who demonize Vodun, most Beninese I spoke with treated the distinction between magic and religion as self-evident. The occult is an individual magical power that one controls, whereas the *vodŭ* may be supplicated, persuaded, or appeased but remain beyond human control. Nevertheless, on deeper questioning, many of my informants revealed a number of ambiguities and connections between Vodun and the occult. This is especially true for healers and others with supernatural expertise who referred to one of two named *àzĕvodŭ* (witchcraft deities). One of these deities, already introduced in chapter 1, is Mĭnɔ̃nằ, a female deity who is considered the creator of *àzĕ*, a protector against *àzĕ*, or the deity of witches and motherhood (Blier 1995; Henry 2008b; Noret 2010). This is unsurprising, given Mĭnɔ̃nằ's symbolic links to feminine sexuality, motherhood, and *àzĕ* (Blier 1995; Herskovits [1938] 1967, 2:260).[33] Still others contended that Mĭnɔ̃nằ is simply a female *vodŭ*, and though she is responsible for witchcraft, many claimed that she is also a good *vodŭ*.[34] In the grandiose, universalizing terms frequently used regarding witchcraft, one healer declared that Mĭnɔ̃nằ presides

FIGURE 9. Mĭnɔ̃nằ shrine outside of Abomey. Shells resembling breasts and a grass skirt mark the deity's female identity. (Photograph by the author)

over Fá divination and is actually another name for Măwŭ, the creator. This
healer's view echoes Herskovits's report of his informants describing Mĭnɔ̃nà
in a range of terms as "the mother of Mawŭ and Lĕgbà, as the sister of Lĕgbà,
and as the mother of Fá" ([1938] 1967, 2:260).[35] These descriptions begin to
hint at the profound complexity of Mĭnɔ̃nà's links to Vodun and àzĕ.

The other àzĕvodũ is Kēnesì, which one informant described as a divinity representing àzĕ (see Blier 1995).[36] The relationship between Kēnesì and
Mĭnɔ̃nà is clouded, as a Sakpatá priest said that Kēnesì is àzĕ and Mĭnɔ̃nà is
the vodũ incarnating àzĕ. But Camille told me that while Mĭnɔ̃nà kills, Kēnesì
only ruins your life and brings suffering, for example, by making you repeatedly fail an exam. She added that Kēnesì is less powerful than Mĭnɔ̃nà and
therefore envious of her.[37] This inequality between Kēnesì and Mĭnɔ̃nà seems
to mirror the envy and wariness that men feel about women's power and sexuality in general. Indeed, a number of informants stated explicitly that Kēnesì
is a masculine counterpart of Mĭnɔ̃nà. Some saw a moral distinction, arguing
that Kēnesì is used especially by men to protect against àzĕ.[38] As with so many
aspects of witchcraft, there is great ambiguity about Kēnesì, and one Cotonou
healer even said that there are two forms of Kēnesì, one that protects and one
that destroys. Furthermore, although informants seemed to associate Mĭnɔ̃nà
with women and Kēnesì with men, Bernard Maupoil (1943) says that in Fá
divination, Kēnesì is also linked to femininity, maternity, and menstruation.

The link between Fá divination and àzĕ is a significant way that Vodun and
àzĕ are connected. For one thing, both of the àzĕvodũ are acknowledged in
the Fá divination system, which is at the core of Vodun religious life. Camille
told me that the bokɔ̃nɔ̃ (diviner) and àzètɔ́ are accomplices, like the pharma-
cist and the doctor. To become a bokɔ̃nɔ̃ one must learn all 256 dù (signs) of
Fá, each dù being represented by a series of lines displayed by the àgũ màgà
chain.[39] Each dù includes stories about animals and vodũ, which also indicate
taboos and acts of supplication to a deity. According to Maupoil (1943), the dù
called turukpē-mɛji is a sign of Kēnesì that is also linked to a number of other
vodũ, one of them being Na, which Suzanne Preston Blier (1995, 33) claims to
be the same as Mĭnɔ̃nà. Maupoil also states that the signs fu-mɛji, sa-mɛji,
and loso-mɛji are likewise connected to Kēnesi or to women's menstruation.[40]
Several of my informants confirmed this connection, stating that fu-mɛji,
sa-mɛji, and turukpē-mɛji are all signs related to àzĕ and Mĭnɔ̃nà. A diviner
explained that finding fu-mɛji during a consultation is a sign of the creator,
the queen mother, or Mĭnɔ̃nà and therefore is an omen of witchcraft. By contrast, he said, when sa-mɛji appears, it means that you are yourself an àzètɔ́:
you do not eat people and cannot be harmed by àzĕ, but you have the power

to kill if you choose.[41] Herskovits ([1938] 1967, 2:260) reported that the children of the deity Gbadu, which interacts closely with Fá, are associated with Mǐnɔ̃nǎ. Thus, within the corpus of Fá, as well as within the larger Vodun culture, there is an acknowledgment that certain vodũ are responsible for creating or controlling àzě.

A related link between àzě and Vodun is that, as with ordinary vodũ, people talk of making offerings to the witchcraft deities. Informants said that both Kēnesì and Mǐnɔ̃nǎ receive offerings, and though these deities are sometimes described as being equivalent to witchcraft, they also combat it. Both deities have shrines dedicated to them in family compounds, and Kēnesì is described as having priests (kěnesìnɔ̀), though I have never heard of a mǐnɔ̃nánɔ̀.[42] My friend Gaston said that Mǐnɔ̃nǎ represents a compound's founding woman, the first one to light a fire in the new house. Blier (1995, 371n29) reports that when a senior woman dies, her family erects a Mǐnɔ̃nǎ shrine in her honor. People leave offerings on Mǐnɔ̃nǎ shrines in supplication for protection from àzě, perhaps even to replace a human target of àzě.[43] Camille told me that she made offerings to Mǐnɔ̃nǎ as a way of gaining protection when she joined the àzètɔ́ society. An early stage in her initiation required her to make a gift of appeasement to Mǐnɔ̃nǎ, after which she received scarification on her wrists. She said the efficacy of the ceremony was evident when she once picked up some peanuts that suddenly felt like a snake, causing her to drop them. The peanuts, she explained, were a thwarted attack. However, Didier, an amateur oral historian in Abomey, told me that offerings to Mǐnɔ̃nǎ are nothing unusual, since every Vodun ceremony must conclude with a ritual called nǎxixɛ (respect/offerings for Nǎ/Mǐnɔ̃nǎ), which involves placing a sacrificial goat atop the akpakpò, a wooden slab with etchings made to resemble the vagina (see also Noret 2010, 173). The offerings are then placed on a roadside for vultures to take the goat's head, after which people remove the akpakpò.[44] In a village south of Abomey, a healer showed me his family's shrine to Mǐnɔ̃nǎ, though, unlike ordinary vodũ, which people rarely object to having photographed, he insisted that I could not take a picture of Mǐnɔ̃nǎ. These functions of the witchcraft deities are similar to those performed by the spirit Lěgbà, who receives regular offerings in exchange for protecting family compounds, markets, and villages from all kinds of dangers.[45] And just as witches and àzě are ambivalently viewed for their good and evil acts, so too is Lěgbà, one of the most unpredictable and fickle of deities (perhaps explaining why missionaries chose him as the equivalent for Satan). But there is more than a cosmological connection between witchcraft and Vodun, because in some ways witches themselves are likened to gods not only in their superhuman powers but in their desire for sacrifices. For example, when healers or *vodũnɔ̃* detect a witch's attack, they may intervene by asking the attacking witch to accept an animal offering in place of the human victim (a rite called *kuɖiɔ*, or "death exchange"; see chapter 5). It is likely due to this practice that one Celestial Church member stated that Vodun and witchcraft are "inseparable" and that witches and *vodũnɔ̃* "speak the same language." If witches are given animal sacrifices, this means that they are themselves being treated as divinities who must be appeased.

Another similarity between the Vodun religion and the occult is the process whereby one becomes a practitioner. As explained in earlier chapters, acquiring *bŏ* involves a straightforward apprenticeship whereby one obtains the knowledge of plants and recipes. In the case of *àzĕ*, many people said that it is acquired involuntarily, but a significant number of informants portrayed it in a way that resembles the secret but voluntary initiation for adepts of a spirit troupe. Some described their own attempts to initiate into *àzĕ*, claiming that there are different stages, ranked hierarchies, and a sacred language and other esoteric knowledge to be learned. Some had begun the initiation and learned how to teleport or how to detect malevolent witches. These reports suggest an initiation process very much like that used for the official Vodun secret societies.

An important connection between Vodun and *àzĕ* is that many people see the supernatural forces behind them as the same. In fact, informants frequently attributed the power of both *àzĕ* and *vodũ* to the virtues of leaves (see Brand 1981, cited in Blier 1995, 212). While *bŏ* are commonly said to employ leaves and other natural ingredients, there is less public discussion of recipes for *àzĕ* or *vodũ*. Yet just as the neighboring Ewe and Yoruba do, Fon people acknowledge that they create their deities (Barber 1981; Herskovits and Herskovits 1933, 37; Rosenthal 1998). Informants often told me that *vodũ* are made by burying a collection of leaves and other ingredients beneath a shrine.[46] I have never attended the installation ceremony for one of the older Vodun, but in the Trɔ̃ ceremony previously described, I witnessed the creation of a new deity, a process that may differ from other *vodũ* installations in the exact ingredients but whose basic principles are otherwise similar. In one sense, this was not a new deity, since the *xunɔ̃* was purchasing Trɔ̃ from the Ouidah priests who came to perform the ceremony. In other words, it was a new manifestation or a replica of the donor Trɔ̃ in Ouidah. Yet in another sense it was a new deity, for each temple represents an independent site of worship and consultation managed by the presiding *xunɔ̃*. And each time a deity is installed, there is a required set of components. In this case, I observed the collection of sacrificial cats, sacred stones, knives, and countless kola nuts, along with some items that I was not permitted to see, all of which were buried under the floor of the new shrine where the deity was to reside (see figure 10).

If a deity's power actually lies in the collection of material objects, then in some ways the deities are façades, with powers resembling *bǒ* hiding just below the surface. This suggests that deities are magical human creations rather than divine entities. As a testament to the materiality shared by supernatural powers, one informant told me that both *bǒ* and *vodũ* are purchased. And two young Cotonou men explained that *bǒ* are related to *vodũ* because the spirits come and work through *bǒ*. Maupoil is instructive here: "Every *vodũ* possesses specific amulets whose secret is part of the priests' education; they cannot actually command the *vodũ* and initiate *vodũ-si* (wife of the *vodũ*) without a serious magical training" (1943, 64). Others suggested that *bǒ* are created in conjunction with deities. For example, Gaston told me about using Lɛ̆gbà to make a *bǒ* to ensure his fiancée's commitment. Bruno Gilli (1982, 14, 16, cited in Blier 1995, 385n16) also sees important connections between

FIGURE 10. Trɔ̃ priests prepare ritual objects during an installation ceremony. Kola nuts sit atop a collection of sabers and other items over which is dripped sacrificial blood. (Photograph by the author)

Vodun and *bǒ*, calling magical acts *bǒvodǔ*, which, however, he distinguishes from what he calls the cosmic *vodǔ*. By *bǒvodǔ*, Gilli may be referring to something like Gaston's *bǒ* or to another phenomenon whereby malicious individuals use a *vodǔ* to harm an innocent person. For example, someone might feed a *vodǔ* with food or drink that it dislikes and tell it that another person is responsible. A prominent healer said that an aggressor could put hot pepper on Lĕgbà and direct the deity's anger toward a third party. Philippe LeMay-Boucher, Joël Noret, and Vincent Somville (2011) report that this strategy is embodied in the expression "ɛ́ na fɔ́ vodǔ do ji nu mɛ" (one will wake the *vodǔ* against someone). The angered deity takes its vengeance on the unsuspecting victim. Though this differs from the usual understanding of how a *bǒ* is made, some informants still label this a *bǒ*, and it reinforces the idea either that *vodǔ* and *bǒ* employ similar magical acts or that they are two labels for the same power. Others referred to this practice as a type of *àzě*, suggesting that certain *vodǔ* can be used to launch witchcraft attacks. For example, the god of iron and war (Gǔ) is responsible for red *àzě*, which can kill by causing car accidents or making a tree fall on someone. Another form of *àzě* is invoked by pouring alcohol on the twin deity and blaming someone else. There are other kinds of *àzě* linked to the gods of Sakpatá, *gorovodǔ*, Trɔ̃, Molu, and Gbagbo.

As noted in chapter 2, a few people even stated that, like *bǒ*, *àzě* is created through recipes that are said to be placed in a special calabash. Calabashes are also common receptacles for the creation of new deities, for the containment of spiritual power associated with Fá, and for other rituals, all of which reflect additional similarities between *vodǔ* and *àzě* (Apter 1991; Bertho 1951; Brand 1981, 7, cited in Blier 1995, 259).[47] For some people, *àzě*, *bǒ*, and *vodǔ* are all rooted in these formulae. Following this conception, the deities and the occult derive from natural and scientifically verifiable processes. Informants added that all religions and deities the world over are part of the same universal force (see Brown 2001, 306). Some call it *àzě* or *sorcellerie*, but others think of it as a science. Thus, in addition to the claims that Christianity and Trɔ̃ have *àzě* at their foundation, some informants confided that Vodun, *àzě*, Fá, nature, and science are all the same thing. By this reasoning, they claimed that any healers, *bokɔ́nɔ̃*, *vodǔnɔ̃*, *xunɔ̃*, Catholic priests, and evangelical pastors all make use of this universal force in performing their religious services and in combatting occult attacks.

The Intersection of Religion and the Occult

Given the increasingly public airing of witchcraft ideas in the religious communities of Benin and elsewhere (Geschiere 1997, 217; 1998, 811; 2000), academics must examine the place of the occult in the religious landscape, taking into account how it interacts with both Christianity and indigenous religion. As I have suggested, Benin bears a striking resemblance to Haiti in the ambivalence with which people view religious leaders. On both sides of the Atlantic, ritual specialists walk a fine line between what we call "religion" and the "occult," prompting questions about the validity of anthropological distinctions between religion and magic and between legitimate and illegitimate supernatural powers. While ignoring Vodun's occult links may serve the ethical objective of protecting the religion's reputation, the occult appears to be an important part of a broader cosmology that belongs to Vodun.

Though Voduisants (Vodun practitioners) may demonstrate no interest in Jesus, and some devout Christians claim utter contempt for Vodun, people are united in their belief in and fear of àzě. These underlying parallels, along with Christianity's overt opposition to the occult and Vodun's implicit links to witchcraft, may help explain Christianity's appeal and foreshadow its eventual replacement of Vodun as the dominant religion. Yet the newcomers Trɔ̀ and the Celestial Church of Christ are popular for similar reasons and may serve as viable "local" alternatives to the foreign Christian denominations. As I have shown, Christianity is itself inescapably linked to witchcraft both in its role in opposing witchcraft and in the suspicions that witchcraft lies at the very heart of churches. Religions benefit from spiritual insecurity, partly in terms of the moral and ideological contrast that helps define religion in relation to evil but also in terms of the revenue generated through people's quest for supernatural protection and worldly success. Therefore, no matter what religions take hold in Benin, I predict that magic and witchcraft will continue to play an important role. Even those who condemn religious profiteering do not question the existence of God, the vodũ, or witchcraft. Healers, ritual specialists, and those intellectuals with a healthy dose of religious skepticism are more likely to embrace a universal spirituality than to reject the relevance of religion altogether. And as I have demonstrated, many Beninese tend to believe that whatever name is used to refer to God, witchcraft, science, religion, magic, and nature, all concepts are integrally related. As I reveal in the next chapter, this universalizing tendency is nowhere more apparent than in the business of spiritual healing, which in recent years has broadened the international scope of local conceptions of witchcraft.

chapter five

Healing and the
Globalization of Witchcraft

The previous chapter outlined some of the efforts people use to oppose witchcraft, efforts that involve both folk techniques and organized religion, but this chapter focuses on how healers, the most prominent spiritual warriors, treat witchcraft and its victims. While some Christian pastors and Trɔ̃ priests perform healing ceremonies, other healers are unaffiliated with a particular religion. Of course, some healers maintain connections with the Vodun religion by serving as *vodúnɔ̃* (Vodun priests) or *bokɔ́nɔ̃* (diviners). However, by and large, healers operate in an indeterminate space that occasionally intersects with other supernatural domains. They perform both spiritual and medicinal healing, bringing them into the world of biomedicine as well. With their herbal medicines, they treat a range of simple and complex illnesses. As I have stated, illnesses, particularly chronic ones or those that medical doctors are unable to cure, are usually a sign of supernatural harassment, so healers are nearly always in the business of spiritual protection.

One feature that sets healers apart from other religious leaders is that while others deny any association with *àzě*, many healers openly acknowledge that they have *àzě* and that they employ it in their healing practice. Their use of *àzě* puts them into direct contact with the nocturnal world of witches. Healers, therefore, come close to representing local images of superheroes or "super-witches" (Geschiere 1998, 827) going toe-to-toe with villains. They also possess esoteric expertise, and they engage in their own research, so they occupy the role of spiritual scholar or scientist. Healers are at the forefront of research into international traditions like Hindu mysticism and Chinese healing, some of which they incorporate into their cosmology as foreign varieties of witchcraft. Given healers' use of *àzě* and their blurring of the lines between spiritual and physiological knowledge and research, they are a powerful example of the convergence of science and witchcraft. In this chapter I offer a close view of spiritual healing beliefs and rituals while also examining how healing's international influences have engendered universalist principles and the globalization of witchcraft ideas.

Healing Witchcraft

The heading for this section has an ambiguous meaning that captures the duality of healers' relationship to àzĕ. As noted, healers are responsible for treating witchcraft victims and for healing illnesses caused by àzĕ. At the same time, as in other parts of Africa, most people suspect, and many healers admit, that only witchcraft can combat witchcraft (see Kahn 2011; West 2005). Thus, witchcraft is a source of both illness and healing power. Though healers may also be vodŭnɔ̀ or bokɔ́nɔ̀, their profession is a distinct category, indicated by the titles àzɔ́gblétɔ́ (destroyer of illness), amǎɖatɔ́ (preparer of leaves), and amǎwatɔ́ (maker of leaves). As described in previous chapters, leaves and other plant products are medicines, but they also possess mystical or magical qualities that make a preparer of leaves well suited to deal with both natural and "provoked" illness. Typically, healers acquire their skills through a long and possibly expensive apprenticeship, during which they learn the properties of leaves, roots, and bark along with the techniques of diagnosis and treatment. Many informants learned their profession from a father or a grandmother who was also a healer, while others spent time as apprentices in other parts of Benin or as far away as India and China. However, one informant said he was born with the gift.

Although this chapter focuses on the supernatural aspects of healing and its connection to witchcraft, it is worth describing briefly the secular side of healing work. Because àzɔ́gblétɔ́ see patients for mundane health concerns, their work rivals that of medical doctors. In fact, the healers that I met often claimed to see dozens or even hundreds of patients per day, and I usually observed between five and fifteen people at a time waiting to see a healer. In interviews àzɔ́gblétɔ́ told me they treated a range of illnesses. For example, one healer said he treats adĭgbè (epilepsy), taɖu (mental illness), tazɔ̀ (head illness), huɖu (rheumatism), sĩxã (edema), xomɛjizɔ̀ (ulcer), and dãnũmɛ (snakebite). Others identified working on the following common ailments: adɔvivi (diabetes), akpadoxomɛ (typhoid), tafẽmɛ (headache), xomɛwli (stomach cramps), conception problems, hemorrhoids, liver trouble, swollen feet and stomach, backache, hypertension, pregnancy complications, constipation, erectile dysfunction, gout, malaria, anemia, cancer, diarrhea, sickle cell disease, and postnatal hemorrhaging. Most simple illnesses are treated routinely with herbal infusions, though for serious conditions, patients may follow a regimen that can last months, prompting patients to be hospitalized in the healer's home. Some healers are also *vodǔnɔ̀*, and they prescribe animal sacrifices to ask for the *vodǔ*'s assistance in curing someone.[1] Most healers employ some type of consultation to diagnose conditions; the most common method is Fá divination, though some healers said they use dreams or their intuition. A Cotonou healer said that he sees patients' problems and the solutions in his sleep. He had been interested in plants since his youth, and then one day, in his sleep, he saw a *yovó* (white person / foreigner) wearing a long white robe and carrying plants and mango pits to treat the sick. Ten years later, during his apprenticeship, he learned about mango pits' medicinal properties as a vermifuge. Healers generally charge a small fee, between 100 and 500 FCFA ($0.20 to $1) for an initial consultation, but subsequent treatments can cost from 20,000 FCFA ($40) to one million FCFA ($2,000), depending on the severity of the condition and the duration of the treatment.[2]

Some healers said they treated AIDS, though many admitted that they cannot. Hervé's healer friend Cyrille held an ambiguous position; although Hervé reported that Cyrille can cure AIDS, the healer himself said that AIDS does not really exist. Perhaps this discrepancy is explained by the fact that Hervé admitted to me that Cyrille is wary of revealing his discovery for fear that Western pharmaceutical companies might kill him to keep him silent. However, Cyrille did say that there is a condition called *kpalaba gohogoho*, which is a thinning disease that may be mistaken for AIDS. He described this as an ancient illness rather than something new, and he told me that the disease develops when a loose woman sleeps with many men, whose fluids mix inside of her, making her and her partners sick. As noted in chapter 2, another healer, Philibert Dossou-Yovo, is well known throughout Benin for his claims of developing a cure for AIDS. Because of his distrust of Westerners, he would not meet with me, but I spoke to his secretary, who told me that foreign doctors and pharmaceutical companies tried to buy his formula for 30 billion FCFA ($60 million), but he refused to sell it.

Aside from AIDS, which most healers do not treat, the most difficult (and expensive) ailments are epilepsy and mental illness, though stomach problems are also complicated. A female *àzɔ̌gblétɔ́* said that male sterility can cost a patient one million FCFA ($2,000). According to informants, stomach problems and mental illness are frequently diagnosed as having supernatural causes (*àzě* or *bǒ*), so it is unsurprising that these are the most difficult and expensive to treat. As the female healer told me, natural sicknesses from God ("Mǎwǔ's illnesses") are easy to cure, compared to witchcraft ("people's

FIGURE 11. Ritual items deposited on a road outside Abomey, likely a request for witchcraft protection. (Photograph by the author)

illnesses"). Her opinion was shared by other healers, including one who stated, "Àzèzɔ̃ syɛ̃̌!" (Witchcraft illness is tough!). The main strategy for treating àzě illness is for a healer to intervene in the attack and negotiate with the àzètɔ́ to release the victim. These negotiations usually take the form of the àzɔ̃gblétɔ́ promising to give an animal to the àzètɔ́ in place of the human victim. The exchange of an animal or other offering for a human is a widespread phenomenon called kuɖiɔ (death exchange). In other cases, the kuɖiɔ involves replacing the intended victim with another person rather than an animal. As one man put it, "E flí jè mɛɖɛvo jì" (It bounces off and lands on somebody else). An electronics technician in Cotonou told me that as a twelve-year-old, he suffered from uncontrollable crying. His mother took him to a healer, who washed him and made animal sacrifices to the àzètɔ́, after which he was released from the spell. Many healers said that they can see the àzètɔ́ attackers at night and talk to them about the patient. Some claim to visit witches during their nocturnal travels to negotiate for the release of a victim in exchange for a goat, chicken, or pig, along with money, all funded by the patient. The àzètɔ́ instructs the healer to take a portion of the money for himself and then leave the package of offerings somewhere to be claimed by the àzètɔ́, frequently under a tree in the forest.[3] (As noted in chapter 1, the iroko and baobab are sacred trees associated with witches.) A healer who is a Trɔ̃ priest showed me a round object that he had removed from a victim as part of a kuɖiɔ (see figure 12). The nut was the source of the patient's illness, and the healer ritually transferred the nut to the belly of a goat, which was then slaughtered to remove it.

Given healers' claims to see and interact with àzètɔ́ at night, it stands to reason that people recognize this ability as a feature of àzě. Indeed, many àzɔ̃gblétɔ́ freely admitted that àzě is what gives them this power. Some healers and diviners even called themselves àzètɔ́, though they qualified this by stating that they use àzě exclusively for healing, and they never eat people. A healer outside of Abomey told me that he uses àzě to see the source of illness and identify the attacking witches before intervening on the patient's behalf. As one man explained the relationship between àzètɔ́ and àzɔ̃gblétɔ́, "A thief knows a thief."

Still others suggested that vodũnɔ̃ are also intimately involved in healing witchcraft. Maurice, the healer who threatened my children, said that he is a vodũnɔ̃, and sometimes the spirits speak to him about his patients, though he prefers to consult a bokɔnɔ̃. A vodũnɔ̃ of the Kútítɔ́ (ghost) cult told me that he performs healing by contacting the àzètɔ́ to ask what formula can cure a patient.[4] A Trɔ̃ adherent said that vodũnɔ̃ are often àzètɔ́ who negotiate with malevolent witches. He was referring primarily to a vodũnɔ̃ of the spirit Kɛ̃nesì (a kɛ̃nesìnɔ̃), and another healer corroborated that kɛ̃nesìnɔ̃ are àzètɔ́ who travel at night and negotiate with witches. (Recall from chapter 4 that Kɛ̃nesì is often described as an àzěvodũ, a witchcraft vodũ.) A Cotonou diviner told me that he also uses àzě to negotiate for a victim's release with Mĩnɔ̃nà, the other àzěvodũ. Others use Fá divination to identify a witch, and some said they ask a vodũ to intervene in a witchcraft attack, and the vodũ will prescribe offering a goat or a chicken as a substitute for the victim. Parts of the animal are left in whatever place the vodũ indicates, and their disappearance the next day indicates that the witches have accepted the offering.[5]

One Cotonou healer said he does not possess àzě, nor does he believe there is such a thing as positive àzě. He told me that he was born with healing knowledge and has never studied with anyone. When he looks at a patient, he can picture the illness immediately. He said he sees six to seven hundred patients each day, and his supernatural treatment follows a series of three

FIGURE 12. A healer shows me the object he removed from the victim. (Photograph by the author)

steps. In the first step, the patient purchases a powerful ring of protection from him for 10,000 FCFA ($20). When the ring changes color, the wearer will know that he or she is under attack from an aggressive *bǒ*. (The healer specified *bǒ*, but presumably this is true for an *àzètɔ́* attack as well.) Step two involves the ritual application of water, soap, and perfume, costing 70,000 FCFA ($140). This gives an individual protection. But if someone wants protection for the whole family, the healer charges 140,000 FCFA ($280) to perform the ritual for all of them. Another Cotonou healer said his treatments begin with a consultation using a deck of cards. Although he respects Fá divination and advises all his clients to learn their *kpɔlí* (personal Fá sign), he said that because the *bokɔ́nɔ̃* manipulates the *akplé* chain, he can rig the reading. Therefore, the healer allows his clients to handle the cards by themselves, producing a more accurate reading. When clients come to him after learning their *kpɔlí*, he performs a life consultation, mapping out their future trajectory, a process lasting a couple of hours. He has treated patients in Europe and once traveled as far as California for his work. He said his clients pay whatever amount they can afford; sometimes this is only 1,000 or 5,000 FCFA ($2 or $10), but it could be 5 million FCFA ($10,000). Not all *àzɔ̃gblétɔ́* are wealthy international travelers, but there is obviously an important market for healers' services. Philippe LeMay-Boucher, Joël Noret, and Vincent Somville (2011) conducted a survey in Cotonou in which nearly half of surveyed households paid for magico-religious services in the preceding year, and of these, the average household's religious costs constituted 5.6 percent of all expenses. Because people recognize the financial rewards of the healing profession, some are skeptical of healers' motives and abilities. Although one may mistrust an individual healer or diviner, witchcraft is an ever-present threat acknowledged by rural farmers and Western-trained doctors alike, so the healing profession is generally regarded as essential and therefore beyond reproach.

Trɔ̃ Healing

Spiritual and physiological healing is a complex process that is usually initiated as a result of a persistent illness. For serious problems, healers perform complicated and costly rituals. Because healing is often a private affair, and because I did not apprentice with anyone or undergo a ritual initiation, I was rarely present or welcome at elaborate healing rituals. However, on one occasion in 2009, Gaston took me to visit his friend, a Trɔ̃ *xunɔ̃* and healer in a village near Abomey. I had met the *xunɔ̃* on several prior occasions, and he had always been extremely hospitable and willing to share his views with me. This was partly because he was a close friend of Gaston, who acted as my

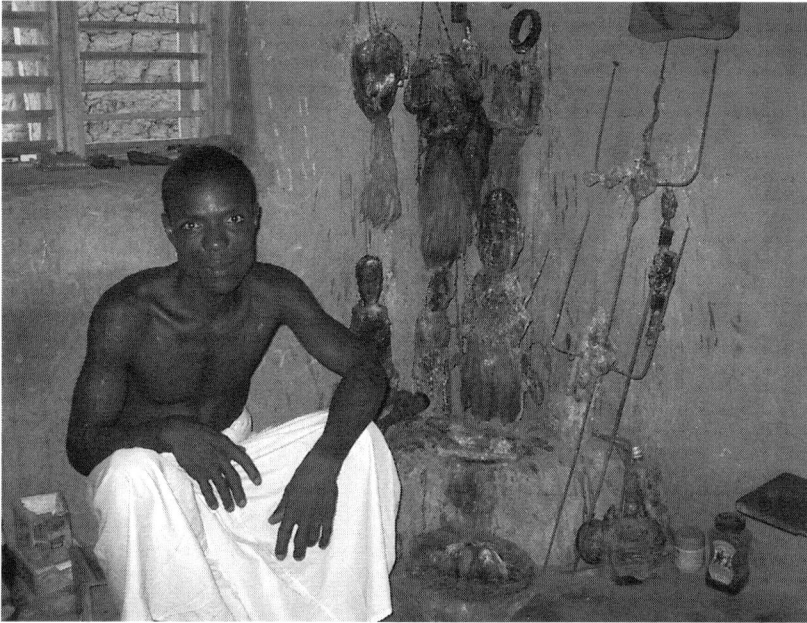

FIGURE 13. A xunɔ̀ (Trɔ̀ priest) who is also a healer seated by his shrine, near Abomey. (Photograph by the author)

"sponsor" on visits like this. Gaston's educated status, membership in a respected royal family, and calm demeanor gave him an air of credibility and trustworthiness as a person with discretion. Personally, I always felt Gaston to be a good judge of character, and so I was comfortable talking to the people he introduced me to. But the xunɔ̀ was unusually open-minded and unassuming, because he did not exhibit the secretive manner of other healers and religious specialists.

On this particular day, Gaston and I arrived unannounced, but the xunɔ̀ received us warmly and with a broad smile. He brought out a special bottle of soɖabì (palm liquor)—the good kind that everybody knows is made in Aja—which he had been saving for a special occasion. We each had a couple of shots of the strong drink, and I acknowledged like a proud connoisseur that his soɖabì was indeed of superior quality. Though I was hoping for an interview, Gaston and I learned that the xunɔ̀ had no time because he was preparing to start a healing ceremony within a few minutes. Although I was accustomed to seeing family, patients, and friends of the xunɔ̀ gathered around his house, I had not realized at first that there was a larger crowd with more purpose.

The ceremony was a pleasant surprise, and the *xunɔ̃* invited us to stay. Only later did we learn the serious circumstances that prompted the day's ritual. The patient was a little boy about two years old. His mother was originally from Ivory Coast but had moved to a nearby village. She told me and Gaston that she was uneasy about the ceremonies, saying that she had never believed in witchcraft in Ivory Coast. But since arriving in Benin, her opinion had changed. When her son became sick with a fever, she first took him to the hospital, where he was diagnosed with malaria. The doctor prescribed medicine, which helped initially. But later that night, the fever returned. The following day, they returned to the hospital, and the child received injections. These also helped temporarily, but sometime later, her son grew sicker and could barely breathe. She said he had looked like he would die. People suggested she visit the *xunɔ̃*, and she was desperate enough to try anything. The healer's preliminary efforts had an immediate effect, and the child's mother said these experiences forced her to believe in witchcraft and traditional medicine. Although the boy was feeling better, this ceremony was supposed to contribute to his complete recovery.

The ritual began with drumming by a group of teenage boys. Some also played cowbells. The atmosphere was relaxed, and the drumming was not strictly coordinated or consistent, as it can be in other ceremonies. Like the other twenty people in attendance, I was seated on the periphery of the ceremonial space, a bare patch of ground adjacent to the *xunɔ̃*'s house and to the area of his Trɔ̃ shrine. The shrine was a sleek cement pillar about six feet high with smooth surfaces on which there were sculpted reliefs and blue designs resembling a cat's face (see figure 14). Gaston had been chatting with some other people before sitting next to me and greeting a second *xunɔ̃* beside him. Within seconds and without warning, the *xunɔ̃* beside Gaston was somersaulting in the ceremonial space, possessed by Trɔ̃. Trɔ̃ rolled around and then stopped directly in front of our friend, the main *xunɔ̃*, who was seated on the opposite side of the ceremonial space from me. The deity was on all fours, rocking slightly, with his hands pointed inward. An attendant brought powder and spread it over Trɔ̃'s head, face, and chest, ritually distinguishing him from ordinary people. The deity rose and started dancing, holding a small-bladed ax. He danced for a few moments until the woman, with her two-year-old son in her lap, was placed on a chair in the center of the space. A small goat and two chickens were tied up nearby, obviously offerings for the deity. The animals were meant to replace the boy's soul as a *kuɖiɔ* (death exchange). One chicken was given to Trɔ̃, who held it up and then placed it against the child's face and chest. This act serves to bind the child and animal spiritually,

FIGURE 14. A recently constructed Trɔ̃ shrine without the usual building to house it, near Abomey. (Photograph by the author)

for the animal would soon be sacrificed on behalf of the child. This happened several times, and each time the boy squealed and squirmed. With Gaston beside me helping to explain what was happening, I learned that a discussion arose between the *xunɔ̃* and some others about money and the fact that the family was 1,500 FCFA ($3) short of the requirements. There was some question about whether the ceremony would even work. Trɔ̃ repeatedly approached the boy in his mother's lap. Gaston and I were summoned to sit next to the *xunɔ̃*, from whom we learned that the chicken was supposed to have died already. Trɔ̃ repeatedly walked around a small building and to the shrine behind it and then returned, holding the chicken belly-up. But the small white bird continued to protest and squawk. By the look on the deity's face, he was obviously discouraged. During these tense moments of uncertainty, Gaston told me that Trɔ̃ was acting as an intermediary, asking the spirit Dã to accept the sacrifice, intervene on behalf of the child, and block the witchcraft that troubled him.

After about fifteen minutes but what seemed like much longer, I grew concerned as well and began to hope that Trɔ̃ or Dã would finally take the chicken. All eyes were on the bird, with everyone waiting for it to die. In those tense moments, it did not matter to me whether I believed in what I saw. If things did not go well, everyone around me knew that the boy's life was in jeopardy. I could not help saying a silent prayer for Trɔ̃ or Dã to accept the exchange. Within thirty seconds, Trɔ̃ began cooing "aaahh, aaahh" approvingly. I took this to mean that the chicken was about to expire. Indeed, its head dropped back and hung down, and a couple of minutes later it was completely limp and lifeless, a delayed but successful sacrifice. Trɔ̃ dropped it to the ground, and the main ceremony was over. The deity retired from the space, and a man who had been whittling a sharp point onto a three-foot-long stake picked up the dead chicken and skewered it with the stake. I left the ceremony a bit confused about what was to be done with the chicken. But the following day, with me on the back of Gaston's motorcycle, we happened to drive past a nearby path about one hundred yards from the *xunɔ̃*'s house. There beside the path we saw the stake with one end in the ground and with the chicken still skewered at the top. Gaston said nonchalantly that it was left there for Dã. The next day, apparently, the goat was sacrificed as well.

Like all ceremonies, this was a unique event and cannot be considered representative of all healing practices or even all *kuɖiɔ*. Nevertheless, it captures some important and recurring themes surrounding healing. For example, supernatural causes are not always the first diagnosis of someone's illness. Indeed, frequently it is only after repeated failed efforts at medical treatment that people consult a ritual specialist. Thus, when the stakes are high, the question of "belief" can become a matter of necessity, even for people previously unfamiliar with the occult, as in this case of the Ivorian woman. Furthermore, there are many stages of healing work, including consultations, herbal infusions, possession, sacrifices, and supernatural intervention. These rituals can occur in several stages and last days or weeks, which means that any irregularity or breach of protocol (such as insufficient payment or a chicken that will not die) could jeopardize the outcome. Lastly, as described in chapter 4, there are ambiguous ties between witchcraft and Vodun. Though nobody at this ceremony would have blamed the boy's illness on Dā or Trɔ̃, the deities' ability to intervene can leave questions about their role just below the surface, particularly given the claims that, whether good or bad, àzě is responsible for causing and stopping supernatural problems and for the creation of vodũ themselves.

One other point that warrants consideration is that the moral ambiguity surrounding witchcraft and healers can often erupt in unexpected and damaging ways. While one person may trust a healer with his life, another may suspect the same healer of carrying out malevolent or antisocial activities. According to Gaston, such a tension regarding this xunɔ̃ nearly destroyed the relationship between Gaston and his brother David. Gaston was the first of the brothers to become friends with the xunɔ̃, and he used the xunɔ̃'s services regularly. Gaston introduced David to the xunɔ̃, and David began ordering bǒ from him as well, including one particular object that was supposed to protect David and his family. Meanwhile, others told David that the bǒ was dangerous and that Gaston and the xunɔ̃ were trying to harm him. David threw the bǒ away and called Gaston an àzètɔ́. Soon after that, David's child died mysteriously, and he began to rethink his actions. Gaston convinced him once again to visit the xunɔ̃, who told him that in discarding the bǒ, he had left his child vulnerable to the àzètɔ́ in the family. A possessed Trɔ̃ deity later identified David's grandmother as the àzètɔ́ responsible for the child's death. Subsequently, David became very close with the xunɔ̃ and worked with him regularly, though he never asked forgiveness from Gaston. Gaston resolved to remain friends with the xunɔ̃ but not to hire him anymore for fear of reigniting tensions with David.

A Spiritual Healing in Abomey

Another healer I know is not a vodũnɔ̃ or xunɔ̃ and does not claim to represent any religion. I first heard about Daǎ Adegbenon through his radio shows, during which he offers listeners recipes for spiritual protection. Unlike the village *xunɔ̀* discussed above, Adegbenon is wealthy and cosmopolitan. He told me he studied mysticism in India, Tibet, and China and returned to Benin so he could apply his new skills to liberate people from witchcraft. Like other healers, he is a staunch advocate of the power of leaves, and he has formed a nongovernmental organization to promote the virtues of plants. He also performs public exorcisms to prevent witches from using their power. He has a healing center in Cotonou where he sees dozens of patients each day, but he performs more complicated ceremonies at his family home in Abomey. Although I had met Adegbenon in 2008, it was not until my 2009 visit that I was able to attend one of his healing ceremonies. He told me by phone that he had two Cotonou patients who were accompanying him to Abomey for witchcraft protection and that I was welcome to join them.

I arrived at Adegbenon's Abomey home at 9:00 p.m. on May 31. Like other visitors, I was first greeted by the large mural painted on a wall of his house depicting Adegbenon flanked on either side by both kinds of owls (with and without tufted ears). I waited with the two patients in the living room, which housed leather couches, a television, and an elaborate stereo system. The walls were adorned with photos of family leaders, an appliquéd cloth bearing the insignia of the precolonial kings, a smaller painting of Adegbenon with two owls on his shoulders, and a large black wall mural of the deity Lɛ̌gbà with an erect penis. I discussed my research with the male patients and obtained their permission to attend the ceremony. The healer entered carrying large pieces of red and white cloth and then asked his patients to step behind a curtain and put them on in place of their regular clothes. They emerged with the white cloth wrapped around their waists. Adegbenon touched their heads three times with the red cloth and draped it around their necks and over their bare chests. Then he took a smaller white cloth and tied it around their heads.

When the healer stepped out of the room, I took the opportunity of asking the two young men about their condition and their reason for entering treatment. The first man was a carpenter in his early thirties who said that in earlier consultations Adegbenon had predicted that he would have trouble with his in-laws. He then lost a child, followed by the deaths of many of his sheep. At that time, he also had contracts for two carpentry jobs, but neither of them produced any profits. When his wife became sick, he finally approached Daǎ Adegbenon, who suggested the carpenter perform a *kuɖiɔ* ceremony. The price was 65,000 FCFA ($130), but the carpenter could not afford it, and he said his situation grew more dire. Adegbenon told him his problem was *envoûtement* (French for "bewitching"; this word usually implies the work of aggressive *bǒ*, but in this case, the *kuɖiɔ* ceremony suggests *àzě*).

Besides the *kuɖiɔ*, he was expecting to receive another ritual called "delivery of luck and the star."

The second patient was a thirty-two-year-old man who did odd jobs for a living. He told me that his problem is a general lack of luck or success. He still had no regular job and no wife. None of the projects he undertook produced any success. He had visited Adegbenon three to four years prior to this ceremony after hearing him on the radio. The healer gave him a provisional product, which helped somewhat, but like the other man, he lacked the funds to perform the complete ceremony. Bad luck continued to plague him and those close to him. His sister suffered difficult births and had two cesarean deliveries, after which both babies died. He brought his sister to Adegbenon, who performed a treatment prior to the delivery of her next child. Again she had a cesarean birth, but with the healer's treatment, the child survived. Returning from another room of the house, Adegbenon contributed to the man's story. He said that the newborn child was sick and did not have enough blood. Even the doctors had given up hope until Adegbenon intervened. I presumed that the man's sister's experience is what prompted him to move forward with his own treatment. He was scheduled to undergo the same two ceremonies as the other patient.

The first part of the ceremony was to take place in Adegbenon's living room, where he discussed some of his techniques. He said he works with snakes, birds, and vultures, but in particular he said he called on the Queen Mother of India, the cobra. But the first animal he brought out was a large brown bird, which I presume was a vulture. He dealt with each patient in turn, and both of them performed the same sequence of events that I report here. The patient was handed the bird and instructed to hold its wings outstretched. Adegbenon spread a white sheet on the ground and asked the patient to stand on it and say what he wanted. Each man complied in soft whispers, pronouncing a type of prayer requesting assistance for his particular problems. This lasted for about ten or fifteen minutes, and the patient was visibly tired, with his arms growing heavy from the weight of the bird. Finally, Adegbenon told him he could lower his arms but then told him to hold the bird out in each of the four directions and continue asking for success. At this stage, the second patient spoke a bit louder, and I was able to make out some of what he asked for: good work, success for his family, the ability to buy land and build a home, and money to buy food. With each man the bird struggled, contributing to the men's fatigue. The healer came and went during this process, which lasted another thirty minutes.

When both men had finished, Adegbenon came back and told them to put the bird down. He handed each in turn a long, black snake and showed them how they were to hold the snake's tail underfoot while Adegbenon touched their heads with the snake's head. Next, he wrapped the snake around the patient's arm for a minute (see figure 15). Both men were noticeably nervous about this, and they alternated between wincing and chuckling at their situation. Most people consider snakes to be dangerous, and they would never attempt to hold them or manipulate them.[6] Once both men had finished with the snake, singing began outside, accompanied by clapping and shakers. Because this traditional music, which resembled Vodun ceremonies, was so distinct from the somber, private, and unusual ceremonies I had just witnessed, I wondered aloud if the musical event was connected to the men's rituals. The patients admitted that they were also uncertain. While we listened to the troupe perform, Adegbenon came to each patient and gave him a beaded necklace with a large talisman attached. Then with a black cat in his hands, the healer instructed the patients to fold the floor sheet in half and put it down. The healer held the cat to the patient's chest and instructed him to place the amulet against the cat's head. Next Adegbenon took a similarly decorated armband and attached it to one patient's upper arm, though the second man received none (I did not learn why).

FIGURE 15. Adegbenon (*right*) places a snake on a patient's arm. (Photograph by the author)

We followed Adegbenon outside and saw his followers dancing and singing under the hut in the courtyard. We walked past them into another building, where a calabash, the bird, and the snake had been placed on a long table against the back wall. The bird and the snake were surrounded by masses of beaded necklaces. Adegbenon and his assistants instructed the two patients to hold the bird and the snake atop the beads while a female assistant drew white marks on each man's arms, chest, and back. The men were asked to put their hands on the different items while Adegbenon and his assistant monitored and guided them from one spot to the next, switching places. Afterward, the men were led out to the hut, and each one held the snake and the calabash in turns while sitting on the ground covered in a red cloth. Next a stiff mat was placed on the ground, and each patient lay down while the attendants wrapped him up within it. The performers lifted him up and swung him back and forth as they continued their song.

When this was complete, the ceremony moved to a nearby walled area of the compound. On one side of the space there was a mat covered by a collection of perfumes, presumably for healing ceremonies, though they were not used in this ritual. At the far end of the enclosure was a rectangular tiled pit resembling a tomb. The patient, still cradled in the mat, was placed in the pit while a pigeon was sacrificed. The blood was spread on the man's neck and shoulders. He was then asked to get out of the pit and walk forward over a series of cylindrical bundles. At the end of his path was a basket positioned upside down on the ground. Adegbenon lifted the basket to reveal a pile of live snakes, and he instructed the patient to put his foot on the writhing mass. As the snakes moved, Adegbenon occasionally herded them back into the pile. After both men had undergone this procedure, they were led out of the enclosure near the hut. Adegbenon poured a black powder on the ground and then placed a lit candle next to it, causing the powder to burst into flame and quickly burn out. As the smoke rose, the patient was told to wave his hands up repeatedly as if helping the smoke rise. After both men had performed the rite, a third man took a turn and joined them for the remainder of the ceremonies.

The next phase of the ceremony began after 11:30 p.m. I was already growing tired and had mistakenly assumed that the events were drawing to a close. Instead we all climbed into a car and followed the dirt road to the nearby blacktop route that skirts Abomey's southern periphery. I learned that we were headed to the sacred forest, only half a mile away. The singers walked ahead of us, and to allow them to arrive first, we parked on the side of the road until they reached the forest. Like most sacred forests in populated areas of southern Benin, this one was quite small and consisted of a collection of bushes and small trees surrounding one large tree—in this case, a medium-sized baobab, though it is often an iroko tree. Two assistants took over the ceremonies while the healer and the rest of us waited a short distance away. With a red cloth on his head, each of the three men was brought before the baobab, which had a cloth stretched vertically against it. The patient faced the tree with both hands on the cloth while the attendants prayed. Next they led the patient around the tree several times carrying bowls of water. As he walked, he put his hands in the water and splashed the tree while praying. Though I was a few yards away from one of the men, I could make out enough of the prayers to know that he was asking for good luck, health for his family, and an end to àzě. When all three men had finished this ritual, our whole entourage walked across the road to a cultivated field. Each patient was lain beneath a mat, and more prayers were recited. The ritual assistants walked around the patient several times, then started plucking weeds and dropping them upon the mat. The patient was instructed to burst out of the mat and run to the car without looking back. At around 12:30 a.m. we all climbed back into the car and headed to Adegbenon's house for the final rite: a bath. The patients were led back to the enclosure, where a large calabash held water. The first patient was stripped nude and bathed by assistants. When he finished, I exited the enclosure and told Adegbenon that I did not need to watch the remaining baths. Between 1:00 and 1:30 Adegbenon asked his driver to take me home.

Although both of the healing rituals I recount in this chapter were classified as kuɖio, there were some dramatic differences. For example, while both healers were attempting to relieve their patients' witchcraft suffering, the xunɔ̃ was treating a physical and perhaps life-threatening ailment. On the other hand, Adegbenon was trying to overcome what we might call general misfortune. The first one involved Trɔ̃ and Dã, both well-known deities in southern Benin, but the second bore no obvious connection to any deities or Beninese religion. Both rituals made use of animals and sacrifice, but the second one employed exotic and perhaps frightening snakes and a bird (one of which was unharmed, though pigeons were also sacrificed). And while the first ritual was not necessarily representative of healing work in general, it would be familiar to many people because it included music, spirit possession, and animal sacrifice in order to request assistance from the deities. Even though Adegbenon's ceremony featured music and the invocation of the sacred forest—a traditional site of spiritual power—it was otherwise a novel and possibly foreign procedure. These two ceremonies by no means encompass the entire spectrum of supernatural treatments, but they do give a sense of the varied ways that healers develop to deal with the threat of witchcraft. And they both demonstrate how new and old elements are marshaled in the quest for spiritual security.

Global Witchcraft

While the Vodun religion has always been receptive to foreign influences, the domains of *àzě* and healing appear to have accelerated the connections to foreign spirituality. *Vodǔnɔ̃*, *bokɔ́nɔ̃*, and *azɔ̃gbletɔ́* all perform healing services, many of which are based on indigenous practices of herbal medicine, divination, and the appeasement of *àzètɔ́*, but healers and others also incorporate foreign elements into the category of witchcraft. As noted in previous chapters, some people suggested that witchcraft encompasses not only science and magic but Vodun, Christianity, and all religions. In this section, I expand on these ideas through discussion of how healers and ordinary people draw parallels between witchcraft and foreign esoteric traditions, resulting in the universalizing tendencies surrounding witchcraft in Benin.

Some years ago in Abomey, two teenagers whom I did not know approached me on the street and asked what I knew about ninjas and how they could acquire ninja power. At the time, I was confused by their request, mainly because I had no idea why they thought I knew anything about ninjas but also because they seemed to suggest that ninjas possessed mystical talents rather than simply trained physical abilities. I told them I knew little of ninjas but that there must surely be martial arts experts in Cotonou if the teenagers were interested in learning more. They were clearly disappointed by my answer, but it would be a few years until I understood why. Although they never told me directly, it occurred to me later that they probably saw ninjas as superhuman warriors akin to healers or *àzètɔ́*. They must have felt that true ninja power was something that only came from far away, so surely I would be more likely to know something about ninjas than anyone in Benin. The boys never explicitly equated ninjas with *àzètɔ́* nor expressed an interest in acquiring foreign *àzě*, but in my subsequent research on *àzě* I have encountered many others who look to foreign inventions and spirituality to fulfill a longing for exotic powers.[7]

During my fieldwork I have heard countless laypeople and healers alike talk about foreign witchcraft and the desire to take advantage of international contacts to acquire new supernatural knowledge and skills. People explained that witchcraft exists in every country, though perhaps in different forms. At a meeting of a village healers' association where I interviewed the group, one man said that people bring different kinds of *àzě* from other countries, which explains why *àzě* is evolving so rapidly. An Abomey man told me that *àzě* and *bŏ* from Burkina Faso and other countries have reached Benin. As if he were quoting from a textbook on globalization, he stated that mobility and communication have brought many changes to the occult in Benin, and he described *àzĕ*'s global network as an "interplanetary characteristic." Given people's interest in acquiring spiritual armaments and foreign *àzĕ*, and given the value they place on witchcraft research, it is no surprise that long-distance connections have emerged. The Ouidah healer who threatened me (chapter 3) called himself a researcher and claimed that he is constantly studying and acquiring new abilities. When I met him in 2008, he said that the previous week he had just spent 450,000 FCFA ($900) on professional training. He told me that he had originally learned his profession in various towns in Benin, including Save, Dassa, and Agonlin. He then did research with Indians and later bought a mystical ring in France for 400,000 FCFA ($800). Though one Cotonou healer confided that he had no international contacts but wanted to cultivate them, it was common for healers to tell me that they either had studied in Togo or had contacts with healers in Togo and other West African countries. More rarely, they said they had contacts in Europe, North America, and Asia, but as I will show, these more distant lands also figure prominently in local conceptions of *àzĕ*.

An Abomey friend and *sakpátánɔ̀* (*vodũnɔ̀* of the spirit Sakpatá) named Serge once reacted defensively when I told him about my interest in studying the occult in Benin. He asked why I came all the way to Benin to study witchcraft, arguing that a researcher must first understand his own society before endeavoring to learn another. I was taken aback, because I had known him for some time, and he was a good friend of Gaston. I tried to respond that I had chosen Benin as my research area, and while there were many important things I could learn about the United States, I had selected a foreign geographic specialty. But clearly I had not followed him, and he pushed on. Why was it, Serge asked, that I had not tried to learn about American witchcraft? Again, though I started feeling inadequate about my knowledge of my own country, I protested that witchcraft (Wicca, I was thinking) was a minority religion and that I had little contact with people of that faith. Exasperated, he finally said that America's witchcraft societies were the Freemasons, Rosicrucians, and followers of Eckankar. Once again, I felt ignorant because I knew even less about these than I did about Wicca. Of course, I had a vague understanding that Freemasons and Rosicrucians were secret societies, but it was only in my visits to Benin that I had begun to understand why they might be considered equivalent to witchcraft. And for some years I had been hearing about Eckankar in Benin, but I had originally assumed it was a marginal religion or money-making scheme from abroad rather than a magical society. Beninese had shown me the pamphlets distributed by the Eckankar organization, and one of the features that people always mentioned was that Eckankar was "from America," so surely I would know about it. Out of curiosity, I had glanced at the pamphlets and learned that Eckankar was a spiritual movement founded in Minnesota, but beyond that I knew little and had no reason to think it was *àzě*. But when my friends began saying that Eckankar and the other societies were American forms of witchcraft, I took notice. These "spiritual science movements," as Rosalind Hackett (1992) observes in Nigeria, rarely catch the attention of scholars, but they are increasingly important because they are perceived as a more advanced scientific knowledge but with correlates in indigenous culture.[8]

In the last few years, I have learned from informants that Eckankar teaches people how to engage in nocturnal travels and spiritual journeys. The association with soul separation makes plain why some understand it as a variety of *àzě*. Gaston's brother David said he began training in Eckankar's chanting practice and felt himself spinning, as if he were going to fly. He abandoned the training out of fear of where he would go and whether he would be able to return.[9] One Eckist friend of mine said that his initiation into the order was gradual. He was well-off and knew that envious witches in his family were attempting to bring him down. He was introduced to Eckankar by a friend gradually, and he spent three or four years chanting the sacred word "hu" before he declared his membership.[10] During this time, he experienced multiple thefts and lost nearly all the material wealth he had accumulated. He said that he understands his losses now as a result of karma and suggested that he was undeserving of his success. Eckankar wanted him to purify himself and start anew, which led him to regain his footing and establish a comfortable but modest lifestyle. He now feels protected from witches, claiming that he sees them in his nocturnal travels. He added that an *àzètɔ́* attempting to enter an Eckankar meeting would be immediately detected, though he is unaware of this happening.

Another Abomey man told me that Eckankar is a powerful force of protection against *àzě*. He said that once he began chanting the Eckankar spiritual word, "hu," all the *àzètɔ́* in his family fled and no longer came to his house. Because others had told me that only *àzě* can counter *àzě*, I asked him if Eckankar is *àzě*. He replied that it is similar in that it allows you to travel in your dreams, except that Eckists do not eat people. Of course, this description of Eckists also resembles benevolent *àzètɔ́* (healers) who use *àzě* to fight witchcraft. He added that Eckists keep a notebook by their bed so they can record their dreams. And after I pressed him on whether others would interpret such dream travel as *àzĕ*, he agreed and explained that this is why Eckists do not discuss these dreams with others. David offered another piece of information that suggests comparisons of Eckankar to witchcraft. He said that Eckists reportedly promise to donate a body part to the society when they die. He noted that Eckists deny this, but he argues that this transaction is what accounts for the fact that Eckists all begin to acquire wealth after being initiated into the society.

Some people told me that Freemasons and Rosicrucians engage in similar spiritual journeys or teleportation; therefore, they claimed, both of these secret societies teach and practice *àzĕ* or something akin to it. Still others portrayed these esoteric traditions as part of a broader, shared spiritual heritage. For example, my friend Serge the *sakpatánɔ̀* told me that he once attended an open house with the Rosicrucians and noticed a drawing on the wall of an *akplé* (Fá divination chain). Seeing this, he said, revealed Rosicrucianism as a façade and convinced him that if other religions rely on the same techniques as Vodun, then he would stay with his original faith. Although his experiences discouraged him from seeking further foreign religions, they did not prevent him from seeing spirituality through the lens of a universal principle. Indeed, he also told me that *bŏ*, *àzĕ*, Jesus, Rosicrucianism, and Eckankar are similar because they all have their own waves, like cell phones. And several healers made similar claims of connections between these foreign societies and other supernatural practices both local and international.

Although Western esoteric societies represent an important part of the foreign influence on Beninese conceptions of religion and *àzĕ*, Eastern mysticism is by far considered to be the most powerful spiritual import. The two primary Eastern traditions are Hindu mysticism and Chinese healing. I met few people with knowledge of Chinese medicine, and it appears less widespread, though the growing presence of Chinese people through commerce and international aid is likely to feed future interest in Chinese healing techniques. Unlike Western esoteric movements, Chinese healing is not generally interpreted as a form of witchcraft. Indeed, the focus on plants and herbal medicine is central to my informants' characterization of this foreign practice. For example, as described in chapter 3, one Cotonou man used a book on Chinese healing to find an herbal treatment for headaches. A Cotonou healer told me that he obtained a diploma in Chinese medicine, and his training consisted of the study of plants and herbal remedies. Another technique he adopted from the Chinese is to massage his patients in order to diagnose their problems. Despite the expressed focus on plants and a de-emphasis on the supernatural, because of the links between health and the occult in Benin, those who follow Chinese medicine are likely to use it in the treatment of *àzĕ* attacks. Furthermore, both Chinese medicine and *bŏ* are characterized by the study of leaves, which suggests ambiguity as to whether this practice is considered purely physiological or supernatural.

By contrast to Chinese healing, Hindu and Indian healing and mysticism were familiar to most people, and they were frequently classified as a form of witchcraft. Indeed, Indians were often (though not always) regarded as possessing the most powerful witchcraft in the world (Drewal 2008; Meyer 1999). As evidence, people often cited the widespread claim that India's national soccer team is barred from international competition because their prowess in magic would make any match unfair (see also Leseth 1997). However, Didier argued that it is only people's desire to see Indians as spiritually strong and to be associated with their powers that makes people believe a false story about their soccer team. Nevertheless, India's reputation as the world leader in mysticism is a prominent feature of occult discourses. This reputation is cultivated through media and personal appearances by Indian spiritualists. People say *yovó* (Indians) appear on TV and the internet talking about spiritual power.[11] Although they may not call it witchcraft, many believe Indians possess incredible abilities to see the future or to bring good fortune. Indians not only appear on foreign programs but also come to Benin to establish a spiritual practice. Although I have never met any of these spiritualists, I have been told they travel around Benin, and one Indian man makes a regular appearance on Beninese television.

However Indian spiritualists might understand their role, many Beninese readily place them in the category of *àzètɔ́*. Much like the claims about Western esoteric movements discussed above, a young Cotonou woman told me that Indian spiritualists travel at night using the same power as *àzètɔ́* but that they only use it for good purposes. Some people who have conducted personal research into Eastern mysticism used New Age imagery, talking of vibrations, auras, and astral voyages. The healer Daă Adegbenon told me he takes voyages to the astral world, where he sees *àzètɔ́* and bargains on behalf of their victims. Cyrille the healer showed me designs in his temple and told me they were from India. He said that Indians use white *àzĕ*, in the form of particular patterns, to fight evil *àzĕ*.

My friend Claude told me about a group of Indians who traveled throughout Benin offering a one-week course in Pranic Healing for 5,000 FCFA ($10). Many of those invited ended up refusing to participate because they understood the training as an initiation into witchcraft. Claude took the course and told me it consisted of instruction in a series of exercises, like yoga, allowing you to see someone's aura. The aura appears either thick and healthy or too thin, indicating the patient's condition. He learned to put his hands on someone and feel the pressure of the aura pushing back. Some exercises were intended to develop the ability to see energy, like tiny stars in the air that belong to energy that is normally invisible. Finally, the instructors taught the group how to heal with their hands. At the end of the week, Claude received a book and cassettes with additional information.[12] He tried the method successfully on his son, who suffered from earaches. But after a few months, the pain returned. Claude told me he discontinued the treatments because they exhausted him. He worried that if his own aura became too weak, then he risked jeopardizing his health. Furthermore, he noted, if evil àzètɔ́ saw him as a healer and opponent, then they might attack him.

There are other examples of people who have studied Eastern mysticism and spirituality. I have already described Daǎ Adegbenon's healing ceremony as a product of his research in Asia. He told me that as a child he had come across some documents about Indian mysticism and contacted someone in New Delhi. Eventually, he traveled to Asia and spent years studying mysticism and the esoteric properties of plants in India and Tibet, as well as in other African countries. He said his treatments derive inspiration from the Bible, Qur'an, and Bhagavad-Gita. An Abomey retiree told me that he has studied spirituality, and then he showed me a book he owns on Hinduism. He told me he follows spiritualism rather than occultism, explaining that spiritualists do not need the occultists' ingredients and incantations; instead, they have a deeper understanding of universal forces.[13] He added that even though this knowledge was developed in spiritual schools and clubs in India, it represents universal truths.

Whether they call it spiritualism or àzě, many amateur researchers use a similar universalist discourse. For example, another Abomey retiree told me that he is Catholic but explores other spiritual knowledge and interests. He told me he believes in reincarnation, saying the soul leaves the body but never dies. He spoke of initiation into supernatural societies, where one acquires knowledge in the same way that seminarians study the Bible and learn prayers. He continued, saying that initiation creates vibrations and gives one power. He told me he had read spiritualist books but avoids telling people for fear they would not understand (i.e., they would think he practices witchcraft). He said that every religion is valid and that he practices them all, including a secret mystical society based in Europe (whose name he did not offer). And even though his church opposes traditional religion, he told me he values Fá divination and called it an art, much like Indians' use of tarot cards. The mayor of a small municipality outside of Abomey told me that he once met an American who claimed to have been reincarnated several times. The reincarnated man reported that his current life has lasted 250 years and that his knowledge of a previous life in France was verified by people who went there and located the places he mentioned. The mayor told me he knows that Indians have *àzě* because he has read articles about their religion and how they worship the cow. Then he declared that Buddhism, Shintoism, and Hinduism are all witchcraft. He concluded our interview with the universalist claim that all religions include a form of divination equivalent to Fá.

These universalizing conceptions of religion and witchcraft not only have the effect of dissolving the boundaries between different religions and between witchcraft and religion but also pave the way for the religious tolerance and experimentation that characterize Benin's religious landscape. As noted in chapter 4, people's quest for spiritual security fuels religions' popularity. But for many, the universalism contributes to a lack of religious allegiance, which means people are free to try out multiple religions and to change regularly. This is why Afro-based religions are often regarded as fundamentally practical rather than ideological or theological. Jérôme, the headache sufferer I introduced in chapter 3, is a good example of someone who has experimented with multiple spiritual options. In 2008 I had a series of long conversations with him about *àzě* and religion. He told me that he had done quite a lot of reading in spiritualism and esoteric arts and then showed me two of his books: *Les clés du Nirvana* (The keys to Nirvana) by T. Lobsang Rampa and *Sorcellerie et magie* (Witchcraft and magic) by Meinrad Hebga.[14] There are other similar publications circulating in Benin, some of which may be inspired by academic works but many of which are popular occult works. Jérôme explained that most people cannot understand this information, but it constitutes the knowledge possessed by *àzètɔ́*.[15] He talked at length about the seven different components of a person, each one a type of body (*corps*): the *corps physique, corps hétérique, corps causal, corps mental, corps spirituel,* and *corps astral* (he could not remember the seventh). He said the soul is different; it is something with vibrations that belongs to the cosmic consciousness. The *corps hétérique,* he told me, is the one that travels or can enter trance.

Jérôme recounted some pieces of his life story, saying that he began as a follower of Eckankar but later withdrew because he was frustrated at not having learned to engage in nocturnal travels to the astral world. But he expressed ambivalence about this because although he desperately wanted to travel, he was afraid that he would like the astral world so much he would never come back. He was worried that without a spiritual master to bring him back, he would never return to his *corps physique* and would die. He further explained that after death, the other bodies leave the *corps physique* and continue to exist in some hidden place, perhaps on another planet. He told me that the karmic law states that bodies are reincarnated in some other body. He speculated that Jesus may have had several incarnations, and if he has finished his mission on Earth, he can now become fused with God to become part of the cosmic consciousness. At some later point, Jérôme became a member of Gambada, an antiwitchcraft deity associated with Trɔ̰. Though he said he no longer belongs to Gambada, his elderly female patron insisted to me that he remains a member, but he prefers to keep it a secret. He also mentioned that he was interested in Kabbalah and Hinduism and that as a child he had done some reading in Chinese medicine. Like some other young educated people today, Jérôme is strongly influenced by Eastern spirituality and its connections to witchcraft. However, his membership in Gambada shows a willingness to entertain other religious options. Though he may have experimented with more than the average number of religions, it is common for people to try out multiple traditions in their quest for spiritual security. As Christine Henry (2008a) notes, Beninese change regularly between Vodun and various churches and then often back again.

A Cotonou healer named Clotaire had a similarly diverse spiritual background, giving him knowledge of the widest range of spiritual knowledge I had ever witnessed. My 2008 encounter with him was like a whirlwind as I tried to keep up with his rapid citation of countless deities and spiritual concepts, many of which were unknown to me. Along the way, I collected the main elements of his life story. Clotaire was a former Catholic who had had an unpleasant experience with the church at the time of his confirmation. Later, at thirty-five, he chose to be baptized in the Celestial Church of Christ. While working in Ivory Coast, he began a spiritual quest, taking forty-one days of solitary reflection. During this time a voice told him to go to Benin to get his *kpɔlí* (personal Fá sign). When he returned to his family village, he was told his *kpɔlí* was the sign of death. The next part of his story was vague, as Clotaire explained that he kept searching and found his true sign, which spoke to him and set him on the right course. I do not know why his *kpɔlí* would have been wrong initially, and I do not know what it means for a *kpɔlí* to speak. Nevertheless, he told me he was also influenced by a trip to China and by his discovery in France of the book by Corneille Agrippa (Cornelius Agrippa) titled *La philosophie du culte*.[16] Then in a rapid-fire monologue, Clotaire laid out his philosophy of witchcraft and religion, and I attempt here to re-create some of what he told me, preserving the disjointed style of his lesson. He began by calling *àzĕ* a marriage, the union of two opposing principles or people. He compared it to yoga being the fusion of two beings. He referred to Mĭnɔ̃nǎ as the queen mother, Mother Nature, the woman who carries humanity, and the Virgin Mary. Jesus was the son who was kept inside her womb, demonstrating the theme of fused interior and exterior components. Thus marriage or fusion is what gives someone limitless power to become a superman, to be an *àzètɔ́*. He then compared Fá divination to what he called the *tché* of Eastern meditation (perhaps referring to Chinese Qi life force) before continuing to describe *àzĕ*. An *àzètɔ́*, he said, symbolizes justice and karma because he is linked to God and the cosmic consciousness. *Àzètɔ́* eat people just as Jesus's body is transformed into food during Communion. The sign X represents multiplication and the link to God; it is also the sign of Fá, and its totem is the hyena, a predator who must eat, just like an *àzètɔ́*. The sound a hyena uses to capture another person and transcend space is *hu*. The sound gives it power, the same sound chanted in Eckankar, a tradition much like Rosicrucianism and Freemasonry. Clotaire then spoke of tarot cards, saying the last card represents King Tut. The Egyptian gods Ra/Mat are equivalent to Lisá/Măwŭ. Venus is Măwŭ, and Eve is Mat. He finished the private sermon with vague references to Kabbalah and Hinduism.

   In 2009 I sought out Clotaire again, and he performed a similar monologue with an assault of deities' names and esoteric notions, but this time it was even more technical. He first spoke of the *Yi King*, describing it as a sacred book of China, and then mentioned that teaching the Fuji tradition in Japan was the same as Fá.[17] He told me Lĕgbà corresponds to the Hebrew god Samekh, while Măwŭ and Lisá correspond to yin and yang.[18] In the Hebrew alphabet, Yahweh had four letters (y, e, v, e), and the letters' positions in the alphabet are 10, 5, 6, 5. When these are added together, they make twenty-six, but since the alphabet only has twenty-two letters, it must instead be 2 + 6 (8). The eighth Hebrew letter is heth, equivalent to the deity of Elohim, also a couple like Măwŭ and Lisá. The letter 8 turned on its side becomes the symbol of Venus and infinity. Venus is the source of witchcraft. Deities from other traditions are all the same as Venus: the Egyptian Aset (Isis), the Babylonian Astarte, the Canaanite Anat, Anna (mother of Mary), and Eve. All these female deities are different manifestations of Mĭnɔ̃nǎ. Clotaire then criticized esoteric movements like Eckankar, Rosicrucianism, Freemasonry, and the Illuminati, arguing that they and all other religions are exploiters because they fail to liberate people. He said the only true religion is the Egyptian deity Ptah, represented by the monkey; Fá's totem is also the monkey, the *bokɔ́nɔ̃* (diviner) is equivalent to the Buddha, Fá's sign is *aklā-mɛji*, and its number is 8. As with our first meeting, I left this one reeling from the scope of religious linkages he enumerated.

Though Clotaire's understanding of foreign deities may be vague at times, his interviews involved a dizzying display of his knowledge of world religion, probably designed in part to impress and mystify me so that I would be unable to ask questions. In fact, when I did attempt a brief question, it usually prompted even more expansive explanations and technical information about diagrams and numeric symbols. On a couple of occasions, taking an even more active teacher's role, Clotaire reached over and took my pen and notebook to record the symbol of infinity and the image of an eight-pointed star that he called the Star of the New Jerusalem. Although both he and Jérôme derive some of their knowledge of Eastern religion from sources regarded as questionable in the West, this does not negate the importance of these discourses for uniting global elements, particularly Eastern ones, with local religious understandings. Particularly for Clotaire, his conceptions of Christianity and Vodun tie in seamlessly with Fá, nature, yin and yang, *àzě*, the ancient Near Eastern gods, and contemporary Asian religions. By this thinking, there is a single universal force in the world that comprises all other systems of knowledge, both natural and spiritual. This is in keeping with physicist Fritjof Capra's (1975) bold treatise on the similarities between physics and Eastern mysticism.[19] Though these observations pertain to Eastern spirituality, my findings show that these parallels obtain also in the universalist terms some informants use to link Eastern mysticism to African witchcraft.

Inviting the Foreign

From a Western perspective, the tension between scientific and supernatural perspectives is nowhere more apparent than in the domain of healing. When faced with the decision of whether to seek biomedical treatment or a traditional healer, Westerners are likely to see this as a question of science versus superstition. In Benin people also make these choices, and they recognize the different approaches to natural and provoked illnesses. Indeed, many people prefer to visit medical doctors and to use pharmaceuticals or herbal medicine rather than face the possibility that someone they know is trying to harm them. At the same time, because medical diagnoses and treatments are often insufficient for restoring health, people also value spiritual strategies that fall in the domain of healers, *bokɔ́nɔ̌*, and other religious leaders. However, as Peter Geschiere points out for Cameroon, healers are anything but "traditional" these days. Instead, they are "emphatically modern figures with sunglasses, speaking fluent French, armed with a wide array of books on magic (especially Indian occult knowledge) and mixing all sorts of modern elements" (1998, 821). In Benin and other parts of Africa, these elements include astrology, Rosicrucianism, and other movements that belong to New Age spirituality (see Geschiere 2008b; Hackett 1992).

What is striking about these new spiritual influences is their apparently seamless incorporation into local understandings of witchcraft. This should come as no surprise, given the history of African religious borrowings (Tall 1995b). The desire for new exotic and foreign spiritual forces is an especially powerful driver in the religious realm, and Geschiere (2013) has suggested that this may even be a universal feature of witchcraft. In Benin observers have long noted the receptivity to foreign gods and religions (Bay 1998, 2008; Falen 2016; Henry 2008a; Herskovits [1938] 1967; Le Herissé 1911; Maupoil 1943; Mercier 1954; D. Rush 2013). This receptivity is perhaps part of a general exoticism, a romance with the foreign. For instance, the West African deity Mami Wata owes her existence to the encounter with Europeans, and she is symbolically linked to foreignness through her association with European travelers, mirrors, and mermaids (Drewal 1988; D. Rush 2013). Henry John Drewal (1988) argues that Mami Wata is the product of West Africans studying the "other" and incorporating foreign attributes into local religious life. Foreign people, objects, ideas, customs, and commodities are symbols to be appropriated and reconfigured to meet local needs (Apter 2005; Drewal 1988; Meyer 1999; D. Rush 2013; J. Smith 2008).[20] Much as the European foreigner is now incorporated into Beninese discourses on morality and identity (described in chapter 2), foreign others also figure into local manifestations of religion and witchcraft. In other words, Beninese and other Africans find the "other" a productive idea to think with, and this exoticism is a source of creativity and syncretism in the domains of religion and the occult as much as in the domains of morality, politics, and international development (J. Smith 2008).

Another feature that unites the local and foreign belief systems and opens the door for the introduction of foreign elements is the holistic approach to healing that acknowledges physical, social, and spiritual facets (Hackett 1992, 225). Holism is a philosophical principle found throughout Africa, defying the compartmentalization of science and religion, or natural and supernatural, that is so common in the West (Horton 1967a, 1967b; Styers 2004). As I have shown, this principle is borne out in the ways my informants talk about àzě as a universal force found in other parts of the world, a force that undergirds the domains of healing, religion, the gods, and divination. I once drove past a sign on the side of the road that read, "Cercle de la Sorcellerie Universelle:

Avec Dieu tout est possible" (Society for Universal Witchcraft: With God, everything is possible). I have no information about this specific organization, but their motto certainly corresponds to what many others repeatedly told me—that witchcraft is everywhere and everything. Therefore, I take inspiration from those Beninese friends and informants who regard witchcraft as a supercategory comprising science and nature, religions and gods, esoteric and occult movements, and systems of knowledge like Fá divination. Though not all laypeople see witchcraft in such universalizing terms, this view is held by a growing segment of the population who conduct research on witchcraft, including young, educated individuals and especially those in the healing professions.

Conclusion

Throughout this book, I present an admittedly inconsistent picture of witchcraft, sometimes examining it through a more distant theoretical lens while other times reporting on my own and others' emotional responses and anxiety regarding supernatural phenomena. As a social scientist, I am drawn to analytical approaches that attempt to capture witchcraft's symbolic associations and its sociological manifestations, but I also have an obligation to show respect for how people in southern Benin think about witchcraft. In anthropological terms, the difference between these two approaches can be crudely reduced to the tension between emic and etic perspectives. Which perspective is correct? For me, this is an unproductive question, because a variety of viewpoints can be useful for different purposes. On the scientific side, I have used a number of sociological interpretations. For example, my research supports scholarly claims that in competing for membership, authenticity, and the moral upper hand, Christian churches focus on the eradication of evil and on the demonization of traditional religion, contributing to the persistence and relevance of witchcraft today. Witchcraft discourses also intersect with gender ideology, since men's expressions of mistrust, admiration, and fear of women are recurring themes that find expression in the assertion that witches are quintessentially female, while healers are nearly always male. In addition, I have drawn on analyses depicting witchcraft as an idiom of power or the mystery of power. *Àzě* is a limitless force that defies understanding, and witchcraft discourses are an important way that people talk about death, wealth, and political abuse. Achille Mbembe (1992) suggests that in the African postcolony, magic and the occult are instruments of power, whereby magical ideas and fears serve to mystify the people and inspire fear and respect for authority (see also Fanon 1963). Although my analysis has not dealt primarily with witchcraft's articulation with political power, my remarks about politicians' presumed use of witchcraft and their search for supernatural advantages tend to support this interpretation.

At the same time, there is no question that power and wealth are related to witchcraft's emphasis on selfishness and inequality, which have become significant sources of tension in newly independent countries increasingly shaped by a neoliberal capitalism that allows elites to become rapidly wealthy on the backs of the desperately poor. Although these processes began long before most African nations achieved independence, the modernity theorists have rightly insisted that we cannot talk about contemporary African witchcraft without acknowledging the role of economic inequality and social upheaval. This has led to envy and jealousy between wealthy and poor individuals scrambling for a piece of what they perceive as a zero-sum pie. Another aspect of that upheaval is economic and social transformation driven by migration and wage labor, which have undermined the gerontocracy and communalism of rural, kin-based agricultural production. This economic individualism has coincided with the spread of Christianity's message about individuality, freedom from family deities, and the dangers of kin-based witchcraft (Meyer 1999). These processes help explain the recent rise in child witches and the motives for wealthy elites to distance themselves from their village kin. I have also offered evidence that African witchcraft expresses postcolonial frustrations with modernity, state governance, development, and the unequal relationship between black and white peoples.

This is an ethnography of a particular place, and we must be cautious about using these theories to develop a metanarrative about worldwide manifestations of witchcraft. However, the fact that occult fears seem to preoccupy so many people in Africa and other regions of the world begs the question of how to explain these trends. One common thread that seems to tie together anthropological accounts of witchcraft and sorcery is the significance of inequality, social tension, and the ways that either society or personal psychology reflect this sense of "spiritual insecurity" (Ashforth 2005). For both Bronisław Malinowski and E. E. Evans-Pritchard, supernatural thought was an attempt to explain the inexplicable and to wrestle with uncertainty. Similarly, Peter Geschiere (2013) has emphasized that witchcraft in Africa and elsewhere expresses a human reaction to uncertainty—an emotional and culturally conditioned response to the inexplicable or "uncanny" (see Siegel 2006). Nils Bubandt (2014) describes witchcraft among the Buli of Indonesia as an entirely mysterious, unknowable phenomenon, and Geschiere (2016) acknowledges that, cross-culturally, witchcraft is a feature of a world in disarray, a world that is fundamentally unpredictable. This is compatible with

Beninese views of *àzě* as a limitless, dynamic, and unknowable power that defies classification and comprehension. Death is a poignant example of a human experience that is uncanny and unfathomable, so it is unsurprising that witchcraft articulates with local theories for and defenses against death. Bruce Knauft (1985) reports that among the Gebusi of Papua New Guinea, every death is attributed to sorcery. Of course, uncertainty is nothing new, but most observers argue that rapid social, political, and economic change, much of it associated with what we call "globalization," may help explain why uncertainty has reached such a fevered pitch.

In a wide-ranging comparative work that tackles witchcraft around the world, Peter Geschiere (2013) offers his broadest theoretical contribution to explaining witchcraft. He suggests that witchcraft everywhere is the manifestation of a universal concern with the tensions inherent in relations between intimates. For Geschiere, intimacy like that found among kin is a powerful node of social connection and is fraught with anxiety because it carries both positive and negative potential. While intimacy might be desirable and beneficial, Geschiere points out that beneath the veneer of apparent comfort and trust among close individuals lies the possibility of competition and treachery. Indeed, mistrust of kin and moral ambiguity are key features of *àzě* in Benin. As noted, families are increasingly under strain from economic competition, migration, and Christianity's emphasis on the nuclear family at the expense of larger kin networks. Therefore, intimacy is heavily laden with ambiguity and ambivalence, and Geschiere believes witchcraft is a means of expressing the uncertainty related to intimacy, trust, and betrayal. Sewing together the idea that witchcraft reflects insecurity in a changing world with Geschiere's observation about the uncertainty inherent in kin relations, we might conclude that witchcraft erupts at times when dramatic social change refigures the conceptions and obligations of kinship. These theoretical approaches advance our understanding of witchcraft's significance in relation to changes in Benin's kinship and political economy, and such interpretations are appealing because they make sense of a disorderly and confusing situation. But as Geschiere (2013) himself notes, these interpretations are often meaningless to our interlocutors. For my Beninese friends and informants, most social science theories appear irrelevant or even misguided because they overlook the Beninese side of the story, creating an unfortunate sense that African and Western peoples have fundamentally different outlooks and thought processes. One side reflects a world governed by science and rationality, while the other appears governed by superstition and fear. And this is why, despite my reference to theory, I have also written this book with my Beninese friends in mind. This is why, regardless of my own epistemological training, I have attempted to explain, justify, and defend their claims that witchcraft is an African science.

The moral dimension of witchcraft is one domain where my informants' views have guided this study. As I have shown, witchcraft discourses contain a symbolic commentary on good and evil and their inevitable duality in both the human and supernatural worlds, and these points are made explicit by Beninese themselves. They recognize that people and gods alike cannot be defined in simple, one-dimensional terms. I hesitate to say that witchcraft represents a moral lesson any more than it represents social inequality or family tensions, yet I believe that witchcraft discourses capture important moral themes that also happen to play out in other domains like family and business dealings, health, postcolonial social justice, the role of public leaders, and the relationships between people and their deities. In thinking about $àzě$'s relationship to justice and morality, I am often reminded of conversations with Beninese friends about corruption and the diversion of public funds by government officials. While people often decried the frequent embezzlement by politicians, my friends freely admitted that in similar circumstances, they would do the same thing, arguing that they have needy relatives like everyone else; therefore, they would happily take advantage of the system. With respect to both $àzě$ and corruption, there is a fluid sense of morality, but even more than that, people have an explicit awareness of this fluidity without judgment or pretensions of moral superiority. Of course, the abstract acceptance of evil as a part of the world does not mean that Beninese celebrate evil or condone an individual's reprehensible actions. On the contrary, scandalous behavior is still shocking and will invariably attract criticism and hand-wringing, especially when it involves a public figure.

This point became apparent when I returned to Benin in 2012 and learned that Daǎ Adegbenon was being held in Abomey's prison. In a poignant example of a benevolent healer suspected of being corrupted by the dark side of witchcraft, Adegbenon was arrested for allegedly using human body parts in his healing rituals. Police had reportedly found children's bones at his home, and although this news was appalling, it was not altogether surprising, for everyone knows that healers tread a fine line between benevolent and nefarious activities. I asked friends whether he was accused of digging up gravesites or of murdering children for the magical use of their bones, and many of them said that he must have killed them, because there were stories circulating about girls from out of town who had mysteriously disappeared. Furthermore, people found these accusations to be revelatory of how he could have become so powerful; achieving that level of success could only have come through availing himself of dubious instruments.

When I first met Daă Adegbenon a few years prior to his imprisonment, my impression was that he was a friendly and reasonable person. He was a fast talker, and I considered him something of an operator who might have been willing to manipulate his clients for his own profit, but he did not strike me as dangerous, and I certainly would never have suspected him of such a gruesome crime. I was troubled by the accusations, trying to reconcile this image of the monster with my own recollection of a self-serving but relatively benign person. Despite my wariness, I gathered my courage to visit the Prison Civile of Abomey. Although I had passed by it dozens of times, this was my first time within its walls. For ten minutes I waited for Adegbenon to be brought to the visitation room, and I watched shoeless and poorly clothed prisoners being escorted to meet their visitors on the benches that lined the room. Beninese prisons have a reputation for brutality and poor conditions, and people have always told me that the prisons are so poorly funded that the only decent meals the prisoners receive are those delivered to them by their families; those prisoners without family nearby who are willing to bring food suffer from undernutrition and malnutrition. I was so conditioned by these stories that I expected to see my old acquaintance in a wretched condition. As I sat there staring at the door in anticipation of his arrival, one disheveled prisoner of Adegbenon's size and build was led out. I nervously jumped up and shook his hand, unconsciously thinking that prison had indeed taken a toll on him. The confused man greeted me with an unknowing look, and I was suddenly embarrassed to realize that I had mistaken him for Adegbenon. When Adegbenon finally arrived, I was surprised not only that he was well dressed in clean clothes but also that the guards treated him with remarkable respect. While all the other prisoners carried out their visitation in the one common room, a guard immediately escorted us to a private room containing a table and chairs and then checked with Adegbenon to make sure he approved of the arrangement. It seemed to me that Adegbenon was the one in charge, and I could not help thinking of Hollywood movies about wealthy Mafia bosses who govern the prisons and give orders to the guards. Adegbenon's wealth was no doubt an asset he could use to buy more comforts than the ordinary prisoners. Yet he did not have his freedom; in fact, before visiting the prison, Claude told me that Adegbenon was being held without trial. He pointed out that a powerful healer like Adegbenon would clearly inspire fear in anyone responsible for his incarceration. Nobody was willing to testify against him and risk supernatural reprisal, so the courts were unable to proceed with the case. If he was so powerful, I asked Claude, why could he not simply change into a bird and escape? He admitted that this was a vexing problem that defies comprehension, but he surmised that there might be something about identifying and apprehending àzètɔ́ that robs them of some of their power. However, as I have emphasized, the ambiguity and uncertainty surrounding àzě ensured that court officials and witnesses alike were probably hesitant to bring Adegbenon to trial or testify against him.

Adegbenon was eventually released, and I saw him again in July 2017, a couple of years after being liberated. He said that he was never tried and that there was never any evidence against him. The reason for his incarceration, he said, was that he was planning to run for political office, which had alarmed the local politicians, so they fabricated the charges against him. He claimed the municipal government leaders were further trying to punish him for refusing to sell his land to the city of Abomey. He also confirmed his privileged treatment in prison, even claiming that he succeeded in amassing greater wealth in prison by buying the rights to manage the prison's telephone booth, as well as conducting real estate deals with prisoners who were eager to sell off assets in exchange for the cash needed to fund their legal defense. Ever the businessman, Adegbenon told me that the contacts and government officials that he met in prison proved to be lucrative; in fact, he was able to sell the land he acquired in prison to the city of Abomey. Although it now seems that Daǎ Adegbenon's income derives from diverse sources, he told me that he maintains his healing craft and even maintains partnerships with the government to promote his plant pharmacopeia.

When I asked Claude about the outcome of Adegbenon's case, he said that unfortunately nobody could prove anything, so justice was not served. But he added that because the healer was accused of dealing in human blood, his crimes were sufficiently reprehensible that he will never regain his former prestige: "I think that for him, nothing will be as before, but in today's world evil is gaining on good, so he will not lack any clientele for his dirty business. He will continue to be feared and avoided, but he will always be important because others will always come to him for his devilish works." Indeed, although Adegbenon does not appear to be suffering since his release from prison, there is still a degree of mistrust and suspicion. For example, during my stay with Claude in 2017, Claude's friend Didier approached us to announce his concern that Adegbenon had reportedly rented a house in our neighborhood. I asked, "Why is he renting a house on this side of town when he has his own home on the other side of Abomey?" "Exactly," said Didier. "Who knows what he's doing, but it's suspicious."

As I have demonstrated, the ambiguity between good and evil also figures into Beninese constructions of *àzĕ* as a science or a technological tool. One of the challenges to seeing *àzĕ* as a science is the positive connotations associated with scientific progress. Science is recognized to accomplish wonderful things like medicine, computers, and space exploration. But my Beninese friends have pointed out that science is also responsible for the creation of guns and bombs, which can kill mercilessly in the hands of a villain. Science and technology are associated with failed international development projects that seem to allow wealthy foreigners to get wealthier while Beninese remain poor. In this regard, Beninese might have a more honest view of science's ambivalence. In short, Beninese do not necessarily equate science solely with benevolent practical technology, because they conceive of both science and *àzĕ* as tools or instruments of power that are guided by the moral disposition of those who wield them rather than by an inherent quality in the tool. This does not strike me as too absurd for those outside of Africa to comprehend. Although there are limits to using Western popular culture as an analogy to African occult beliefs, I have tried to show that the themes of good and evil *àzĕ* are similar to contemporary Western portrayals of omnipotent superheroes and supervillains who are vulnerable to corruption and whose moral standing is often depicted as flexible and circumstantial. Whereas we are tempted to dismiss the comparison of fiction with real life, in a telling example of its usefulness, Rodrigue the artist once responded to my question of whether Westerners have witchcraft by saying that the Harry Potter stories show that the occult has a deep history in the West, so witchcraft must be universal.

Àzĕ also offers a model for causality and innovation and a universal language that touches on the source of the divine in people and in gods. Because of its reach into so many facets of life, *àzĕ* is a key window into Beninese culture; to examine witchcraft is to investigate much of what it means to live in Benin. *Àzĕ* is an overarching concept forcing observers to reckon with the connections between science, religion, morality, and the unpredictability of life. Such broad themes summon comparisons of *àzĕ* discourses not only to science but also to philosophical perspectives. Paulin Hountondji (1996) expresses unease at conflating lay perspectives with philosophy, especially if there is an implication that African peoples exhibit uniform consensus.[1] In fact, despite the general patterns I report, one of the points that I have stressed in this study is that my informants disagree about many aspects of *àzĕ* and *bŏ* in terms of whether they are related or not, voluntary or involuntary, potentially benevolent or solely evil, independent or connected to Vodun, psychic or material forces, similar to or different from Western witchcraft, and many other ways. Hountondji (2008) acknowledges that we may speak broadly of native conceptions of the world as a philosophy as long as we distinguish this from the professional academic discipline of philosophy. His point is well taken, and I do not mean to imply that *àzě* itself is a systematic philosophical discipline or that everyone is a philosopher. While ordinary people possess many of the basic ideas I mention, including the philosophical notions about *àzě* morality, it is especially professional healers and diviners who articulate the philosophical universalism that I discuss. Perhaps it would be better to follow V. Y. Mudimbe (1988) in using the term "gnosis" rather than "philosophy" to refer to African wisdom and ways of knowing. The notion of universality is a central feature of this gnosis. Those ritual specialists who espouse this universal view envision witchcraft as a supercategory comprising not only *àzě* but possibly also science, technology, the Vodun deities, Trɔ̃, Freemasonry, Christianity, Hindu mysticism, and Chinese healing.

Witchcraft is a dynamic category responding to and incorporating global flows of people and ideas. In reporting on the globalization of witchcraft, I am not merely conforming to an academic fad. In fact, although it is now axiomatic to see all cultures and religions as syncretic (Mary 2000), I was surprised to learn how intentionally people blended indigenous supernatural categories with foreign spiritualities. *Àzě* and *bǒ* are indigenous terms with local origins, but today it is impossible to understand them without reference to other parts of the world. Moreover, Beninese and African identities are undeniably defined by comparisons between local witchcraft and that of foreign, often white, others. The domain of *àzě* brings together foreign and local, traditional and modern, emphasizing the creative potential of reversal and continuous transformation. *Àzě* proves to be a vibrant, adaptive, and expansive concept that threatens to engulf religions and spiritual movements like Christianity, Trɔ̃, and Freemasonry. Thus, while it is common for Westerners to view African religion and witchcraft as ancient, timeless, traditional, and backward, Beninese people's tendency to redefine and reinvent in this very sphere illustrates instead a more postmodern understanding of life's indeterminacies, challenges, and opportunities. This is in keeping with Geschiere's (2013) observation that foreign borrowing and healers' deliberate associations with other places heighten their prestige and presumed power.[2] In fact, he adds that innovation and exoticism may be universal features of witchcraft, highlighting the modern and hybrid characteristics of the occult that I have described in this book. If *àzě* behaves in some ways like religion and appropriates both foreign and local religions, it becomes difficult to distinguish between religion and magic (Styers 2004). While Western sensibilities about religion's benevolence might hamper our ability to conceive of *àzĕ* as a religion, I hope this account has demonstrated that religious thought, like science, can carry a deep moral ambiguity, and this has not prevented other previously fringe beliefs like Wicca, Brazilian Candomblé, and Haitian Vodou from gaining religious legitimacy.

Although I acknowledge important differences in American and Beninese cultures and systems of thought, after years of interacting with Beninese people, I have come to believe that we are more similar than we are different. The early twentieth-century anthropologist Lucien Lévy-Bruhl recognized that one of the most important and challenging questions of the human sciences is to understand how others think. He concluded that other peoples with magical beliefs have a fundamentally different type of rationality, though "not wholly incomprehensible to us" (1926, 72). His approach provides a narrow opening through which an outsider can attempt to empathize with the Other, but I tend to agree with Stanley Jeyaraja Tambiah's (1990) more ambitious belief that some form of psychic unity is a feature of humanity. If we cannot understand or at least empathize with the Other, then the ethnographic study of challenging topics like witchcraft would be pointless, and we would have to accept that others are unknowable and that our worlds are incommensurable.

African witchcraft presents a serious challenge to cross-cultural understanding, reminding us that the questions raised by Lévy-Bruhl and Evans-Pritchard remain at the core of the anthropological enterprise. I admitted in chapter 3 that there are important barriers to understanding others' views of witchcraft, and it is impossible for me to feel or believe exactly what my Beninese friends do. However, the humanist side of me, with the aid of a phenomenological stance, has embraced my Beninese friends' perspectives and found they are not so foreign or inaccessible. By accepting the idea that we can adopt different modes of thought and entertain the existence of different types of realities, anthropologists can perhaps lessen the gap between African and Western worlds. I think the most significant contribution that anthropology can make is to bridge cultural divides by emphasizing our shared humanity and the need for respect across difference. British Ghanaian philosopher Kwame Anthony Appiah convincingly declares that reconciling the realities of African and Westerner, scientist and religious adherent, is crucial, because "unless all of us understand each other, and understand each other as reasonable, we shall not treat each other with the proper respect" (1992, 134). At a time of heightened racial tensions, anti-immigrant sentiment, terrorism, xenophobia, and the demonization of the Other, the anthropological potential to

reduce these barriers is more important than ever. These matters are especially pressing in light of the unequal relationship between more powerful
countries and those formerly colonized nations that have historically been
the targets of racist Western ideologies. That is why, in this text, I endeavor
to take my friends' positions seriously as a commitment to understand and
treat them with respect. For them, witchcraft does not "mean" or "represent"
something. It is simply a fact of life. They regard witchcraft as a phenomenon of nature, as something that can be understood through scientific examination. This is why nearly everybody calls *àzě* a science. Despite my social
scientific tendencies, I have tried to present their views of the natural and
supernatural worlds they inhabit and show that witchcraft forms an important part of their reality, one that is compelling and convincing for anyone,
including a foreign anthropologist. I have attempted to portray how people
both fear and crave witchcraft power and the ways that Beninese themselves
see witchcraft playing a pivotal role in the religious marketplace. Finally, I
have discussed how healers and others actively cultivate their knowledge of
both local and foreign versions of witchcraft in their quest for healing power.
For them, witchcraft, science, and religion are ultimately the same universal
force found throughout the world.

One of the intellectual and ethical challenges of this work has been to
reconcile two apparently different versions of reality, one based in scientific
rationalism and the other built on collective experiences with invisible forces.
As noted in chapter 2, the strain between these two versions of reality erupted
during a 2016 seminar at the University of Cape Town, where a student was
captured on social media arguing that Western science is a colonial enterprise
(UCT Scientist 2016). When the video went viral, it generated heated debate,
with numerous racist comments discrediting the woman as ignorant and
crazy or the product of delusional or leftist propaganda. The student pleaded
for a drastic decolonization of science and even proclaimed that science must
fall. I am sympathetic to this student's frustrations, and I condemn the offensive reactions to her views, but I am also cognizant of the line between re-
specting other lived worlds and advocating an extreme relativism where any
thought constitutes its own reality. Bruno Latour (2004), one of the most outspoken critics of science, has expressed regret over his earlier enthusiasm,
cautioning that arguing for a constructed view of reality may unintentionally
provide ammunition to fundamentalist extremists such as climate deniers
and other opponents of scientific evidence who deploy the same postmodern
constructivist arguments to advance their political agendas by undermining
the notion of scientific truth. I agree with Latour that science does contain its

own biases and subjective claims, but we should not throw out the baby with the bathwater. Instead, it is more useful to consider both realities as a form of construction. Therefore, I am not at war with science, and neither are my Beninese friends. Rather than see the debate between science and constructivism as an either/or decision, I prefer to accept that different viewpoints can coexist and that they provide a useful corrective to a one-sided reality. This is the kind of corrective to which I hope this book can contribute by providing Beninese people's alternative and widely held understandings of witchcraft, science, and religion.

Knowing what we know about the ravages of witchcraft fears in Africa, as well as about the colonial and missionary legacy on the continent, it is tempting to ask what we should "do" about witchcraft. Should *we* do anything at all? Asking such questions alone betrays an enduring paternalism in the West, whose neocolonial objectives continue to produce mixed results and plenty of resentment among African peoples. Nevertheless, the imprisonment and vigilante killings of accused witches appear so profoundly wrong that many observers feel compelled to take a stand. In the mainstream media and some academia, witchcraft is presented as a problem to be fixed, a social pathology that paralyzes people and destroys civil society (Topanou 2009). I follow Randall Styers (2004) in suggesting that such perceptions may derive from the inability to take seriously the ideas of others. I am sympathetic to those who devote time and energy to saving the lives of accused witches, but it is hard to avoid the specter of historically racist judgments about the "irrational" or "magical" thought of the inhabitants of the "Dark Continent." However, I am not advocating an extreme moral relativism that absolves any culture of brutal killings. Even if I accepted Westerners' responsibility to intervene in African affairs, I confess I have no foolproof recommendations for how to deal with the issue. However, as part of the corrective endeavor I mentioned above, I suggest that any policy, African or foreign, must take into account the Beninese lived world. Westerners cannot maintain a patronizing discourse about the African occult, as if witchcraft were a childish fantasy. We cannot continue to treat supernatural systems inconsistently, offering respect for established religions and disdain for witchcraft and other occult beliefs. Perhaps we should abandon once and for all the imaginary distinction between magic and religion and accept that witchcraft is a religion or even a science. This might add strength to a growing movement in Benin and elsewhere that seeks to legitimate witchcraft and bring it into the public domain, a process that could eliminate the secretive, negative aspects while still validating the experiences of millions of people on the African continent.

Glossary of Fon Terms

acɛ̀: power, signifying strong character, but also refers to mystical or supernatural power

àgǔ màgà: the chain used in Fá divination, also called *akplé*

Ajavodǔ: term for any deity deriving from the Aja region of Southwestern Benin, considered a stronghold of mystical power

akpakpò: wooden slab upon which offerings are made to Mĭnɔ̀nà̀

akplé: the chain used in Fá divination, also called *àgǔ màgà*

Alɔtɔdekɛ̀: religious court in Abomey that adjudicates transgressions by Vodun priests and adherents

amǎ (or *mǎ̀*): generic term for leaf, but also implies leaves used in magical and medicinal recipes

amǎɖatɔ́ (amǎwatɔ́): maker (preparer) of leaves; traditional healer

amasì̀: "leaf water," infusion or liquid medicine

atákǔ̃: a pepper used during incantations and in magical recipes

Atchigali (Atingale): an antiwitchcraft deity found throughout West Africa

atíkɛ̀: "tree powder"; pills or other dry medicine

àzɛ̌: supreme occult force; "witchcraft"

àzɛ̌-ká: calabash associated with *àzɛ̌*, perhaps the receptacle in which one's witchcraft power is held

àzètɔ́: one who possesses *àzɛ̌*; "witch"

àzɛ̌vodǔ: a divinity associated with *àzɛ̌*

àzɛ̌ wewé: benevolent (white) *àzɛ̌*

àzɛ̌ wiwi: malevolent (black) *àzɛ̌*

àzɛ̌-xɛ̀: witchcraft bird, especially owls and other night birds; spirit familiar of a witch

azɔ̃ɖatɔ́: literally, preparer of illness; "sorcerer"

àzɔ̃gblétɔ́: destroyer of illness; traditional healer

Banguele: one of several deities in the Trɔ̀ pantheon

bǒ: magical object or force; "sorcery"

bocíɔ̃: statuette imbued with supernatural power

bǒgbe: literally, "*bǒ* language"; incantation

bokɔ́nɔ̀: diviner initiated in the Fá divination system

botɔ́ (boɖatɔ́, bowatɔ́): master (preparer or maker) of *bǒ*; "sorcerer" *bŏvodū*: a magical force, perhaps reflecting a link between *bŏ* and the Vodun religion

cakatú: mystical "gun," an aggressive *bŏ* used to attack an enemy

Dã: in the Vodun pantheon, the deity associated with water, snakes, and wealth

Daǎ: honorific title for the head of a family collective

dù: sign in the Fá divination system; there are 256 *dù*

Egungun: Yoruba ancestor cult adopted by Fon people; Kútítɔ́

Fá: the Fon divination system; a means of communicating with deities

fu-mɛji: one of the Fá divination signs associated with *àzĕ*

Gambada (Garbala/Gabada): one of several deities in the Trɔ̃ pantheon

Gbadu: deity associated with the Fá divination system

Gbigbɔwèwé: the Celestial Church of Christ, or a member of this church

gorovodū̃: "kola nut deity"; generic term for Trɔ̃ and related deities

Gŭ: in the Vodun pantheon, the deity of iron

Hoxo: twin, considered a divine being

jɔtɔ́: ancestral soul inherited by a descendant of the deceased

ká gohŭ: bumpy calabash, used to make the *àzĕ-ká*

Kēnesì: one of two *àzĕvodū*; Kēnesì seems to be associated more with men

kloloɛ (kulele): owl

kpējigā: first-stage initiate into the Trɔ̃ society

kpetɔ deka (and *kpetɔ ve*): first (and second) versions of the Trɔ̃ order

kpɔlí: a person's individual sign in the Fá divination system

kuɖiɔ: "death exchange"; refers to any ritual meant to save or replace the soul of a witch-craft victim

Kunde: one of several deities in the Trɔ̃ pantheon

Kútítɔ́: ghost or ancestor; Fon equivalent of the Yoruba Egungun cult

Lɛ̆gbà: key deity in the Vodun pantheon; an intermediary between people and other deities

lĭdɔ̃́: one of the components of the soul

Lisá (or Sɛgbo-Lisá): sun deity, often considered male, of the Vodun pantheon; sometimes regarded as part of a duality with the deity Mǎwŭ

Mami Wata: deity of the sea, beauty, and wealth

Mǎwŭ: supreme creator god, though sometimes regarded as part of the Mǎwŭ-Lisá duality

Mewi Hwendo: native custom; refers to Benin's Catholic Church policy of adapting Christianity to local culture

Mĭnɔ̃nǎ: with Kēnesì, one of two *àzĕvodū*; regarded as the *vodū̃* associated with *àzĕ*, female sexuality and motherhood

Nēsúxué: ancestor cult of the royal family in Abomey

Oro: a secret spiritual society popular in Yoruba-speaking regions

Sakpatá: in the Vodun pantheon, deity of the earth and smallpox

sa-mɛji: one of the Fá divination signs associated with *àzĕ*

sé: one component of the soul; the part that is displaced during spirit possession and that is attacked by an *àzètɔ́*

soɖabì: palm liquor

Tɔxósú: in the Vodun pantheon, the water deity associated with deformed and stillborn children

Trɔ̀: a pantheon of deities, borrowed from Togo for its power in combatting *àzě*

turukpē-mɛji: one of the Fá divination signs associated with *àzě*

vɛvɛ: corn flour design sprinkled on the ground, used in some Vodun rituals

Vodou: Haitian Afro-Caribbean religion, derived from West African Vodun

Vodun: the indigenous animistic religion of Southern Benin

vodũ̀: deity

vodũ̀sì: literally, "wife of the *vodũ̀*"; an initiate into a Vodun secret society

vodũ̀nɔ̀: owner, or guardian of a *vodũ̀*; a Vodun priest

Voodoo: the African-derived religion practiced in Louisiana and other parts of North America

wēnsagũ: a component of one's soul, or perhaps a spiritual "messenger" that helps carry out occult actions

wútútú: one of several birds associated with *àzě*; it makes a series of sharp hooting noises, leading to its name

Xɛbiosò: in the Vodun pantheon, the deity of thunder and lightning

Xuélú: a deity that protects the home and its residents

xunɔ̀: term for a priest of Trɔ̀

xunɔ̀gā: the leader of all Trɔ̀ *xunɔ̀* in Benin

yɛ̀: an aura or "shadow" of one's soul

yovó: European, white person, or generic foreigner

Zàgbétɔ́: deity that guards the community at night

zemijā: motorcycle taxi

Notes

Introduction

1. With the exception of my friend and assistant Chams Linkpon and his mother, Mouni, all names used in this book are pseudonyms.

2. Griots are traditional bards who sing songs to honor individuals or families.

3. Many scholars of Africa note the apparent increase in witchcraft concern and discourse, though Henrietta Moore and Todd Sanders (2001) point out that similar claims were reported beginning in the 1930s and that it is difficult to accurately measure whether witchcraft preoccupations are truly on the rise.

4. Latour (1993) similarly argues that the distinction between modern and premodern is more a myth of wishful thinking.

5. Although Geschiere (1997) is closely associated with modernity studies in witchcraft, he does not employ the same functionalist framework to explain witchcraft's manifestations.

6. Birgit Meyer (1999) reports that *adze* existed in precolonial times among the neighboring Ewe.

Chapter 1. *Àzě* and *Bǒ*

1. Though Fon is the dominant language and a lingua franca of southern Benin, there are fifty-four different languages spoken in Benin (Ethnologue.com), so there are other language-specific terms for the various occult forces.

2. But, as noted above, kinship is never far removed from witchcraft discourses, since the primary motive for witchcraft (i.e., envy) is a preeminent family affair, which means that fear and suspicion nearly always fall along kinship lines. And Geschiere (2013, 21) points out that membership in the witchcraft society typically requires the sacrifice of a relative, another theme I address in this book.

3. There are different components of the soul: the *sé* (life force), the *yè* (shadow), the *jɔtɔ́* (ancestral soul), and the *lìdɔ́* (spirit). Some people admitted to me that they do not know the difference between the *sé* and *lìdɔ́*, and in my experience, most people tend to use *sé* as the basic term for soul. Bernard Maupoil (1943, 379) identifies an additional component of the soul, known as *wēnsugū*, probably referring to *wēnsagū*, which I was

told is a sort of messenger spirit that animates the actions of *àzĕ*, *bŏ*, and the deities and that acts as a force of justice to settle a score, like a guardian angel. One diviner characterized Fá (the divination deity) as God's *wĕnsagŭ* or spokesperson, and another friend said that deceased individuals are also *wĕnsagŭ* because they can take a message to the world of the dead.

4. Beginning in the 1970s, the former Marxist president Kérékou repressed religion and launched antiwitchcraft campaigns, ordering the imprisonment of suspected witches and the destruction of sacred trees (Bierschenk and Sardan 2003; Kahn 2011; Tall 1995a).

5. In fact, Melville Herskovits ([1938] 1967, 2:299) referred to *àzètɔ́* as "vampires," and there is an obvious correlation between the European and African traditions' preoccupation with birds of the night and the extraction of blood or life force. As Katharina Wilson (1985) notes, some speculate that the word "vampire" derives from the Turkish word *uber*, meaning "witch." In referring to *àzètɔ́* today, people place more emphasis on owls and other birds than on bats. And yet, elsewhere Herskovits ([1938] 1967, 2:243–44, 287) discusses evil people whom he calls *azɔ̌ɖatɔ́* (literally, "preparer of illness") and who are responsible for zombie slaves and other nefarious acts. He writes that these people are "organized into a close guild. They exercise power over the souls of those who have not had a proper burial and therefore wander about the earth discontented, and over those souls procured by 'killing' their owners in the manner described above. These *azɔ̌ɖatɔ́* are to be recognized by their blood-shot eyes, and Dahomeans stealthily point out two or three such persons in the market-place who usually may be remarked to be doing somewhat better business than those who sit near them. These dangerous individuals change into bats at night, or assume other animal forms and go forth to hold council together or to perform their dark deeds" (2:287). While people rarely mentioned anything like zombies to me, Herskovits's *azɔ̌ɖatɔ́* are otherwise remarkably similar to *àzètɔ́*.

6. But one informant claimed that using *àzĕ* allows *àzètɔ́* to extend their lives by usurping their victims' life force.

7. Another informant said that an *àzètɔ́* attempting to attack someone who is naturally immune will find the magic turning back on herself or himself.

8. A healer added that witches must confess or they will defecate on themselves in their bed. A few informants suggested that those who have murdered through *bŏ* (rather than *àzĕ*) are the ones who confess on their deathbeds. And still others claim that both categories of people will confess, provided that they have committed evil deeds and provided that their death is slow and predictable rather than a sudden accident.

9. In "Anthropologie du bo," Beninese scholar Jean-Marie Apovo (1995) describes *bŏ* in detail.

10. Blier's primary interest is *bocɔ́* sculptures, which are anthropomorphic *bŏ*, but she gives a thorough account of the logic and meaning of *bŏ* more generally. Blier acknowledges *àzètɔ́* as people who travel mystically at night but otherwise says little about them and at times seems to collapse the two powers under the term "sorcery."

11. Incantations are generically called *gbesisa*, and those used for *bŏ* are *bŏgbe* (literally, "*bŏ* language").

12. See Herskovits ([1938] 1967, 2:264) for a list of *bŏ* (which he calls *gbŏ*) and their purposes.

13. Other formulae are reported by Gbenoukpo Bodehou Dah-Lokonon (1997) and Herskovits ([1938] 1967, 2:264–88).

14. Caribbeanists will note that this usage of *vɛvɛ* differs from that in Haiti, where a distinct corn flour design is made for each deity prior to a possession ceremony and, to my knowledge, has no connection with twins (see Brown 2001; Desmangles 1992; Herskovits [1937] 1971). In the Abomey area where I have interacted most with religious specialists, I have never witnessed *vɛvɛ* used for possession ceremonies, but Pierre Fatúmbí Verger (1954, 88) mentions the use of *vɛvɛ* during a Sakpatá possession ceremony in Abomey.

15. As noted above, birds and owls have an important connection to *àzĕ*, and although this is a recipe for a *bŏ*, it is logical that sympathetic magic would be employed to allow birds and owls to also be used to protect against *àzĕ*.

16. As with the example of owls (see the previous note), this is another illustration of *bŏ* using sympathetic magic.

17. Herskovits ([1938] 1967, 2:109) also suggests an important connection between the sacredness of trees (and the tree god Lokó) and the fact that tree leaves are used for magical and medicinal purposes.

18. Herskovits ([1938] 1967, 2:258) uses the term *azɔ̃ɖatɔ́* (preparer of illness) for one who kills by magic or *bŏ*, though he later conflates *azɔ̃ɖatɔ́* with individuals who control zombies and shapeshift (2:287).

19. See Augé (1976, 130) for a discussion of methods for transmitting witchcraft in Ivory Coast.

20. Another informant said that anyone with supernatural powers must transfer them to someone; before dying, his father warned people that three things would fall from him at the moment of his death, and the family was to guard these things well. And just as his father had foretold, three magical objects (*bŏ*) fell from his body: a string he wore, a ring, and another string that was inside his arm. A university student said that an *àzètɔ́* who kills someone while the victim is pregnant will automatically transfer the power to her unborn child.

21. A female teacher in Cotonou also said that the perceived gender imbalance in the number of *àzètɔ́* could be a false impression due to the fact that men are more secretive in their use of this power.

22. There was incomplete consensus on this topic; some claimed ignorance about the gender of the leaders or held the opposite—that men sat atop the *àzètɔ́* hierarchy.

23. R. P. B. Segurola's dictionary (1963) and Christine Henry (2008b) both offer the same translation, though an ordinary translation of "our mothers" would be *nɔ̃ mĭtɔ́ lɛ*. Some informants suggested that Mĭnɔ̃nà̀ must be an archaic syntactic construction. Herskovits ([1938] 1967, 2:260) translates Mĭnɔ̃nà̀ as "our mother Na." Andrew Apter (1991, 222) says that the Yoruba expression for witch, *ìyá wa*, also means "our mothers," and witchcraft is symbolically linked to the fertility deity Yemoja.

24. One healer said that the name Mĭnɔ̃nà̀ means *àzètɔ́*, and their leader is called Nā Ayinɔ̃ (literally, "princess owner of the land").

25. The *atákũ* pepper holds mystical properties and is frequently chewed while one recites incantations as a way of boosting the power of a *bŏ* (Blier 1995, 79–80). The left hand is employed for magical and religious purposes because, as one man put it, it is the opposite hand and therefore should be used for things of the other world (164).

26. One village man said that after giving birth, a woman touches the umbilical cord, and it transmits power to the child to become successful and wealthy. But, he said, if the child grows up and fails to show his mother respect, she can ruin his life, and he concluded by saying that her angry response is the manifestation of *àzĕ*.

27. See also Brandes (1981), Gilmore (1990), and Swartz (1982) on women's informal or behind-the-scenes exercise of power.

28. When prompted, this man acknowledged that older menopausal women can enter the sacred forest and become diviners.

29. Brain (1982) uses a combination of structuralist and psychoanalytical approaches to explain the gender asymmetry contained in witchcraft. While my data tend to support his interpretation, particularly the feminist implications, I avoid the universalist claims and psychological assumptions in favor of a more modest reliance on my specific data and the imagery evoked by the discourse.

30. Maupoil (1943, 447) cited an expression from the *yeku-mɛji* divination sign about the deity Sɛgbo-Lisá never wearing only one cloth. He wrote that it represents the reversal between the status of rich and poor people.

31. *Àzè-xè* may be a generic term for night birds, but it is the most common term for owls. Nevertheless, one informant offered the word *kloloɛ*, and another mentioned *kulele* and *agbigbi* as referring to owls. Blier (1995, 310, 420n49) cites birds with similar significance: *kolele* (*kloloɛ* or *kulele?*) *agbidi* (*agbigbi?*), and *avesikpui*, the first two of which she says are nocturnal. Blier (227, 410n56) also identifies the association between witchcraft and weaver birds and vultures.

Chapter 2. Black and White

1. Birgit Meyer (1999, 90) reports that the nearby Ewe people of Togo probably formerly had a more ambiguous conception of witchcraft (*adze*) that allowed for both good and evil.

2. Some people named a third variety—red *àzĕ*—which resembles black *àzĕ* in performing evil deeds. One informant said that the red type is what destroys people's possessions and causes them to lose their money.

3. The currency in Benin is the franc of the Communauté Financière Africaine, abbreviated as FCFA. During the period of fieldwork, the exchange rate was roughly 500 FCFA per US dollar.

4. A similar duality is found in related religious traditions, as in Haiti and Togo, where hot and cold, male and female, and other binary oppositions are central to ordering the religious world (see Brown 2001; Rosenthal 1998).

5. By contrast, as discussed in chapter 1, one of the most frequent changes reported in *àzĕ* was the fact that today's *àzètɔ́* are often children.

6. Although I have not heard of zombies in Bénin, Herskovits ([1938] 1967, 2:243) reported that sorcerers possess the ability to transform people into zombie slaves, which

does bear a striking resemblance to Haitian folk culture. Geschiere (1998) and Jean-François Bayart (1993) also note a new type of *ekong* witchcraft, whereby witches transform victims into zombies rather than eating them. Some informants report that the Yoruba secret society of Oro performs a similar regulatory function. This is separate from the Alɔtɔdekɛ̃ court, which is a religious court in Abomey whose purpose is to adjudicate violations of religious protocol among Vodun priests and adepts. Wade Davis's (1985) somewhat controversial reports of Haitian secret occult societies emphasized the possibility of a link to the Efik traditions in Nigeria, though there are other possible origins in the secret religious societies of present-day Benin and Nigeria.

7. And *àzĕ* clearly parallels European alchemists' merging of magical and scientific theories.

8. Geschiere (2013, 10) encountered similar contradictory views from his Cameroonian informants, and he argues that this "elasticity" may be the source of witchcraft's ability to adjust and survive in new and dynamic situations.

9. One healer told me of a special lotion to put on your face, saying it gives you good *àzĕ* (*wewé*), which allows you to see witches in your sleep and talk to them. But if you touch it to your tongue, you automatically become evil and are forced to eat people.

10. The recipe is provided in chapter 4.

11. However, as noted in the previous chapter, there are other French terms that can be used to distinguish between the two occult forces.

12. An elderly man defined *bŏ* as medicine and said that people must adhere to the specific ingredients to produce medicines with clearly marked labels, the way that white people do with pharmaceuticals.

13. One informant said that he was once thinking about his mother when she phoned him, a demonstration of the invisible forces that operate between people.

14. Numerous informants referred to *àzĕ* in connection with wavelengths, cell phone technology, or other special communicative methods. For example, a woman told me that *àzètɔ́* can send a spell over the phone to make you go crazy, so she is often wary of answering a call from an unknown number. She said that in such cases, she will answer the call but just listen, because malevolent magic can only work when voices are in direct contact.

15. She added that today's *àzètɔ́* no longer demand only sacrifices in return for releasing a human victim; instead, they increasingly require money or technology like telephones and videos as gifts of appeasement.

16. Among the neighboring Yoruba, Barry Hallen (2001) reports that witches are also understood as superintelligent.

17. Similarly, a judge remarked on airplane technology, saying, "C'est du genie. . . . Ce genie existe en sorcellerie, en Afrique ici" (It's genius. . . . This genius exists in witchcraft here in Africa). Interestingly, similar views of witchcraft are found in European traditions of the occult, since Carolyn Morrow Long (2001, 10) reports that the Old English meaning of witchcraft (wiccecraeft) suggested a witch's "knowledge."

18. Although most *yovó* are white foreigners, and light-skinned or albino Africans are playfully called *yovó*, the term does not solely index skin color. African Americans

are often called *yovó*, which suggests that the word carries connotations of non-African identity and culture.

19. One village man reassured me that since *yovó* do not have *àzĕ*, I have nothing to fear from witchcraft.

20. Similarly, Camille the entertainer said that Beninese could learn from *yovó* how to use *àzĕ* to help society advance.

21. Keith Basso (1979) presents another example of the way discourses of the "other" define self and morality for Western Apache while they humorously parody the dominant white ethnic group.

22. Although he did not provide details, this divination may have been performed by consulting the spirit Mami Wata, whose divination frequently uses mirrors.

23. However, Crystal Biruk (2011) observes in Malawi that white researchers are often rumored to be "bloodsuckers" whose work extracts both wealth and life force from African people (see also Isichei [2002] and White [1993] on vampire suspicions in East Africa). She notes that witchcraft is attributed to kin, while bloodsucking is attributed to foreigners.

24. Stephen Ellis and Gerrie ter Haar even suggest that "the evolving political language of Africa tends to regard politics as a metaphor for movements in a spirit world rather than vice versa" (1998, 186).

Chapter 3. Whose Reality?

1. Friedson (1996) offers another example of a courageous phenomenological account of belief and spirit possession in Timbuka religion and healing in Malawi.

2. Although Geschiere's (2000, 2003) work deals with witchcraft's relationship to modern socioeconomic changes, he does not use the same distancing theory; instead, he insists on the need for anthropologists to engage with African notions of reality.

3. Elsewhere, Ashforth (2008) has stated that he made a conscious effort to "suspend disbelief" and "remain agnostic" in order to carry out his research.

4. Ashforth has expressed similar dissatisfaction with the inadequacy of social science interpretation: "Framing of the problem as located in the realms of discourse, idiom, or ideation failed to comprehend either the complexity of the politics of relations among forces shaping my Sowetan friends' lives . . . or the possible implications of these ways of living with and managing relations for governance and politics in a democratic African state" (2008, 5). Niehaus (2013) also critiques current anthropological theory on witchcraft, suggesting that it is too deterministic and fails to address microlevel explanations. His biography of a friend who died amid fears of witchcraft attacks is an example of the fine-grained, idiosyncratic factors involved in witchcraft phenomena.

5. Although West does not adopt the same view of reality as his audience, he concludes that "sorcery constituted a language through which the Muedans with whom I worked comprehended and—even if euphemistically—commented on the workings of power in their midst" (2007, 11).

6. Douglas (1970) finds similar fault with some functionalist anthropologists, who, while they may not believe in witchcraft, justify others' beliefs by virtue of their functions. She suggests that anthropologists have a duty to be more critical of beliefs like witchcraft.

7. Siegel (2006, 14) points out that in many African cases, accused witches are in fact executed, rather than pardoned, so confession would be illogical in such cases. He also notices that Stevenson's account offers evidence that it was more likely her intervention that spared the boy rather than his confession.

8. Here I distinguish consensus regarding the existence of witchcraft from consensus over the definition and understanding of witchcraft. As noted before, there is little agreement among informants over what witchcraft is and how it works, but there is wide agreement that witchcraft exists. In that regard, I concur with Fields about the power of socialization to shape people's beliefs.

9. Geschiere (2000) finds that magical apprenticeship is increasingly common among today's anthropologists. Castaneda (1968) is one notable, though notorious, example of magical apprenticeship. He has been criticized for misrepresenting and even falsifying his account of apprenticeship with a Yaqui sorcerer.

10. Nyamjoh (2001) believes that African elites are equivocal, preferring to keep one foot in each world rather than choose.

11. Or worse, that rumor is a social pathology, a symptom of anxiety and uncertainty (see Aldrin [2003] for a review of theoretical approaches to rumor).

12. During my interview with one of the court employees, a man knocked on the door and came in to exchange a few words. In an odd coincidence, after the man left, my interviewee told me the visitor was himself an *àzètɔ́* and that he admits it freely.

13. In fact, James ([1890] 1913, 299) equated "primitive" people's thought with the dreams, hallucinations, and uncritical thought of children.

14. Franz Boas reportedly had a Kwakiutl friend who was initiated as a shaman with the intent of unmasking the fictional nature of shamanism, but he became so embedded in the work that he eventually became a believer (Lévi-Strauss 1964).

15. It has been suggested that Neopaganism may be an expression of frustration with modernity and rationality (Ivakhiv 1996; Lewis 1996), in which case it bears a resemblance to Africans' fascination with the occult.

16. However, Geschiere also acknowledges that new Pentecostal pastors are reviving accusations that Candomblé is nothing more than black magic.

Chapter 4. Religion and the Occult

1. In contrast to Christianity, Vodun does not evangelize or seek converts.

2. Islam is also a prominent religion, especially among northern Beninese in Cotonou, and it has its own relationship with witchcraft and magic. But in general, Islam is uncommon among the primarily Fon-speaking people whom I encountered in southern Benin, so I am unqualified to offer an analysis of how Islam responds to occult threats.

3. An NGO official told me she knew about two girls who were discovered teleporting from the town of Attogon to Porto-Novo (forty miles).

4. Another person said that when you approach a sleeping *àzètɔ́*, your head swells and you shiver.

5. As described in chapter 2, such a formula could be seen as *àzě* itself, demonstrating one of the ways *àzě* resembles *bǒ*.

6. A *wútútú* bird, though not a nocturnal species, is associated with witchcraft. It makes a sharp sound, from which the bird derives its onomatopoetic name.

7. See Alokpo (1996), Henry (2008b), and Mayrargue (2002) for the history of Christian denominations in Bénin.

8. See Clément (1996), Alladaye (2003), and Bonfils (1999) for the history of the Catholic Church in Benin.

9. Islam is the dominant religion in the north of Benin, so the proportion of Muslims is significantly lower in the southern regions where I worked. For example, in the Atlantic Department, where Cotonou is located, 37 percent are Catholic, 28 percent practice traditional religion, and less than 4 percent are Muslim. In the Zou Department, where Abomey is located, 26 percent are Catholic, 42 percent practice traditional religion, and 3 percent are Muslim (INSAE 2003, 22).

10. An elderly Abomey man declared that pure faith is uncommon, even among priests, and he cited the recent international pedophilia scandals in the Catholic Church as an example of priests' corrupt faith.

11. Henry (2008a, 203) indicates that patients are kept for one, three, seven, or twenty-one days in order to protect them from witchcraft attacks.

12. One informant is now an advocate for self-empowerment and argues that organized religion is unnecessary if people can tap their own inner spiritual strength.

13. In my experience, the relationship between Catholics and Celestial Christians seems particularly heated, though Henry (2008b) claims that evangelicals are especially likely to condemn the Celestial Church for syncretism.

14. A Cotonou businessman held that even Celestial Church leaders who have power eventually find that it fades when they are unable to live up to the expectations to be pure and faithful. Then they are forced to look to *àzĕ* to fill the void. He confided that this is how his own uncle, a Celestial Church member, became an *àzètɔ́*. My informant said that he sees his uncle at night during his nocturnal travels, but they never speak about it.

15. A Sakpatá *vodŭ́nɔ̃* offered a slightly different version of this relationship, claiming that Christian pastors do not possess *àzĕ* themselves; instead, they negotiate with *àzètɔ́* for the liberation of their victims.

16. Although she is a woman, she and her followers insist on the male status of God. While she is possessed by God, she is referred to with masculine French pronouns.

17. Others suspected that she is empowered by the spirit Mami Wata. At the time of this writing (October 2017), Parfaite is also embroiled in a legal scandal following the deaths of a number of her followers in January 2017. According to reports, she instructed her congregation to light incense in their closed homes and to pray through the night. When several people died of asphyxiation near Porto-Novo, some of her priests were arrested. In September 2017 media outlets reported that in the course of the investigation Parfaite was summoned to appear before a judge but that she had failed to appear and might be evading the authorities. One friend speculated that because there are rumored ties between Parfaite and President Talon's administration, she may be receiving assistance from the highest levels of the government.

18. A Celestial Christian told me that God's power is manifest not only in Christianity but everywhere, including in Vodun.

19. I am grateful to my Beninese colleagues Hippolyte Amouzouvi and Didier Dahounto for discussions about this expression and the religious tension it embodies.

20. *Kpetɔ* seems to be an Ewe word, possibly meaning "one who wields the stone" (Judy Rosenthal, personal communication, January 11, 2012, though Montgomery and Vannier (2017) translate *kpetɔ deka* and *kpetɔ ve* as "first prayer place" and "second prayer place," respectively. During Trɔ̃'s divination, the priest bangs a stone on the ground, and the Trɔ̃ installation ceremony I attended involved a number of large rocks being buried. However, my friend Didier claimed that *kpetɔ* means "skull" and refers to the practice of using the powder from ground skull bones to trace the Fá divination signs.

21. Some other Ajavodũ that people cited were Koku, Molu, and the well-known Atchigali (Atingale) that spread throughout West Africa in the 1940s (Apter 1993; Henry 2008a; Rosenthal 1998; Tall 1995b). One informant told me that Molu is particularly effective in identifying witches by possessing an adept who jumps on trees, cuts his own body, and circulates around town pulling *àzètɔ́* out of the crowd. The accused fall to the ground and confess everything. Although most of the popular antiwitchcraft deities are recent imports, one informant told me that the ancient deity Age also fights witchcraft.

22. A *xunɔ̃* (Trɔ̃ priest) from a village near Bohicon stated that the deity comes from Sahelian regions near Saudi Arabia. A Cotonou day laborer said he used to belong to Gabada, calling it a *vodũ* from Ghana that combined deities from the North and South.

23. Of course, not everyone believes in Trɔ̃'s efficacy, and one unfortunate woman told me that her mother, who suffered from a supernatural attack, sought the aid of Trɔ̃, but it did not prevent her death.

24. One informant showed me a bracelet made by a Trɔ̃ priest to embody Trɔ̃'s power of witchcraft protection.

25. He told me that a foreigner like me with my local ties would easily pay 40,000 or 50,000 FCFA ($80 or $100), still considered a bargain compared to the tourist rate.

26. Other informants reported that both Banguele and Gambada like cigarettes and drink gin.

27. However, one *xunɔ̃* I met boasted to me that he was responsible for chasing off Jehovah's Witnesses missionaries from a village. This was the same *xunɔ̃* who advised me to pay for a ceremony to protect my wife from another man's advances.

28. According to Chams, the previous *xunɔ̃gá* of Ouidah died, leaving two sons. One son, Chams's friend the *xunɔ̃gá*, was illiterate and remained faithful to his father's tradition, *kpetɔ deka*. The second son was literate and split off to form a more modern version of Trɔ̃, *kpetɔ ve*.

29. See D. Rush (2013) for one account by an art historian. See Montgomery and Vannier (2017) and Rosenthal (1998) on Togolese Vodu.

30. I do not offer an extensive description of Vodun and divination, which have received thorough treatment by Herskovits ([1938] 1967), Herskovits and Herskovits (1933), and Maupoil (1943). Since these scholars' research in the 1930s, Vodun has certainly changed and been confronted by competing religious influences, but the core concepts and practices remain largely intact in terms of ritual specialists' roles, the initiation process (though it is much shorter), spirit possession, sacrifices/offerings, and the role of

divination as a source of supernatural knowledge. For a more recent account by an art historian, see D. Rush (2013).

31. See Blier (1995, 38–40) for a discussion of the possible etymologies of the word *vodú*.

32. Christians often refer to Măwŭ as Aklúnɔ̀ (Lord). Măwŭ was previously (and still sometimes is) regarded as one part of a creator couple named Măwŭ-Lisá, but, perhaps because of Christian missionaries' translation of God as Măwŭ, the term Măwŭ now typically refers to a supreme creator god (Claffey 2007). Other possible creator deities are Dada Ségbó and Nană-Bulukŭ. Despite these uncertainties, most people today use Măwŭ to refer to the highest spiritual entity, though Olabiyi Yai (1993) argues that the notion of a monotheistic creator god is a foreign introduction from Christian missionaries.

33. See Apter (1991) for similar associations regarding Yoruba witchcraft.

34. A Sakpatá priest said that Mĭnɔ̀nà̀ is the female equivalent of the important male deity Lègbà.

35. While Herskovits acknowledges the connection between the witch-like *azɔ̀ɖatɔ́* and Mĭnɔ̀nà̀ ([1938] 1967, 2:287), he also claims that Mĭnɔ̀nà̀ is responsible for *bŏ* (260), thus implicitly conflating *àzě* and *bŏ*.

36. Blier (1995, 34) contends that Kēnesì literally means a "wife who knows grudges," derived from the words *kē* (grudge), *ne* (to know), and *si* (wife). Though I agree that Kēnesì as witchcraft is closely related to rancor and envy, I am unfamiliar with this meaning of *ne*, and I wonder instead if *ne* might be *nē* (male genitalia), reflecting the gender dichotomy between Kēnesì and Mĭnɔ̀nà̀.

37. But a *vodŭnɔ̀* healer said that Kēnesì can be lethal if its owner fails to initiate a successor before his death. In such cases, he said, Kēnesì can kill the whole family.

38. A Cotonou diviner said that men do more good with *àzě*, but when they perform malevolent *àzě*, they are actually called Akunā. He explained that Akunā is not a *vodú* but rather something you eat. But then he informed me that Kēnesì means Akunā and that these are equivalent to the deity Gbadu. However, a *vodŭnɔ̀* told me that Akunā is the same as Mĭnɔ̀nà̀.

39. The *àgŭ màgà*, also called the *akplé*, is a string to which are attached eight split seed pods (from mango or *asrɔ́* fruit). Bokɔ̀nɔ̀ cast the *àgŭ màgà* and read the orientation of face-up and face-down seed pods as one of the 256 possible divination signs (*dù*). Cowry shells and kola nuts can also be used for divination.

40. Maupoil (1943, 508) reported that *sa-mɛji* is derived from the Yoruba *asa-mɛji*, meaning "two thighs," evoking the vagina, which *sa-mɛji* commands.

41. Another informant offered a different interpretation, saying *sa-mɛji* means that somebody is being attacked by witchcraft.

42. A female informant said that Mĭnɔ̀nà̀'s shrine is constructed from red earth and must have a flag nearby to bring air to the shrine. She said that the shrine's material components symbolize all menopausal women in the home.

43. A Porto-Novo man told me that Mĭnɔ̀nà̀'s preferred offerings include certain parts of the chicken, along with powdered pepper and red corn dough.

44. An Abomey friend noted that his father owns a Mĭnɔ̀nà̀ shrine, but he keeps it in a calabash under his bed rather than exposing it in the open (evoking accounts of the *àzě*

calabash). Other informants in Abomey showed me a Kēnesì shrine to which they said they made offerings to protect their household from *àzě*.

45. In addition to Mǐnɔ̄nǎ, Kēnesì, and Lɛ̆gbà, there is another protective domestic spirit named Xuélú. Gaston said that Xuélú is the same as Mǐnɔ̄nǎ, but another friend denied this, saying they are distinct and have their own shrines. A healer told me that Xuélú is a guardian of the house, which corroborates claims that Xuélú keeps justice in the home. Like an ordeal, if people are suspected of adultery or some other wrongdoing, they can be made to swear before Xuélú. If they lie, they will suffer serious consequences. (Another man told me that a woman suspected of adultery must perform this ritual before the Mǐnɔ̄nǎ shrine.) A similar role of protection and adjudication is also performed by a family's Tɔ́xwiɔ́, a deity associated with the founding ancestor. Still another informant argued that Xuélú is not a deity but a ritual performed when a new house is built.

46. Melville Herskovits and Frances Herskovits (1933, 37–38) and Jacques Bertho (1951) provide detailed lists of the leaves and other ingredients and rituals involved in the installation of new *vodǔ*.

47. In fact, the deity Gbadu, which is so important in the operation of Fá, is etymologically linked to the calabash, since the term is derived from the Yoruba expression "Igba Odou" (calabash of odu), that is, calabash of the Fá signs (*dù* in Fon) (Bertho 1951).

Chapter 5. Healing and the Globalization of Witchcraft

1. But in one case, a Cotonou healer told me that his government identification card says he is a *vodǔnɔ̄*, though he denies any association with the deities and makes no sacrifices. This is a telling example of how *vodǔnɔ̄* and healers are often conflated, especially by outside authorities.

2. One cannot necessarily take the claims of such large payments at face value. Though I believe healers can charge exorbitant amounts, other informants told me that healers probably exaggerate their fees to brag or to impress the *yovó* (white person / foreigner).

3. When shown the photo of ritual items on the road (see figure 11), informants explained that the terracotta blocks are known as *vɔkɔ* and are often carved with features representing the victim. Most people identified the items collectively as a *kuɖiɔ*.

4. *Kútítɔ́* is the Fon equivalent of the well-known Yoruba Egungun, or Egun, masquerade cult. A Kútítɔ́ *vodǔnɔ̄* is usually addressed by the title Baale.

5. My friend Didier agreed that only those initiated into *àzě* can heal *àzě* illness, but he argued that the animal offering is only a symbolic gesture; people may leave food at a crossroads or under a baobab or iroko tree, but in reality dogs, rather than *àzètɔ́*, will eat it. According to him, the only thing that matters is that negotiation leads to the *àzètɔ́* releasing the victim. Another man denied altogether that *àzɔ̄gblétɔ́* have *àzě*, stating that they get results solely through negotiation.

6. It is true that a certain species of snake is sacred in Ouidah, and people there may hold or carry snakes to the temple, but in my experience most other people are fearful of snakes and generally kill them whenever possible.

7. Interestingly, James Siegel (2006, 164) observed a fascination with ninjas in Indonesia, where they were associated with foreign, hidden powers.

8. There are other esoteric movements in Benin, such as the Fraternité Universelle Blanche, though I know little about them and therefore restrict my comments to the three societies discussed here.

9. He also told me about a similar religious order called Mikaly, in which the master controls a light emanating from his hand that provokes spiritual experiences in the followers.

10. He described Eckankar as lacking a formal leadership, with only an Eck master to advise and guide people in their spiritual activities. Members, known as chela, pay an annual fee—in his case, about 45,000 FCFA ($90) per year.

11. The Indians I have seen on TV are relatively light-skinned; therefore, the label of *yovó* (white person) is understandable. But in general, most Beninese do not perceive racial distinctions between Europeans and Indians. Indeed, people are often unaware of the country of origin of a *yovó* visitor and tend to lump all *yovó* into a single undifferentiated category (much in the way Americans tend to do with all Africans).

12. The book was *Miracles de la Guérison Pranique* (Sui 2003), a translation of *Miracles through Pranic Healing*.

13. His explanation bears a similarity to the distinctions between *àzě* and *bǒ*: *bǒ* are regarded as tangible creations, and *àzě* is conceived as a psychic force. But in this case, he held that occultists, more than spiritualists, are *àzètɔ́*. This is perhaps unsurprising, given that he identifies with spiritualism and would want to distance himself from the label of *àzètɔ́*.

14. Rampa (born Cyril Hoskin) was a controversial figure in Britain who wrote widely on Tibetan-inspired occultism and spirituality (Dodin and Räther 2001; Germano 2001). Hebga was a Cameroonian priest and theologian with research interests in witchcraft. The Hebga document Jérôme showed me was published by Pirogue in 1981, though library searches suggest that there are different versions with vague publication information, perhaps suggesting the dissemination of this work through nonscholarly channels.

15. He said his father was a Rosicrucian who used to say that there were more powerful things than *àzě*, and this was one of the rare times that I heard that *àzě* might not be the strongest force.

16. Heinrich Cornelius Agrippa was an influential sixteenth-century figure in the domain of magic, the occult, and astrology. Although there may be popular versions of his books with various titles, it is possible that Clotaire misspoke (or I misheard) in referring to Agrippa's *La philosophie occulte*. Like many of my informants, Agrippa himself represented a holistic approach to life through the study of astrology, alchemy, philosophy, theology, and medicine (Van der Poel 1997; Yates 1972).

17. *Yi King* possibly refers to the *I Ching*, the Chinese divination text. I am unaware of the Fuji tradition and could find no reference to it, unless it refers to Mount Fuji.

18. I was unable to identify a Hebrew god named Samekh, though samekh is the name of a Hebrew letter with mystical associations.

19. See also Caribbean physician Reginald Crosley's (2000) book on the connections between physics and Haitian Vodou.

20. In addition to her associations with Europeans, Mami Wata has also appropriated Hindu iconography (D. Rush 2013).

Conclusion

1. Hountondji (1996) uses the term "ethnophilosophy" to refer to an ethnographic account of a philosophical system of thought attributed uniformly to an African people. In his view, ethnophilosophy is inherently colonialist, essentialist, and objectifying. As a white, American anthropologist, I am cognizant of the dangers of representing others' thoughts and participating in the same colonialist discourses, but I approach this topic with the commitment to allowing my informants' voices to be heard by the primarily Western readership that this book will reach.

2. James Siegel (2006) observes that Indonesian sorcery has also changed and now emphasizes foreign origins.

References

Adjido, Clement T. 1997. "Links between Psychosomatic Medicine and Sorcery." In *Endogenous Knowledge: Research Trails*, edited by Paulin Hountondji, 265–78. Dakar: Codesria.

Adogame, Afeosemime U. 1998. *Celestial Church of Christ*. Frankfurt: Peter Lang.

Adoukonou, Barthélemy. 1993. *Vodun, démocratie et pluralisme religieux*. Cotonou: Sillon Noir.

Agossouza, Doyitin Mêhou Jonathan. n.d. *Plus de peur pour la sorcellerie*. Self-published.

Aguessy, Honorat. 1992. *Cultures vodoun*. Cotonou: Institut de Développement et d'Échanges Endogènes.

Ahyi, Gualbert R. 1997. "Traditional Models of Mental Health and Illness in Bénin." In *Endogenous Knowledge: Research Trails*, edited by Paulin Hountondji, 217–46. Dakar: Codesria.

Akrong, Abraham. 2007. "A Phenomenology of Witchcraft in Ghana." In *Imagining Evil: Witchcraft Beliefs and Accusations in Contemporary Africa*, edited by Gerrie ter Haar, 53–66. Trenton, NJ: Africa World Press.

Aldrin, Philippe. 2003. "Penser la rumeur: Une question discutée des sciences sociales." *Genèses* 50:126–41.

Alladaye, Jérôme. 2003. *Le catholicisme au pays du vodun*. Cotonou: Éditions Flamboyant.

Alokpo, Michel. 1996. "L'histoire des églises et missions évangéliques au Bénin." In *Nos racines racontées*, edited by James Krabill, 37–108. Abidjan: Presses Bibliques Africaines.

Apovo, Cossi Jean-Marie 1995. "Anthropologie du bo." PhD diss., Université de Paris V, 1995.

Appiah, Kwame Anthony. 1992. *In My Father's House: Africa in the Philosophy of Culture*. Oxford: Oxford University Press.

Apter, Andrew. 1991. "The Embodiment of Paradox: Yoruba Kingship and Female Power." *Cultural Anthropology* 6 (2): 212–29.

———. 1992. "'Que Faire?': Reconsidering Inventions of Africa." *Critical Inquiry* 19 (1): 87–104.

———. 1993. "Atinga Revisited: Yoruba Witchcraft and the Cocoa Economy 1950–51." In *Modernity and Its Malcontents: Ritual and Power in Postcolonial Africa*, edited by Jean Comaroff and John L. Comaroff, 111–28. Chicago: University of Chicago Press.

———. 2005. *The Pan-African Nation: Oil and the Spectacle of Culture in Nigeria*. Chicago: University of Chicago Press.

Ashforth, Adam. 2005. *Witchcraft, Violence, and Democracy in South Africa*. Chicago: University of Chicago Press.

———. 2008. "Relational Sociology Run off the Rails, or: How Chuck Tilly Helped Me Understand Spiritual Insecurity in Soweto." Paper presented at the conference "Contention, Change, and Explanation: A Conference in Honor of Charles Tilly," Social Science Research Council, New York, October 3–5, 2008.

Augé, Marc. 1976. "Savoir voir et savoir vivre: Les croyances à la sorcellerie en Côte d'Ivoire." *Africa* 46 (2): 128–36.

Austen, Ralph A. 1993. "The Moral Economy of Witchcraft." In *Modernity and Its Malcontents: Ritual and Power in Postcolonial Africa*, edited by Jean Comaroff and John L. Comaroff, 89–110. Chicago: University of Chicago Press.

Ayegboyin, Deji, and S. Ademola Ishola. 1997. *African Indigenous Churches*. Lagos: Greater Heights.

Aza, David Koffi. n.d. *Le créateur est une femme*. Cotonou: Printed by Siag.

Azalou, Michel Romaric. 2006. *Qualification des infractions courantes: Crimes, délits, contraventions, peines encourues*. 2nd ed. Cotonou: Imprimerie COPEF

Babatounde, Joseph, and Barthelemy Adoukonou. 1991. "Historique du Sillon Noir." In *Une Expérience Africaine d'Inculturation*, 1: 3–18. Cotonou: Centre de recherche et d'inculturation.

Banégas, Richard. 2003. *La démocratie à pas de caméléon: Transition et imaginaires politiques au Bénin*. Paris: Karthala.

Barber, Karin. 1981. "How Man Makes God in West Africa: Yoruba Attitudes towards the Orisa." *Africa* 51 (3): 724–45.

Bashkow, Ira. 2006. *The Meaning of Whitemen: Race & Modernity in the Orokaiva Cultural World*. Chicago: University of Chicago Press.

Basso, Keith H. 1979. *Portraits of "The Whiteman": Linguistic Play and Cultural Symbols among the Western Apache*. Cambridge: Cambridge University Press.

Bastian, Misty L. 2001. "Vulture Men, Campus Cultists and Teenaged Witches." In *Magical Interpretations and Material Realities*, edited by Henrietta L. Moore and Todd Sanders, 71–96. London: Routledge.

Bay, Edna G. 1998. *Wives of the Leopard: Gender, Politics and Culture in the Kingdom of Dahomey*. Charlottesville: University of Virginia Press.

———. 2008. *Asen, Ancestors, and Vodun: Tracing Change in African Art*. Urbana: University of Illinois Press.

Bayart, Jean-François. 1993. *The State in Africa*. London: Longman.

Beattie, John. 1963. "Sorcery in Bunyoro." In *Witchcraft and Sorcery in East Africa*, edited by John Middleton and Edward H. Winter, 27–55. New York: Frederick A. Praeger.

Bertho, Jacques. 1951. "Le Gbadou chez les Adja du Togo et du Dahomey." *Comptes rendus: Première conférence internationale des africanistes de l'Ouest*, 2:331–50. Dakar: Institut Français d'Afrique Noire.

Bierschenk, Thomas, and Jean-Pierre Olivier de Sardan. 2003. "Powers in the Village: Rural Bénin between Democratisation and Decentralisation." *Africa: Journal of the International African Institute* 73 (2): 145–73.

Birman, Patricia. 2011. "Sorcery, Territories, and Marginal Resistances in Rio de Janeiro." In *Sorcery in the Black Atlantic*, edited by Luis Nicolau Parés and Roger Sansi, 209–31. Chicago: University of Chicago Press.

Biruk, Crystal. 2011. "The Production and Circulation of AIDS Knowledge in Malawi." PhD diss., University of Pennsylvania.

Blanes, Ruy Llevera. 2006. "The Atheist Anthropologist: Believers and Non-believers in Anthropological Fieldwork." *Social Anthropology* 14 (2): 223–34.

Blier, Suzanne Preston. 1995. *African Vodun: Art, Psychology, and Power*. Chicago: University of Chicago Press.

Bond, George Clement. 2001. "Ancestors and Witches: Explanations and the Ideology of Individual Power in Northern Zambia." In *Witchcraft Dialogues: Anthropological and Philosophical Exchanges*, edited by George Clement Bond and Diane M. Ciekawy, 131–57. Athens: Ohio University Press.

Bond, George Clement, and Diane M. Ciekawy. 2001. "Introduction: Contested Domains in the Dialogues of 'Witchcraft.'" In *Witchcraft Dialogues: Anthropological and Philosophical Exchanges*, edited by George Clement Bond and Diane M. Ciekawy, 1–38. Athens: Ohio University Press.

Bonfils, Jean. 1999. *La mission catholique en république du Bénin*. Paris: Karthala.

Bongmba, Elias K. 1998. "Toward a Hermeneutic of Wimbum Tfu." *African Studies Review* 41 (3): 165–91.

Bowie, Fiona. (2000) 2006. *The Anthropology of Religion*. Malden, MA: Blackwell.

Brain, James L. 1982. "Witchcraft and Development." *African Affairs* 81 (324): 371–84.

Brand, Roger-Bernard. 1981. "Rites de naissance et réactualisation matérielle des signes de naissance à la mort chez les Wéménou (Bénin/Dahomey)." In *Naître, vivre et mourir: Actualité de Van Gennep*, edited by Jacques Hainard and Roland Kaehr, 37–62. Neuchâtel: Musée d'Ethnographie Neuchâtel.

Brandes, Stanley. 1981. "Like Wounded Stags: Male Sexuality in an Andalusian Town." In *Sexual Meanings: The Cultural Construction of Gender and Sexuality*, edited by Sherry B. Ortner and Harriet Whitehead, 216–39. Cambridge: Cambridge University Press.

Brown, Karen McCarthy. 2001. *Mama Lola: A Vodou Priestess in Brooklyn*. Berkeley: University of California Press.

Bubandt, Nils. 2014. *The Empty Seashell: Witchcraft and Doubt on an Indonesian Island*. Ithaca, NY: Cornell University Press.

Capra, Fritjof. 1975. *The Tao of Physics: An Exploration of the Parallels between Modern Physics and Eastern Mysticism*. Boulder, CO: Shambhala.

Castaneda, Carlos. 1968. *The Teachings of Don Juan: A Yaqui Way of Knowledge*. Berkeley: University of California Press.

Chavunduka, Gordon L. 2003. "Notes on African Witchcraft." In *Witchcraft Violence and the Law in South Africa*, edited by John Hund, 136–42. Pretoria: Protea Book House.

Claffey, Patrick. 2007. *Christian Churches in Dahomey: A Study of Their Socio-Political Role*. Leiden: Brill.

Clément, Yacoubou Badorou. 1996. "Histoire de la mission SIM et l'église UEEB au Bénin." In *Nos racines racontées*, edited by James Krabill, 33–36. Abidjan: Presses Bibliques Africaines.

Comaroff, Jean, and John L. Comaroff, eds. 1993. *Modernity and Its Malcontents: Ritual and Power in Postcolonial Africa*. Chicago: University of Chicago Press.

———. 1999. "Occult Economies and the Violence of Abstraction." *American Ethnologist* 26 (2): 279–303.

Comaroff, John, and Jean Comaroff. 2004. "Policing Culture, Cultural Policing: Law and Social Order in Postcolonial South Africa." *Law & Social Inquiry* 29 (3): 513–45.

Constantin, François, and Christian Coulon. 1997. *Religion et transition démocratique en Afrique*. Paris: Karthala.

Cosentino, Donald J., ed. 1995. *Sacred Arts of Haitian Vodou*. Catalog of exhibition organized by and held at the UCLA Fowler Museum of Cultural History and traveling to four other venues in the United States. Los Angeles: UCLA Fowler Museum of Cultural History.

Creppy, G. A. J. 1988. "La pensée négro-africaine traditionnelle et la nyctosophie chez les Africains." *Mondes et cultures* 48 (3): 430–73.

Crosley, Reginald. 2000. *The Vodou Quantum Leap: Alternate Realities, Power and Mysticism*. St. Paul, MN: Llewellyn Publishers.

Dagnon, Gilbert. n.d. *Libérer de la divination, de la sorcellerie*. Cotonou: Printed by Grande Marque.

Dah-Lokonon, Gbenoukpo Bodehou. 1997. "'Rain-Makers': Myth and Knowledge in Traditional Atmospheric Management." In *Endogenous Knowledge: Research Trails*, edited by Paulin Hountondji, 83–112. Dakar: Codesria.

Dalzel, Archibald. 1793. *The History of Dahomy*. London: Self-published.

Davis, Wade. 1985. *The Serpent and the Rainbow*. New York: Simon & Schuster.

De Boeck, Filip. 2005. "Children, Gift and Witchcraft in the Democratic Republic of Congo." In *Makers and Breakers, Children and Youth in Postcolonial Africa*, edited by Alcinda Honwana and Filip de Boeck, 188–215. Oxford: James Currey.

De Sardan, Olivier. 1988. "Jeu de la croyance et 'je' ethnologique: Exotisme religieux et ethno-ego-centrisme." *Cahiers d'études africaines* 28 (111–12): 527–40.

Desjarlais, Robert, and C. Jason Throop. 2011. "Phenomenological Approaches in Anthropology." *Annual Review of Anthropology* 40:87–102.

Desmangles, Leslie. 1992. *The Faces of the Gods*. Chapel Hill: University of North Carolina Press.

Dodin, Thierry, and Heinz Räther. 2001. "Imagining Tibet: Between Shangri-la and Feudal Oppression: Attempting a Synthesis." In *Imagining Tibet: Perceptions, Projections, and Fantasies*, edited by Thierry Dodin and Heinz Räther, 391–416. Somerville, MA: Wisdom Publications.

Douglas, Mary. 1970. "Introduction: Thirty Years after *Witchcraft, Oracles, and Magic*." In *Witchcraft Confessions & Accusations*, edited by Mary Douglas, xiii–xxxviii. London: Tavistock Publications.

Drewal, Henry John. 1988. "Performing the Other: Mami Wata Worship in Africa." *TDR: The Drama Review* 32 (2): 160–85.

———. 2008. "Introduction: Sources and Currents." In *Mami Wata: Arts for the Water Spirits in Africa and Its Diasporas*, edited by Henry John Drewal, 23–69. Los Angeles: Fowler Museum.

Drewal, Henry John, and Margaret Thompson Drewal. 1983. *Gẹlẹdẹ: Art and Female Power among the Yoruba*. Bloomington: Indiana University Press.

Duncan, John. (1847) 1968. *Travels in Western Africa in 1845 & 1846, Comprising a Journey from Wydah, through the Kingdom of Dahomey, to Adofoodia in the Interior*. London: Frank Cass.

Ekoué, Léocadie, and Judy Rosenthal. 2015. "*Aze* and the Incommensurable." In *Evil in Africa: Encounters with the Everyday*, edited by William C. Olsen and Walter E. A. van Beek, 128–39. Bloomington: Indiana University Press.

Elgin, Catherine Z. 2004. "True Enough." *Philosophical Issues* 14 (1): 113–31.

Ellis, Stephen. 1989. "Tuning In to Pavement Radio." *African Affairs* 88 (352): 321–30.

———. 2001. "Mystical Weapons: Some Evidence from the Liberian War." *Journal of Religion in Africa* 31 (2): 222–36.

———. 2002. "Writing Histories of Contemporary Africa." *Journal of African History* 43:1–26.

Ellis, Stephen, and Gerrie ter Haar. 1998. "Religion and Politics in Sub-Saharan Africa." *Journal of Modern African Studies* 36 (2): 175–201.

Ethnologue. n.d. Accessed January 19, 2012. https://www.ethnologue.com/language/fon.

Evans-Pritchard, E. E. 1935. "Witchcraft." *Africa: Journal of the International African Institute* 8 (4): 417–22.

———. 1936. "Customs and Beliefs Relating to Twins among the Nilotic Nuer." *Uganda Journal* 3 (3): 230–38.

———. (1937) 1976. *Witchcraft, Oracles and Magic among the Azande*. Oxford: Oxford University Press.

Evens, Terence M. S. 1996. "Witchcraft and Selfcraft." *European Journal of Sociology* 37 (1): 23–46.

———. 2012. "Twins Are Birds and a Whale Is a Fish, a Mammal, a Submarine: Revisiting 'Primitive Mentality' as a Question of Ontology." *Social Analysis* 56 (3): 1–11.

Everett, Daniel. 2005. "Cultural Constraints on Grammar and Cognition in Pirahã." *Current Anthropology* 46 (4): 621–46.

Falen, Douglas J. 2007. "Good and Bad Witches: The Transformation of Witchcraft in Bénin." *West Africa Review* 10:1–27.

———. 2008. "Polygyny and Christian Marriage in Africa: The Case of Bénin." *African Studies Review* 51 (2): 51–74.

———. 2011. *Power and Paradox: Authority, Insecurity, and Creativity in Fon Gender Relations*. Trenton, NJ: Africa World Press.

———. 2016. "Vodun, Spiritual Insecurity, and Religious Importation in Bénin." *Journal of Religion in Africa* 46 (4): 453–83.

Fanon, Frantz. 1963. *The Wretched of the Earth*. New York: Grove Press.

Farmer, Paul. 1992. *AIDS and Accusation: Haiti and the Geography of Blame*. Berkeley: University of California Press.

Favret-Saada, Jeanne. 1980. *Deadly Words: Witchcraft in the Bocage*. New York: Cambridge University Press.

Ferguson, James. 1999. *Expectations of Modernity: Myths and Meanings of Urban Life on the Zambian Copperbelt*. Berkeley: University of California Press.

Fields, Karen. 2001. "Witchcraft and Racecraft: Invisible Ontology in Its Sensible Manifestations." In *Witchcraft Dialogues: Anthropological and Philosophical Exchanges*, edited by George Clement Bond and Diane M. Ciekawy, 283–315. Athens: Ohio University Press.

Fisiy, Cyprian. 1998. "Containing Occult Practices: Witchcraft Trials in Cameroon." *African Studies Review* 41 (3): 143–63.

Fisiy, Cyprian F., and Peter Geschiere. 2001. "Witchcraft Development and Paranoia in Cameroon." In *Magical Interpretations and Material Realities*, edited by Henrietta L. Moore and Todd Sanders, 226–46. London: Routledge.

Forbes, Frederick. 1851. *Dahomey and the Dahomans*. London: Longman, Brown, Green and Longmans.

Forte, Jung Ran. 2010. "Black Gods, White Bodies: Westerners' Initiation to Vodun in Contemporary Bénin." *Transforming Anthropology* 18 (2): 129–45.

Foster, George M. 1965. "Peasant Society and the Image of Limited Good." *American Anthropologist* 67 (2): 293–315.

Fratkin, Elliot. 2004. *Ariaal Pastoralists of Kenya*. Boston: Pearson Education.

Frazer, James George. 1890. *The Golden Bough: A Study in Comparative Religion*. London: Macmillan.

Freedman, Samuel G. 2009. "Paganism, Just Another Religion for Military and Academia." *New York Times*, October 30.

Friedson, Steven M. 1996. *Dancing Prophets: Musical Experience in Tumbuka Healing*. Chicago: University of Chicago Press.

Geertz, Clifford. 1973a. "Deep Play: Notes on the Balinese Cockfight." In *The Interpretation of Cultures*, edited by Clifford Geertz, 412–53. New York: Basic Books.

———. 1973b. "Thick Description: Toward an Interpretive Theory of Culture." In *The Interpretation of Cultures*, edited by Clifford Geertz, 3–30. New York: Basic Books.

Germano, David F. 2001. "Encountering Tibet: The Ethics, Soteriology and Creativity of Cross-Cultural Interpretation." *Journal of the American Academy of Religions* 69 (1): 165–82.

Geschiere, Peter. 1997. *The Modernity of Witchcraft*. Charlottesville: University of Virginia Press.

———. 1998. "Globalization and the Power of Indeterminate Meaning." *Development and Change* 29:811–37.

———. 2000. "Sorcellerie et modernité: Retour sur une étrange complicité." *Politique africaine* 79:17–32.

———. 2003. "On Witch Doctors and Spin Doctors: The Role of 'Experts' in African and American Politics." In *Magic and Modernity: Interfaces of Revelation and Concealment*, edited by Birgit Meyer and Peter Pels, 159–82. Stanford, CA: Stanford University Press.

———. 2006. "Witchcraft and the Limits of the Law." In *Law and Disorder in the Postcolony*, edited by Jean Comaroff and John Comaroff, 219–46. Chicago: University of Chicago Press.

———. 2008a. Review of *Ethnographic Sorcery*, by Harry G. West. *African Studies Review* 51 (3): 138–40.

———. 2008b. "Witchcraft and the State: Cameroon and South Africa: Ambiguities of 'Reality' and 'Superstition.'" *Past and Present* 199, supplement 3:313–35.

———. 2013. *Witchcraft, Intimacy and Trust: Africa in Comparison.* Chicago: University of Chicago Press.

———. 2016. "Witchcraft, Shamanism, and Nostalgia. A Review Essay." *Comparative Studies in Society and History* 58 (1): 242–65.

Geschiere, Peter, and Cyprian Fisiy. 1994. "Domesticating Personal Violence: Witchcraft, Courts and Confessions in Cameroon." *Africa* 64 (3): 323–41.

Gilli, Bruno. 1982. "Naissances humaines ou divines? Analyse de certains types de naissances attribués au vodun." PhD diss., École des Hautes Études en Sciences Sociales, Paris.

Gilmore, David D. 1990. "Men and Women in Southern Spain: 'Domestic Power' Revisited." *American Anthropologist* 92 (4): 953–70.

Good, Byron J. 1994. *Medicine, Rationality, and Experience: An Anthropological Perspective.* Cambridge: Cambridge University Press.

Goody, Esther. 1970. "Legitimate and Illegitimate Aggression in a West African State." In *Witchcraft Confessions and Accusations*, edited by Mary Douglas, 207–44. London: Tavistock.

Green, Lesley J. F. 2007. "The Indigenous Knowledge Systems Policy of 2004: Challenges for South African Universities." *Social Dynamics* 33 (1): 130–54.

Hackett, Rosalind I. J. 1992. "New Age Trends in Nigeria: Ancestral and/or Alien Religion?" In *Perspectives on the New Age*, edited by James R. Lewis and J. Gordon Melton, 215–31. Albany: State University of New York Press.

———. 2003. "Discourses of Demonization in Africa and Beyond." *Diogenes* 50 (3): 61–75.

Hallen, Barry. 2001. "'Witches' as Superior Intellects: Challenging a Cross-Cultural Superstition." In *Witchcraft Dialogues: Anthropological and Philosophical Exchanges*, edited by George Clement Bond and Diane M. Ciekawy, 80–100. Athens: Ohio University Press.

Hallen, Barry, and J. Olubi Sodipo. 1997. *Knowledge, Belief, and Witchcraft: Analytic Experiments in African Philosophy.* Stanford, CA: Stanford University Press.

Hayes, Kelly E. 2011. *Holy Harlots: Femininity, Sexuality, and Black Magic in Brazil.* Berkeley: University of California Press.

Hebga, Meinrad P. 1979. *Sorcellerie: Chimère dangereuse . . . ?* Abidjan: INADES Éditions.

Henare, Amiria, Martin Holbraad, and Sari Wastell, eds. 2007. *Thinking through Things: Theorising Artifacts Ethnographically.* London: Routledge.

Henry, Christine. 2001. "Du vin nouveau dans de vieilles outres: Parcours d'un dissident du christianisme céleste (Bénin)." *Social Compass* 48 (3): 353–68.

———. 2008a. *La force des anges: Rites, hiérarchie et divination dans le christianisme céleste, Bénin.* Turnhout, Belgium: Brepols.

———. 2008b. "Le sorcier, le visionnaire et la guerre des églises au sud-Bénin." *Cahiers d'études africaines* 48 (1–2): 101–30.

Herdt, Gilbert H. 1982. *Rituals of Manhood: Male Initiation in Papua New Guinea.* Berkeley: University of California Press.

Herskovits, Melville J. (1937) 1971. *Life in a Haitian Valley*. New York: Doubleday.

———. (1938) 1967. *Dahomey: An Ancient West African Kingdom*. 2 vols. Evanston, IL: Northwestern University Press.

Herskovits, Melville J., and Frances S. Herskovits. 1933. *An Outline of Dahomean Religious Belief*. Menasha, WI: American Anthropological Association.

Heywood, Paolo. 2012. "Anthropology and What There Is: Reflections on 'Ontology.'" *Cambridge Anthropology* 30 (1): 143–51.

Holbraad, Martin. 2010. "Ontology Is Just Another Word for Culture: Motion Tabled at the 2008 Meeting of the Group for Debates in Anthropological Theory, University of Manchester." *Critique of Anthropology* 30 (2): 179–85.

Hoppers, Catherine A. Odora. 2002. Introduction to *Indigenous Knowledge and the Integration of Knowledge Systems*, edited by Catherine A. Odora Hoppers, 23–38. Claremont, South Africa: New Africa Books.

Horton, Robin. 1967a. "African Traditional Thought and Western Science. Part I. From Tradition to Science." *Africa* 37 (1): 50–71.

———. 1967b. "African Traditional Thought and Western Science. Part II. The 'Closed' and 'Open' Predicaments." *Africa* 37 (2): 155–87.

Hountondji, Paulin J. 1996. *African Philosophy: Myth and Reality*. 2nd ed. Bloomington: Indiana University Press.

———, ed. 1997a. *Endogenous Knowledge: Research Trails*. Dakar: Codesria.

———. 1997b. "Introduction: Recentering Africa." In *Endogenous Knowledge: Research Trails*, edited by Paulin Hountondji, 1–39. Dakar: Codesria.

———. 2002. "Knowledge Appropriation in a Post-colonial Context." In *Indigenous Knowledge and the Integration of Knowledge Systems*, edited by Catherine A. Odora Hoppers, 23–38. Claremont, South Africa: New Africa Books.

———. 2008. "Une pensée pré-personnelle: Note sur 'Ethnophilosophie et idéo-logique' de Marc Augé." *L'homme* 1–2 (185–86): 343–63.

Houreld, Katharine. 2009. "Witchcraft Poses New Dangers in Africa." CBS News, October 17, 2009. https://www.cbsnews.com/news/nigerian-children-deemed-witches -tortured/.

Hund, John. 2003a. "African Witchcraft and Western Law: Psychological and Cultural Issues." In *Witchcraft Violence and the Law in South Africa*, edited by John Hund, 9–39. Pretoria: Protea Book House.

———, ed. 2003b. *Witchcraft Violence and the Law in South Africa*. Pretoria: Protea Book House

Hurston, Zora Neale. (1938) 1990. *Tell My Horse*. New York: Harper & Row.

INSAE (Institut National de la Statistique et de l'Analyse Économique). 2003. *Troisième recensement général de la population et de l'habitation, synthèse des analyses en Bref*. Cotonou.

Isichei, Elizabeth. 2002. *Voices of the Poor in Africa: Moral Economy and the Popular Imagination*. Rochester, NY: University of Rochester Press.

Ivakhiv, Adrian. 1996. "The Resurgence of Magical Religion as a Response to the Crisis of Modernity." In *Magical Religion and Modern Witchcraft*, edited by James R. Lewis, 237–65. Albany: SUNY Press.

Jackson, Michael. 2013. *Lifeworlds: Essays in Existential Anthropology*. Chicago: University of Chicago Press.

James, William. (1890) 1913. *The Principles of Psychology*. Vol. 2. New York: Henry Holt.

Jorgensen, Danny L., and Scott E. Russell. 1999. "American Neopaganism: The Participants' Social Identities." *Journal for the Scientific Study of Religion* 38 (3): 325–38.

Kahn, Jeffrey. 2011. "Policing 'Evil': State-Sponsored Witch-Hunting in the People's Republic of Bénin." *Journal of Religion in Africa* 1 (1): 4–34.

Kapferer, Bruce. 1997. *The Feast of the Sorcerer: Practices of Consciousness and Power*. Chicago: University of Chicago Press.

———. 2002. "Introduction: Outside All Reason." In *Beyond Rationalism: Rethinking Magic, Witchcraft and Sorcery*, edited by Bruce Kapferer, 1–30. New York: Berghahn Books.

Karimi, Faith. 2009. "Abuse of Child 'Witches' on Rise, Aid Group Says." *CNN*, May 18, 2009. http://edition.cnn.com/2009/WORLD/africa/05/18/nigeria.child.witchcraft/.

Karlström, Mikael. 2004. "Modernity and Its Aspirants." *Current Anthropology* 45 (5): 595–619.

Katz, Jack, and Thomas J. Csordas. 2003. "Phenomenological Ethnography in Sociology and Anthropology." *Ethnography* 4 (3): 275–88.

Kimmel, Michael S. 2000. *The Gendered Society*. New York: Oxford University Press.

Kiniffo, Henry-Valère T. 1997. "Foreign Objects in Human Bodies." In *Endogenous Knowledge: Research Trails*, edited by Paulin Hountondji, 247–63. Dakar: Codesria.

Knauft, Bruce M. 1985. *Good Company and Violence: Sorcery and Social Action in Lowland New Guinea Society*. Berkeley: University of California Press.

Kohnert, Dirk. 1996. "Magic and Witchcraft: Implications for Democratization and Poverty-Alleviating Aid in Africa." *World Development* 24 (8): 1347–55.

Kuassi, Sylvain. n.d. *La science de la félicité ou l'art d'interroger le devin*. Self-published.

Kuhn, Thomas S. 1962. *The Structure of Scientific Revolutions*. Chicago: University of Chicago Press.

Kunhiyop, Samuel Waje. 2003. *Contemporary Issues Facing Christians in Africa*. Lagos, Nigeria: Baraka Press.

Labouret, Henri, and Paul Rivet. 1929. *Le royaume d'Arda et son évangélisation au XVIIe siècle*. Paris: Institut d'Ethnologie.

Landry, Timothy. 2013. "When Secrecy Goes Global: Vodún, Tourism, and the Politics of Knowing in Bénin, West Africa." PhD diss., University of Illinois at Urbana-Champaign.

———. 2015. "Vodún, Globalization, and the Creative Layering of Belief in Southern Bénin." *Journal of Religion in Africa* 45 (2): 170–99.

Larner, Christina. 1984. *Witchcraft and Religion: The Politics of Popular Belief*. London: Basil Blackwell.

Latour, Bruno. 1988. *Science in Action: How to Follow Scientists and Engineers through Society*. Cambridge, MA: Harvard University Press.

———. 1993. *We Have Never Been Modern*. Translated by Catherine Porter. Cambridge, MA: Harvard University Press.

———. 1999. *Pandora's Hope: Essays on the Reality of Science Studies*. Cambridge, MA: Harvard University Press.

———. 2004. "Why Has Critique Run Out of Steam? From Matters of Fact to Matters of Concern." *Critical Inquiry* 30 (2): 225–48.

Le Herissé, A. 1911. *L'ancien royaume du Dahomey: Moeurs, religion, histoire*. Paris: Larose.

LeMay-Boucher, Philippe, Joël Noret, and Vincent Somville. 2011. "Double, Double Toil and Trouble: Investigating Expenditures on Protection against Occult Forces in Bénin." Department of Economics Working Paper 1105, University of Namur.

Leseth, Anne. 1997. "The Use of Juju in Football: Sport and Witchcraft in Tanzania." In *Entering the Field: New Perspectives on World Football*, edited by Gary Armstrong and Richard Giulianotti, 159–74. Oxford: Berg.

Lévi-Strauss, Claude. 1963. *Structural Anthropology*. New York: Basic Books.

———. 1966. *The Savage Mind*. Chicago: University of Chicago Press.

Lévy-Bruhl, Lucien. 1926. *How Natives Think*. London: George Allen & Unwin.

Lewis, James R. 1996. Introduction to *Magical Religion and Modern Witchcraft*, edited by James R. Lewis, 1–5. Albany: SUNY Press.

Littlejohn, James. 1970. "Twins, Birds, etc." *Bijdragen tot de Taal-, Land- en Volkenkunde* 126 (1): 91–114.

Long, Carolyn Morrow. 2001. *Spiritual Merchants: Religion, Magic, and Commerce*. Knoxville: University of Tennessee Press.

Macintyre, Alasdair. 1970. "Is Understanding Religion Compatible with Believing?" In *Rationality*, edited by Bryan R. Wilson, 62–77. Oxford: Blackwell.

Malinowski, Bronisław. 1948. *Magic, Science, and Religion, and Other Essays*. Garden City, NY: Doubleday.

Marie, Alain. 1997. Introduction to *L'Afrique des individus*, edited by Alain Marie, 7–16. Paris: Karthala.

Marshall-Fratani, Ruth. 1998. "Mediating the Global and Local in Nigerian Pentecostalism." *Journal of Religion in Africa* 28 (3): 278–315.

Marwick, Max. 1964. "Witchcraft as a Social-Strain Gauge." *Australian Journal of Science* 26:263–68.

Mary, André. 2000. *Le bricolage africain des héros chrétiens*. Paris: Les Éditions du Cerf.

———. 2002. "Pilgrimage to Imeko (Nigeria)." *International Journal of Urban and Regional Research* 26 (1): 106–20.

———. 2005. "Histoires d'église." In *Entreprises religieuses transnationales en Afrique de l'Ouest*, edited by Laurent Fourchard, André Mary, and René Otayek, 155–81. Paris: Karthala.

Matory, J. Lorand. 1994. *Sex and the Empire That Is No More*. Minneapolis: University of Minnesota Press.

Maupoil, Bernard. 1943. *La géomancie à l'ancienne côte des esclaves*. Paris: Institut d'Ethnologie.

Mayrargue, Cédric. 2002. "Dynamiques religieuses et démocratisation au Bénin: Pentecôtisme et formation d'un espace public." PhD diss., Université Montesquieu, Bordeaux IV.

Mbembe, Achille. 1992. "Provisional Notes on the Postcolony." *Africa* 62 (1): 3–37.

Mbiti, John S. 1969. *African Religions and Philosophy*. New York: Praeger.

Mbuy, Tatah H. 1989. *Encountering Witches and Wizards in Africa*. Self-published.

———. 1992. *Understanding Witchcraft Problems in the Life of an African*. Owerri Imo State, Nigeria: Printed by High Speed Printers.

Mercier, Paul. 1954. "The Fon of Dahomey." In *African Worlds: Studies in the Cosmological Ideas and Social Values of African Peoples*, edited by Darryl Forde, 210–34. London: Oxford University Press.

Métraux, Alfred. (1959) 1972. *Voodoo in Haiti*. London: Deutsch.

Meyer, Birgit. 1999. *Translating the Devil: Religion and Modernity among the Ewe in Ghana*. Trenton, NJ: Africa World Press.

———. 2009. "Response to ter Haar and Ellis." *Africa* 79 (3): 413–15.

Meyer, Birgit, and Peter Pels, eds. 2003. *Magic and Modernity: Interfaces of Revelation and Concealment*. Stanford, CA: Stanford University Press.

Middleton, John. 1963. "Witchcraft and Sorcery in Lugbara." In *Witchcraft and Sorcery in East Africa*, edited by John Middleton and Edward. H. Winter, 257–75. New York: Frederick A. Praeger.

Middleton, John, and Edward H. Winter. 1963a. Introduction to *Witchcraft and Sorcery in East Africa*, edited by John Middleton and Edward. H. Winter, 1–26. New York: Frederick A. Praeger.

———, eds. 1963b. *Witchcraft and Sorcery in East Africa*. New York: Frederick A. Praeger.

Monsia, Marc. 2003. *Religions indigènes et savoir endogène au Bénin*. Cotonou: Éditions du Flamboyant.

Montgomery, Eric J., and Christian N. Vannier. 2017. *An Ethnography of a Vodu Shrine in Southern Togo: Of Spirit, Slave and Sea*. Leiden: Brill.

Moore, Henrietta L., and Todd Sanders. 2001. "Magical Interpretations and Material Realities: An Introduction." In *Magical Interpretations and Material Realities*, edited by Henrietta L. Moore and Todd Sanders, 1–27. London: Routledge.

Moreau de Saint-Méry, Médéric Louis Elie. 1798. *Description topographique, physique, civile, politique et historique de la partie française de l'Île de Saint Domingue*. Self-published.

Mudimbe, V. Y. 1988. *The Invention of Africa: Gnosis, Philosophy, and the Order of Knowledge*. Bloomington: Indiana University Press.

Mukundi, Mubengayi Lwakale. 1983. *La sorcellerie: Existe-t-elle?* Kinshasa: Centre d'Études Pastorales.

Mutwa, Credo. 2003. "The Sangoma's Story." In *Witchcraft Violence and the Law in South Africa*, edited by John Hund, 151–67. Pretoria: Protea Book House.

Nadel, S. F. 1952. "Witchcraft in Four African Societies: An Essay in Comparison." *American Anthropologist* 45 (1): 18–29.

Needham, Rodney. 1972. *Belief, Language, and Experience*. Chicago: University of Chicago Press.

Newell, Sasha. 2007. "Pentecostal Witchcraft: Neoliberal Possession and Demonic Discourse in Ivoirian Pentecostal Churches." *Journal of Religion in Africa* 37 (4): 461–90.

Ngokwey, Ndolamb. 1994. "The President's Illness: Culture, Politics, and Fetishism in Bénin." *Culture, Medicine and Psychiatry* 18 (1): 61–81.

Niehaus, Isak. 2001. *Witchcraft, Power and Politics: Exploring the Occult in the South African Lowveld*. London: Pluto Press.

————. 2013. *Witchcraft and a Life in the New South Africa*. Cambridge: Cambridge University Press.

Nkashama, Pius Ngandu. 1987. "De l'image au mot: Les procédés de lexicalisation dans et par la Radio-Trottoir." *Meta* 32 (3): 285–91.

Noret, Joël. 2008. "Between Authenticity and Nostalgia: The Making of a Yoruba Tradition in Southern Bénin." *African Arts* 41 (4): 26–31.

————. 2010. *Deuil et funérailles dans le Bénin méridional: Enterrer à tout prix*. Brussels: Éditions Université de Bruxelles.

Nyaga, Stephen Nyoka. 2007. "The Impact of Witchcraft Beliefs and Practices on the Socioeconomic Development of the Abakwaya in Musoma Rural District, Tanzania." In *Imagining Evil: Witchcraft Beliefs and Accusations in Contemporary Africa*, edited by Gerrie ter Haar, 247–68. Trenton, NJ: Africa World Press.

Nyamnjoh, Francis B. 2001. "Delusions of Development and the Enrichment of Witchcraft Discourses in Cameroon." In *Magical Interpretations and Material Realities*, edited by Henrietta L. Moore and Todd Sanders, 28–49. London: Routledge.

Obafemi, Olu. 1986. *Pastor S. B. J. Oshoffa*. Ikeja, Lagos: Pathway Publishers.

Omoyajowo, J. Akinyele. 1965. *Witches? A Study of the Belief in Witchcraft and of Its Future in Modern African Society*. Ibadan, Nigeria: Daystar Press.

O'Neil, Marcy Hessling. 2012. "'You Who Have Been to School, What Have You Become?': An Ethnographic Study of University Life in Bénin." PhD diss., Michigan State University.

Oppenheimer, Mark. 2010. "On a Visit to the U.S., a Nigerian Witch-Hunter Explains Herself." *New York Times*, May 21.

Paleček, Martin, and Mark Risjord. 2012. "Relativism and the Ontological Turn within Anthropology." *Philosophy of the Social Sciences* 43 (1): 3–23.

Parés, Luis Nicolau. 2013. *The Formation of Candomblé: Vodun History and Ritual in Brazil*. Translated by Richard Vernon in collaboration with the author. Chapel Hill: University of North Carolina Press.

Pels, Peter. 1998. "The Magic of Africa: Reflections of a Western Commonplace." *African Studies Review* 41 (3): 193–209.

————. 2003. Introduction to *Magic and Modernity: Interfaces of Revelation and Concealment*, edited by Birgit Meyer and Peter Pels, 1–38. Stanford, CA: Stanford University Press.

Pierre, Roland. 1977. "Caribbean Religion: The Voodoo Case." *Sociological Analysis* 38 (1): 25–36.

Piot, Charles. 2010. *Nostalgia for the Future: West Africa and the Cold War*. Chicago: University of Chicago Press.

Pocock, David. 1972. Foreword to *A General Theory of Magic*, by Marcel Mauss. Translated by Robert Brain. New York: W. W. Norton.

Price-Mars, Jean. (1928) 1983. *So Spoke the Uncle*. Washington, DC: Three Continents Press.

Quénum, Maximilien. (1936) 1983. *Au pays des Fons: Us et coutumes du Dahomey*. Paris: Maisonneuve et Larose.

Ram, Kalpana, and Christopher Houston. 2015. "Introduction: Phenomenology's Methodological Invitation." In *Phenomenology in Anthropology: A Sense of Perspective*, edited by Kalpana Ram and Christopher Houston, 1–25. Bloomington: Indiana University Press.

Ranger, Terence. 2007. "Scotland Yard in the Bush: Medicine, Murders, Child Witches and the Construction of the Occult: A Literature Review." *Africa* 77 (2): 272–83.

Rasmussen, Susan. 2001. "Betrayal or Affirmation?" In *Magical Interpretations and Material Realities*, edited by Henrietta L. Moore and Todd Sanders, 136–59. London: Routledge.

Rödlach, Alexander. 2006. *Witches, Westerners, and HIV: AIDS and Cultures of Blame in Africa*. Walnut Creek, CA: Left Coast Press.

Rosenthal, Judy. 1998. *Possession, Ecstasy and Law in Ewe Voodoo*. Charlottesville: University of Virginia Press.

Rush, Dana. 2013. *Vodun in Coastal Bénin: Unfinished, Open-Ended, Global*. Nashville: Vanderbilt University Press.

Rush, John A. 1974. *Witchcraft and Sorcery*. Springfield, IL: Charles C. Thomas.

Sahlins, Marshall. 1999. "Two or Three Things That I Know about Culture." *Journal of the Royal Anthropological Institute* 5 (3): 399–421.

Sargent, Carolyn. 1989. *Maternity, Medicine and Power: Reproductive Decisions in Urban Bénin*. Berkeley: University of California Press.

Schutz, Alfred. 1962. *Collected Papers. Volume 1: The Problem of Social Reality*. Edited by Maurice Natanson. The Hague: Martinus Nijhoff.

Segurola, R. P. B. 1963. *Dictionnaire Fon–Français*. Cotonou: Centre Catéchétique de Porto-Novo, with the aid of the Embassy of France in Cotonou, Benin.

Siegel, James. 2006. *Naming the Witch*. Stanford, CA: Stanford University Press.

Smith, James Howard. 2008. *Bewitching Development: Witchcraft and the Reinvention of Development in Neoliberal Kenya*. Chicago: University of Chicago Press.

Smith, Wilfred Cantwell. 1977. *Belief and History*. Charlottesville: University of Virginia Press.

Spencer, Herbert. 1897. *Principles of Sociology*. New York: D. Appleton.

St. John, Spenser. 1884. *Hayti or The Black Republic*. London: Smith, Elder.

Stevenson, Matilda Coxe. 1904. "The Zuñi Indians: Their Mythology, Esoteric Societies, and Ceremonies." *Twenty-Third Annual Report of the Bureau of American Ethnology*. Washington, DC: US Government Printing Office.

Stewart, Pamela, and Andrew Strathern, eds. 2004. *Witchcraft, Sorcery, Rumors and Gossip*. Cambridge: Cambridge University Press.

Stoller, Paul. 1989. "Speaking in the Name of the Real." *Cahiers d'études africaines* 29 (113): 113–25.

———. 1998. "Rationality." In *Critical Terms for Religious Studies*, edited by Mark C. Taylor, 239–55. Chicago: University of Chicago Press.

———. 2008. *Power of the Between*. Chicago: University of Chicago Press.

Stoller, Paul, and Cheryl Olkes. 1987. *In Sorcery's Shadow: A Memoire of Apprenticeship among the Songhay of Niger*. Chicago: University of Chicago Press.

Styers, Randall. 2004. *Making Magic: Religion, Magic and Science in the Modern World*. Oxford: Oxford University Press.

Sui, Master Choa Kok. 2003. *Miracles de la Guérison Pranique*. Quezon City, Philippines: European Institute for Inner Studies Publishing House.

Surgy, Albert de. 1996. "La multiplicité des églises au Sud de l'Afrique occidentale." *Afrique contemporaine* 177:30–44.

———. 2001. *Le phénomène pentecôtiste en Afrique noire: Le cas béninois.* Paris: Éditions L'Harmattan.

Swartz, Marc J. 1982. "The Isolation of Men and The Happiness of Women: Sources and Uses of Power in Swahili Marital Relationships." *Journal of Anthropological Research* 38 (1): 26–44.

Tade, A. O. 1980. *Celestial Church of Christ.* Akure, Nigeria: Ade-Tade.

Tall, Emmanuel Kadya. 1995a. "De la démocratie et des cultes vodun au Bénin." *Cahiers d'études africaines* 35 (137): 195–208.

———. 1995b. "Dynamique des cultes voduns et du christianisme céleste au Sud-Bénin." *Cahiers des sciences humaines* 31 (4): 797–823.

———. 2005. "Stratégies locales et relations internationales des chefs de culte au Sud-Bénin." In *Entreprises religieuses transnationales en Afrique de l'Ouest*, edited by Laurent Fourchard, André Mary, and René Otayek, 267–84. Paris: Karthala.

Tambiah, Stanley Jeyaraja. 1990. *Magic, Science, Religion, and the Scope of Rationality.* Cambridge: Cambridge University Press.

Taussig, Michael. 1980. *The Devil and Commodity Fetishism in South America.* Chapel Hill: University of North Carolina Press.

Taylor, Philip. 2008. *Modernity and Re-enchantment: Religion in Post-revolutionary Vietnam.* Lanham, MD: Lexington Books.

Ter Haar, Gerrie, ed. 2007. *Imagining Evil: Witchcraft Beliefs and Accusations in Contemporary Africa.* Trenton, NJ: Africa World Press.

Ter Haar, Gerrie, and Stephen Ellis. 2009. "The Occult Does Not Exist: A Response to Terence Ranger." *Africa* 79 (3): 399–412.

Thomas, Keith. 1971. *Religion and the Decline of Magic: Studies in Popular Beliefs in Sixteenth and Seventeenth Century England.* New York: Scribner.

Topanou, Victor. 2009. "La peur du Bó: Pratiques occultes et construction de l'état de droit." In *L'ancien et le nouveau: La production du savoir dans l'Afrique d'aujourd'hui*, edited by Paulin J. Hountondji, 267–301. Porto-Novo, Benin: Centre Africaine des Hautes Études.

Turner, Victor W. 1964. "Witchcraft and Sorcery: Taxonomy versus Dynamics." *Africa* 34 (4): 314–25.

Tylor, Edward Burnett. 1871. *Primitive Culture: Researches into the Development of Mythology, Philosophy, Religion, Language, Art and Custom.* Vol. 2, *Religion in Primitive Culture.* London: John Murray.

UCT Scientist. 2016. *Science Must Fall?* YouTube, October 13. https://www.youtube.com/watch?v=C9SiRNibD14.

Van Binsbergen, Wim. 2001. "Witchcraft in Modern Africa as Virtualized Boundary Conditions of the Kinship Order." In *Witchcraft Dialogues: Anthropological and Philosophical Exchanges*, edited by George Clement Bond and Diane M. Ciekawy, 212–63. Athens: Ohio University Press.

Van der Poel, Marc. 1997. *Cornelius Agrippa, the Humanist Theologian and His Declamations.* Leiden: Brill.

Van Heekeren, Deborah. 2015. "Senses of Magic: Anthropology, Art, and Christianity in the Vula'a Lifeworld." In *Phenomenology in Anthropology: A Sense of Perspective*, edited by Kalpana Ram and Christopher Houston, 248–67. Bloomington: Indiana University Press.

Verger, Pierre Fatúmbí. 1954. *Dieux d'Afrique: Culte des Orishas et Vodouns à l'ancienne Côte des Esclaves en Afrique et à Bahia, la Baie de Tous les Saints au Brésil*. Paris: Paul Hartmann.

Verrips, Jojada. 2003. "Dr. Jekyll and Mr. Hyde: Modern Medicine between Magic and Science." In *Magic and Modernity: Interfaces of Revelation and Concealment*, edited by Birgit Meyer and Peter Pels, 223–40. Stanford, CA: Stanford University Press.

Vigh, Henrik Erdman, and David Brehm Sausdal. 2014. "From Essence back to Existence: Anthropology beyond the Ontological Turn." *Anthropological Theory* 14 (1): 49–73.

Viveiros de Castro, Eduardo. 2004. "Perspectival Anthropology and the Method of Controlled Equivocation." *Tipití: Journal of the Society for the Anthropology of Lowland South America* 2 (1): 3–22.

———. 2013. "The Relative Native." *Journal of Ethnographic Theory* 3 (3): 473–502.

Wagner, Roy. 1981. *The Invention of Culture*. Chicago: University of Chicago Press.

West, Harry G. 2005. *Kupilikula: Governance and the Invisible Realm in Mozambique*. Chicago: University of Chicago Press.

———. 2007. *Ethnographic Sorcery*. Chicago: University of Chicago Press.

White, Luise. 1993. "Cars out of Place: Vampires, Technology, and Labor in East and Central Africa." *Representations* 43:27–50.

Whitehead, Neil L., and Robin Wright, eds. 2004. *Darkness and Secrecy: The Anthropology of Assault Sorcery and Witchcraft in Amazonia*. Durham, NC: Duke University Press.

Whorf, Benjamin Lee. 1952. "Language, Mind, and Reality." *ETC: A Review of General Semantics* 9 (3): 167–88.

———. 1956. *Language, Thought, and Reality: Selected Writings of Benjamin Lee Whorf*. Cambridge, MA: MIT Press.

Wilson, Katharina M. 1985. "The History of the Word 'Vampire.'" *Journal of the History of Ideas* 46 (4): 577–83.

Winch, Peter. 1970. "Understanding a Primitive Society." In *Rationality*, edited by Bryan R. Wilson, 78–111. Oxford: Blackwell.

Yai, Olabiyi. 1993. "From Vodun to Mawu: Monotheism and History in the Fon Cultural Area." In *L'invention religieuse en Afrique*, edited by Jean-Pierre Chrétien, 241–65. Paris: Éditions Karthala.

Yates, Frances. 1964. *Giordano Bruno and the Hermetic Tradition*. London: Routledge and Kegan Paul.

———. 1972. *The Rosicrucian Enlightenment*. London: Routledge.

Zawa, Aïmavo Boniface. 2006. *Médecine traditionnelle et ses luttes contre la sorcellerie*. Cotonou: Éditions CORLAF.

Index